D1595915

Architecture is an art that must be un-derstood to be enjoyed. The pleasures arising from a just perception of its beauties, can only be experienced by those who have obtained some knowledge of its principles, and its historical associations. An architectural object may, it is true, affect to a limited extent, almost every observer; but the refining and ennobling influences to which its peculiar imagery is ad-dressed, are realized by those only who have cultivated a taste for its enjoyment. Hence, it is of no small importance that an art, so pro-lific of intellectual pleasures, should be generally understood and appreciated.

An impression that the study of Architecture belongs exclusively to Architects, has, no doubt, done much to retard the progress of the art, and to limit its humanizing and elevating influences on

THOMAS U. WALTER

THE LECTURES ON ARCHITECTURE, 1841-53

Edited by

Jhennifer A. Amundson

The Athenæum of Philadelphia
2006

Library of Congress Cataloging-in-Publication Data

Walter, Thomas Ustick, 1804-1887.
    Thomas U. Walter : the lectures on architecture, 1841-53 / edited by
    Jhennifer A. Amundson.
        p. cm.
    ISBN 0-916530-20-5
    1. Architecture. 2. Architecture--United States--19th century. I. Title:
Lectures on architecture, 1841-53. II. Amundson, Jhennifer A., 1968- III.
Title.

NA737.W27A35 2006
720--dc22

                                                        2006041203

Published by The Athenæum of Philadelphia
219 S. Sixth Street, Philadelphia, PA 19106
ISBN 0-916530-20-5

CONTENTS

THOMAS U. WALTER
THE LECTURES ON ARCHITECTURE, 1841-1853

ACKNOWLEDGMENTS

The preparation of this publication drew on the generous assistance of a number of institutions and individuals whom I am delighted to have the opportunity to thank here. Financial support for research and manuscript preparation was awarded by the National Endowment for the Humanities, the Graham Foundation for Advanced Studies in the Fine Arts, the Winterthur Museum and Library, and The Athenæum of Philadelphia. I am especially indebted to the board of The Athenæum and its director, Roger W. Moss, for support of my research on Walter through the Charles E. Peterson Fellowship program as well as the opportunity to work in one of the finest and most beautiful architecture libraries in the country. Bruce Laverty, Gladys Brooks Curator of Architecture at the Athenæum, has been a constant source of encouragement, guidance, and enthusiasm. Several people at Judson College provided invaluable assistance in many forms. Dale Simmons, Provost, and Jack Kremers, former Chair of the Architecture Department, arranged for release time that allowed for completion of the manuscript. My colleagues Royce Earnest and Christopher Miller kindly read parts of the manuscript and offered wise suggestions. A team of architecture majors, Jonathan Flager, Byron Gehrig, and Michael Spadafore, assisted the typescript, research, and formatting phases and Peter Iezzi designed the book cover.

Lastly, I owe my deepest thanks to David Amundson for providing both professional guidance and domestic support with consistent and admirable graciousness.

JAA

EDITOR'S PREFACE

Jhennifer A. Amundson

Thomas Ustick Walter wrote and rewrote a series of architectural lectures across a twelve-year time span during which they were delivered at several institutions in Philadelphia and Washington, DC. This edition aims to capture the characteristic content of the Lectures on Architecture between 1841 and 1853, the two most secure dates for the extant manuscripts in the Walter Collection at The Athenæum of Philadelphia.

Walter began writing and lecturing at least by 1840 but only bound and dated the extant manuscripts in 1841, the year he accepted the position of Professor of Architecture at the Franklin Institute and presented a six-part series there. The last certain date for the documents is 1856, the year in which Walter reported that he was "grinding them over" for an upcoming presentation at the Smithsonian Institution.[1] Walter continued to lecture on architecture until the end of his life, most significantly in 1860 for the Columbian College (now George Washington University) and in the 1870s for the American Institute of Architects. No written accounts of these presentations have been located.

Because Walter edited his original manuscripts for over a decade, the pages preserve the progress of his thought on architecture during an important period in his own career during which he served as Architect of the Capitol. It also overlaps a crucial period of American architectural history, considering Walter's construction of the dome and wings of the Capitol Building and establishment of the American Institute of Architects, of which he was a founding member. His alterations to the manuscript record both his judgment concerning what required updating and what remained constant in his thought. The manuscripts have little evidence

---

[1] With plans to offer them in the winter, Walter wrote that "I have them now on my table for revision and rearrangement." Walter to Rev. E. L. Magoon, 16 Sept. 1853.

of whole portions being removed; rather, Walter most often chose to cross out outdated or inappropriate content, and adding new sections on blank backs of pages or occasionally glued-in pieces of paper.

Such a heavily-edited document also presents a certain challenge to an editor who wishes to preserve as much of Walter's thought from both the early and later periods. Where Walter rewrote segments of the manuscript to clarify the prose without altering its meaning (changes to word choice, alterations to verb tense), the later text has been favored, and has been done so without comment. Whole new sentences or paragraphs that introduce material not present in the document as of 1841 are signaled in the editor's numerical endnotes. When long sections of text were struck from the original manuscript during Walter's later editing, they are reinserted here using italics and brackets.

Pagination of the original manuscripts is recorded in bracketed numbers which refer to the original manuscript. Further complicating the document, at times of later revisions Walter inserted additional sheets which he also numbered. The added pages are noted here as Walter numbered them, with a "+" sign to indicate their status as a later addition. Because Walter did not repaginate the original sheets, there can be some duplication, for example pages [3+] and [3] appear sequentially in Lecture I, the former [3+] being the later addition (and the actual third page in the extant manuscript), and the latter [3] being the original page three (and now its fourth page).

Walter's original spelling, grammar and capitalization have been preserved; punctuation has been added only when its absence makes the text difficult to read. Punctuation has been changed only for sake of consistency regarding the relative location of end quotes and periods. Walter's own manner of punctuation—especially the use of long dashes which indicate his speaking style—are preserved. Underlines are Walter's, and indicate emphasis of whole words in sentences as well as syllables to guide his pronunciation; italics are the editor's. All title and dating information at the top of each Lecture appears as it does on the manuscript. Subheadings have been added by the editor. The few diagrams which Walter occasionally sketched within the body of his writing (Lectures I, III, and IV) are positioned here as they appear in the manuscripts.

Both as architect and historian Walter was eager to acknowledge his precedents, and in the lectures recorded scores of source citations, usually in the margins or on the facing pages. These citations have been preserved here as footnotes which employ the same symbolic notations that Walter used. The editor's comments are reserved as numeric notes or, when added to Walter's notes, are bracketed and marked *Ed*. Descriptions of his sources will be found in Appendix A.

Walter's lectures were accompanied by large watercolor renderings which are now lost. Appendix B records as much information as is available on the character of these images. Every effort has been made to employ illustrations that would have been familiar to Walter, and most are drawn from books that he himself used in his preparation for the lectures, and from the sketchbooks of one of his students, John D. Jones. In the cases where such was not possible, contemporaneous images have been included in all but the most obscure cases.

It is hoped that with these strategies that the reader will have the best possible sense of the content and character of Walter's lectures as he presented them between 1841 and 1853.

A Note on the Discovery and Acquisition
of the Lecture Manuscripts

Roger W. Moss,
Executive Director, Athenæum of Philadelphia

Thomas Ustick Walter's lectures on architecture, published here for the first time, were unavailable to scholars until The Athenæum of Philadelphia acquired them in 1982. The story of this discovery, and how the manuscripts were returned to the city where they were written and first delivered, deserves a brief account.

In the early 1970s, the Philadelphia architectural historian Robert B. Ennis, who had selected the career of Thomas Ustick Walter as his dissertation topic at The University of Pennsylvania, set out to discover whether any Walter descendants had drawings or manuscripts. The Baltimore art historian William Sener Rusk had written a biographical essay on Walter for the *Dictionary of American Biography* in the 1930s. As part of the bibliography for that essay Rusk mentioned that "many of Walter's letters, notebooks, sketch books, drawings and account books... are owned by Mrs. C. H. Wegemann of Baltimore, Maryland." Ennis knew that Walter's widow had moved to Baltimore following his death in 1887 to be closer to Congress, where for years, she pressed a claim for unpaid compensation for her husband's government work beyond his contract for the United States Capitol.

Beginning with Professor Rusk's lead, Ennis contacted far-flung Walter family descendants. Eventually the trail led to Isabel Becker, Thomas Ustick Walter's granddaughter who owned Banner Ranch near Larkspur, Colorado. With some reluctance, Mrs. Becker eventually permitted Ennis to examine the archive which remained in the crates into which Walter had packed his papers for shipment from Washington to Philadelphia in 1865. The crates were stored in an unheated wooden bunkhouse on the ranch. Ennis was permitted to make photocopies and photographs of the more than 500 drawings and 30,000 pages of correspondence, diaries, and personal accounts. Included in this trove were the original manuscript copies of the Thomas Ustick Walter lectures on architecture.

Upon his return to Philadelphia, Ennis confided to me what he had found, and I proposed that the Athenæum attempt to acquire the archive, or at least to borrow heavily from it for the first exhibition ever devoted to Walter's career. Robert B. Ennis would serve as curator. The National Endowment for the Arts offered to provide the necessary funding, providing Mrs. Becker would agree to the loan. Initially she had rejected our overtures to purchase the archive, but eventually agreed to lend seventy-four items for the exhibition which opened at the Athenæum on October 26, 1979.

Following the exhibition, Mrs. Becker temporarily left the loans in storage at the Athenæum. Meanwhile, I urged her to consider selling the entire archive, which she finally agreed to do in March of 1982. (I later learned that Mrs. Becker was in part motivated by the desire to acquire some land adjoining Banner Ranch. This is the origin of the often-repeated story that the Athenæum bought and then traded a ranch for the Walter archive.)

At that time, the Athenæum had never purchased an architectural archive approaching the appraised value of the Walter drawings and papers which included the presentation drawings for the United States Capitol. Fortunately the Athenæum's directors recognized the importance of the archive to the library and individually pledged the full purchase price. In May of 1982, the archive was packed and shipped to Philadelphia, except for a few large watercolor renderings which were too fragile to move, and had to be conserved in Denver before shipping. Over the following year the archive was conserved and rehoused with grant funds from the National Endowment for the Humanities and Getty Foundation. The next year, Mrs. Becker decided to sell the John Neagle portraits of Thomas Ustick Walter and Mary Ann Walter, as well as the Emanuel Leutze portrait of Amanda Walter, which hang in the grand stair of the Athenæum. To this day, the Walter archive remains the crown jewel of the Architecture Department at the Athenæum.

LIST OF ABBREVIATIONS

APS   American Philosophical Society,
Philadelphia

JFI   *Journal of the Franklin Institute*

PAT   Athenæum of Philadelphia

Thomas Ustick Walter. Engraving by Albert Newsam after John Neagle portrait, ca. 1835
The Athenæum of Philadelphia

THE CONTEXT AND CHARACTER OF AMERICA'S FIRST ARCHITECTURAL THEORY

Jhennifer A. Amundson

Although America had established its political independence some twenty-one years earlier, Asher Benjamin's *Country Builder's Assistant* of 1797 reveals a continued dependence on Europe for certain cultural traditions, including the writing of books on architecture. The practical character of such early works lends credence to Alexis de Tocqueville's claim that Americans could (and in the case of architects, certainly did) look to the Old World to find "distinguished men of science, able artists, and great writers . . . and so could gather the treasures of the mind without working to produce them themselves."[1] Decades would pass before an American would generate a modern theory of architecture. Architectural theory is defined here as a written account that identifies the means by which a consciously adopted or invented (or, alternately, an unconsciously inherited) philosophical construct is channeled into built form. Architectural theory is a conduit of thought, a filter through which human values are sifted into built form.

Rare is the early-nineteenth-century American lecture or publication on architecture that attempts more than serving the pragmatic interests of builders' guides or transmitting inherited theoretical ideas. When such theory did appear in America it occurred, significantly, at the same time that a critical mass of self-proclaimed professional architects first attempted to carve an exclusive niche by establishing a restrictive professional organization to block the participation of those they deemed to

---

[1] Alexis de Tocqueville, *Democracy in America*, trans. George Lawrence, ed. J. P. Mayer (New York: Harper & Row, 1988), 455.

be unqualified. Additionally, this theory was written by a quintessentially American individual: one born to no special social or financial advantage, but one to whom doors of opportunity opened as a response to discipline, determination and talent; a former mason and life-long Baptist who professed to have an education that was "liberal, though not collegiate."[2] Written in 1841 and revised intermittently over two decades, the Lectures on Architecture by Thomas U. Walter (1804-87) are recorded in six manuscripts preserved in The Athenæum of Philadelphia's extensive Thomas U. Walter Collection. The lectures blend four millennia's historical content with contemporary aesthetic principles to fulfill both professional and sacred objectives that informed Walter's theoretical objectives.

These many strands—historical study, aesthetic essay, professional apologia, and theological proposition—each in their own way related to the calls for improvement that spread through America in Walter's day. It was believed that this striving for personal progress through the application of intellectual and cultural endeavors would ultimately profit the population at large. Improvement prompted the formation of social and cultural societies, mechanic's institutes, and other forward-looking programs in progressive cities. Such was Walter's home town of Philadelphia, which had enjoyed a reputation as a center of intellectual and religious development since the Colonial period, and where, around the turn of the nineteenth century, many cultural, scientific and social organizations were established to serve the aims of improvement.[3]

Historically, the roots of improvement can be traced to the Great Awakening, and indeed its earliest adherents were the followers of several Christian denominations who believed "For the soul to be without knowledge is not good," as the common sentiment was expounded by one nineteenth-century Baptist apologist.[4] The ideals of improvement were certainly in keeping with the general mission of the denomination into which Walter was baptized as an adult in 1824. The Baptist church's tradition of learning was manifest in such activities as the founding of the first Sunday Schools to acquaint students with literacy in general and the Bible in particular. Likewise, in 1843 the American Baptist Publication Society was said to have as its "paramount object" the goal of making their

---

[2] Walter, "Genealogical Sketches and Investigations Relating to Ancestry and Family Connections Embracing Biographical and Historical Notes and Records" (hereafter referred to as "Genealogical Sketches"), Thomas U. Walter Collection, The Athenæum of Philadelphia (hereafter, PAT).
[3] Already the distinguished home of the Library Company, American Philosophical Society, Peale Museum, and Federal Government (1790-1800), Philadelphia would welcome The Pennsylvania Academy of the Fine Arts, Academy of Natural Sciences, The Athenæum of Philadelphia and the Franklin Institute between 1805 and 1824.
[4] The Reverend Robert Samuel Duncan, *The History of Sunday Schools* (Memphis: Southern Baptist Publication Society, 1876), 124.

countrymen "a reading, thinking," and also a "devotedly religious people."[5] The promotion of American society was deemed to rest on developing the two essential aspects of humanity: both the minds and souls of its citizens. Among other denominations, Baptists exercise their devotion through evangelism, a response to the "great commission" recorded by the gospel-writer Matthew, which charges laity and clergy alike to teach their fellow citizens and encourage one another's devotion.[6] This directive was a motivating force of Walter's Christian faith and a hallmark of his character as is evident in not just his regular attendance at several church services every week, but the content of his letters and other writings, and most obviously the hundreds of Bible lessons that he wrote. His piety was not lost on others, as recorded in his obituary:

> He had a great love for the Bible, and studied it with diligence and care. Believing that the system of faith which he early embraced was clearly taught in the Word of God, he held to it with unyielding tenacity. He was to the last degree intolerant of any attempt to modify what he understood to be the teaching of the Bible.[7]

Walter maintained his faith not as an inward spirituality, but rather exercised it as a guiding impetus for his personal relationships and ultimately his architectural practice, which he performed almost as an evangelical pursuit.

Walter began his professional life as a bricklayer under the guidance of his father, Joseph Saunders Walter, a mason who worked on several of Philadelphia's most notable buildings.[8] At some point during his apprenticeship the younger Walter determined to lay aside the mason's trowel and take up to the architect's dividers, perhaps in response to the encouragement or expectations placed upon him by his parents who recognized an intellectual and artistic streak in their eldest son. Or perhaps it was part of the vocational progression available to him as an advocate for improvement; his transition promised that Walter would be able to use his mind more than his hands in his practice. Although it was still possible for a skilled "mechanic" to adopt the title "architect," during Walter's lifetime architectural practice would become recognized as a learned profession

---

[5] John Mason Peck quoted in H. Leon McBeth, *The Baptist Heritage* (Nashville: Broadman Press, 1987), 364.
[6] The biblical mandate and justification for all believers to take part in spreading the gospel is recorded in Matt. 28:19-20.
[7] This obituary was written by Walter's own pastor, the Rev. Warren Randolph. "The Architect of the United States Capitol," *The Standard* (21 June 1888).
[8] In particular, two of William Strickland's most important buildings in Philadelphia: the Second Bank of the United States (1818-24) and the Merchant's Exchange (1832-34).

William Strickland. Second Bank of the United States, Philadelphia, 1818-1824.
The Athenæum of Philadelphia

in America. Walter's establishment as an architect would constitute an advance beyond the tradition of manual employment practiced by both his father and grandfather. Additionally, the nature of architectural practice promised Walter an arena in which to fulfill his social calling before a wider public audience than he could in the brickyard and job site.

Walter's residency in Philadelphia was a fortunate circumstance in the development of his career because it gave him access to two professionals who were responsible both for changing the character of the city's built environment and the education of young hopeful architects as well. Walter enjoyed a privileged association with William Strickland (1788-1854) that seems to have begun on the job site where the elder Walter was leading the crews, including his fifteen-year-old son, constructing the Greek Revival Second Bank of the United States (1818-24). Soon thereafter the younger Walter obtained a position in Strickland's office where he developed his drawing skills and learned "a general knowledge of the professional practice of architects."[9] Strickland's approach to the profession was conditioned by his own experience in the office of European-trained Benjamin Henry Latrobe (1764-1820), the country's first consummate professional. During his two periods in Strickland's charge (1819-ca. 1821 and 1828-30), Walter observed his master's growing involvement in architecture, from his design

---

[9] Walter, "Genealogical Sketches," PAT.

and construction of many of the city's most prominent buildings, including the US Naval Asylum (1826-33), US Mint (1829-33), Arch Street Theatre and Medical Hall for the University of Pennsylvania (both 1829). During the 1820s Strickland also published several works on architecture and engineering, one the product of foreign travel at the behest of an American scientific society.[10] The crown of Strickland's scholarly credentials was his position as the first Professor of Architecture of the Franklin Institute (of which he was a founding member), where he presented a series of architectural lectures in 1824-25.

Established in February of 1824 on the ideals of improvement, the Franklin Institute of the State of Pennsylvania for the Promotion of the Mechanic Arts was the first of its kind in the country, and was distinguished from the many other mechanics' institutes which followed by its varied and stimulating program of teaching, research, and publication. By autumn of 1824 the Institute had established a Drawing School to provide training to artisans and would-be architects and engineers. Walter was one of the first fifty students to matriculate into the Drawing School, which offered lessons, lectures and access to a library after 1829, and would become the most successful unit during the Institute's early history.[11]

At the Franklin Institute Walter established another significant relationship with the school's Professor of Drawing, émigré John Haviland (1792-1852), who, with Strickland, was largely responsible for Philadelphia's status as a center for architectural innovation. Arriving in Philadelphia in 1816, the English-born Haviland had studied under architect-author James Elmes, from whom he received a thorough practical professional education. In Elmes' London office Haviland would also have been exposed to his master's abiding interest in and appreciation for architectural history as an important subject of study for contemporary architects. As Elmes explained in his *Lectures on Architecture, Comprising the History of the Art from the Earliest Times to the Present Day*,

> Ancient examples . . . are the best schools of true architecture [when they are] selected with judgment and pure taste; adapted, with the latitude of genius, to modern necessities; combined with the scientific inventions of modern construction; and perfected by study and practice.[12]

[10] See "A Chronologic, Bibliographic, and Descriptive Catalogue of the Architecture and Engineering Works of William Strickland" in Agnes Addison Gilchrist, *William Strickland, Architect and Engineer, 1788-1854* (New York: Da Capo Press, 1969), 45-118.
[11] Bruce Sinclair, *Philadelphia's Philosopher Mechanics: A History of the Franklin Institute, 1824-1865* (Baltimore: Johns Hopkins University Press, 1974), 120-21; Sydney L. Wright, The Story of the Franklin Institute (Philadelphia: Franklin Institute, 1938), 16-17, 108-09.
[12] James Elmes, *Lectures on Architecture, Comprising the History of the Art from the Earliest Times to the Present Day*, 1821; reprint (New York Benjamin Blom, 1971), 229.

John Haviland. The Franklin Institute (now Atwater Kent Museum), Philadelphia.
Lutz Collection, The Athenæum of Philadelphia

Haviland exercised this historical interest in his buildings, which were designed in a variety of historical styles, and also in his books. His first publication, the *Builder's Assistant* of 1818, was the first American title to include illustrations of the Greek orders. It is probable that Haviland introduced Walter not only to architectural history as a topic for study and appreciation, but also in particular to Elmes's book, to which Walter's lectures owe a debt.

The extent to which Walter modeled his professional life on the careers of Strickland and Haviland is perhaps particularly evident in the self-portrait Walter commissioned in 1835. Clearly modeled on the formula established by earlier European architects and seen in Haviland's portrait from some ten years earlier, it was also painted by the same artist, John Neagle. The architects share a similar pose and are each positioned with an important career-making, competition-winning building design in the background. Haviland and Walter are both shown with the essential tools of their trades, books and drawing instruments: one the device of inquiry and inspiration for the designer, the other the means by which to record and communicate designs. From Strickland and Haviland then, and in the context of the Franklin Institute, Walter was introduced to the idea of the architect as a professional who was distinguished from builders by specific training, specialized education and the practice of an intellectual profession, manifest in the growing importance of books.

On a foundation comprising the interrelated ideas of professionalism, faith, improvement and history Walter launched his architectural career in the late 1820s. Among the dozens of commissions for houses, churches, commercial and institutional buildings that poured into his office during the 1830s, winning entries for two competitions were especially important in establishing his career. His designs for a castellated Philadelphia County Prison (1831) and a "Grecian" Girard College for Orphans (1833) catapulted him into immediate national recognition. His increasing success as an architect (by the end of the decade almost 150 projects passed through his office) and his recognition as a man of learning was honored by his election to the Franklin Institute in 1829, the Academy of Natural Sciences in 1835, and the American Philosophical Society in 1839, all by the age of thirty-five. A home-grown success story, Walter was a natural choice to replace Strickland as Professor of Architecture at the Franklin Institute. After declining several invitations starting in 1836 due to the demands of foreign travel (conducted at the behest of Girard College) and his increasingly busy office, in 1840 Walter finally began to work on a series of essays. These would be the basis for the lectures that Walter presented before a number of audiences in Philadelphia and Washington.

Thomas Ustick Walter. Girard College, Philadelphia. Lutz Collection, The Athenæum of Philadelphia.

On a weekly basis starting in late 1840 Walter presented lectures that he described as "popular," embracing architecture's history, analyzing its principles, and considering its rank as a fine art. At the Franklin Institute Walter spoke to a mixed audience of architectural students and nonprofessionals with an interest in architecture. All of them were welcomed by the Institute's Board members who were dedicated to offering "scientific" lectures to an improvement-focused public, and who were well aware of the lecture series' potential financial advantages.[13] With his conviction that public appreciation of architecture could assist social improvement, Walter was eager to address a varied audience, and remained so through his career. Twenty years after first writing his lectures, Walter still believed in their value to the public, and encouraged thirty-three-year-old Richard Morris Hunt, with whom he had established a mentoring relationship, to deliver similar lectures in New York. Walter believed that architectural lectures presented to non-professional audiences were worthwhile because such presentations

> seem to have been well received, and to have produced as good an effect as I could have anticipated. I don't think we talk enough to the people about our Profession. . . . The influence of the Inst.

---

[13] Sinclair, 109.

[American Institute of Architects] has been felt for good in every part of the country, but we want more familiar talking to the people.[14]

Walter also anticipated professional benefits of enlightening those who exerted a certain control over architects. He considered all Americans as potential patrons, if not through the financial support of their own projects, then in their capacity to hold accountable the government that commissioned buildings in their names and the architects that served them.

To engage his diverse audience Walter illustrated his Lectures with large water color renderings (see Appendix B) in the tradition of John Soane's Royal Academy lectures. Walter tried to avoid "technicalities" and architectural "science" that would be appropriate to professionals alone.[15] Excluding professional jargon and practical minutiae, Walter ornamented his essays with appealing excerpts from modern poetry, ancient texts and the Bible. Foremost, Walter chose historical narrative as the framework through which to communicate his comprehensive view of architecture, including its relevance to contemporary taste and morals, and his hopes for its future as a profession.

Walter's choice to deliver his lectures in the form of history is worthy of note. There was no such directive from his client; the Board of the Franklin Institute left the architect to his own devices to develop the themes and content of a lecture series that would address architecture in whatever way he saw fit. Walter had established a habit of writing on architecture (Appendix D), publishing anonymous notes about his own buildings in newspapers as well as dabbling in diverse architectural topics in articles for the *Journal of the Franklin Institute*. These considered a variety of subjects, including color science, penitentiary design, the history of glass, the Orders and contemporary urban planning, which he termed "street architecture." Walter considered these focused issues the domain of "scientific" readers, professionals, members of the Institute and readers of the *Journal*. For his public lectures he chose to address that aspect of architecture most valuable to a broad audience, including both architects and nonprofessionals alike. In writing a history he also chose a popular literary genre that would appeal to a broad audience. In their geographical and chronological sweep, contemporary commentary, and theoretical insight, the lectures eclipsed any earlier American work on architecture.

---

[14] Walter to Richard Morris Hunt, 16 July 1860, Letterbooks, PAT.
[15] Ideally, students and young practitioners would follow Walter's own example by learning the pragmatic details of the profession through office experience. Walter to Rev. E. L. Magoon, 16 September 1853, Letterbooks, PAT.

Each of the first five lectures relates the story of architectural development in a specific chronological era. The general categories are predictable: the Ancient, Greek, Roman, Medieval and Modern Periods are each treated in turn, explaining the correspondence of famous building projects to political events, matters of culture and climate, and historical figures. On the architecture of antiquity, Lecture I is perhaps the most surprising in its breadth. With an expected emphasis on Egypt, the lecture balances a reasonable coverage of the architecture of the ancient Near East and ancient Americas and takes account of the architecture of the ancient Chinese, Hindus, Persians, Israelites, and Phoenicians. The inclusion of these, and Walter's handling of them, is significant. This comprehensiveness reflects the widening studies in these areas during Walter's life time, even if he would admit to a friend that the lecture included "everything we don't know much about."[16] Greece, the topic of Lecture II, is illustrated by the monuments of Athens delineated in *The Antiquities of Athens* by James Stuart and Nicholas Revett and treated with the kind of admiration that was common in the first decades of the nineteenth century. To this familiar handling Walter adds an uncommon critique explaining the reasons for Greece's preeminence in architecture, constituting part of his contribution to architectural theory. In Lecture III the Romans are admonished for their extravagant architectural practices and their "corruption" of the pure Greek system. The changing opinions about medieval architecture are evident in Lecture IV with Walter's inclusion of Islamic architecture, although his treatment of medieval architecture in Western Europe constitutes the greater part of the lecture. Walter's definition of the Modern period, which is the focus of the final historical essay, Lecture V, begins in the Renaissance and continues in his present day. Indeed, it features his own buildings as examples of contemporary applications of historical principles. Although the other lectures also include references to recent buildings, Lecture V focuses on this material, discussing examples from cities in Europe and the United States, including thirty-five recent examples standing in New York, Philadelphia, Washington, and other American cities.

Walter's writings balance an effort to be inclusive and expansive, yet at the same time were immediately relevant to his audience. He was careful to ground his lectures with local illustrations of styles and principles of far-away buildings, several times editing the American examples to be more recognizable to audiences in his different lecturing venues. He continually updated the lectures, revising them several times between the dates of their binding in late 1841 and their later revisions in 1853, and perhaps after that as well. The many additions, deletions, and even the odd newspaper clipping folded into their pages reveal how Walter stayed abreast of new discoveries

[16] Walter to Rev. E. L. Magoon, 16 Sept 58, Letterbooks, PAT.

across the twenty years during which he developed the lectures.

Walter's interest in history ran deeper than a curiosity about the formal precedents which he used in his architectural design, or an acknowledgment of its popularity as a literary genre. He held an abiding interest in the subject as an indicator of cultivation and civilization; historical knowledge was a potential agent of improvement. Such an attitude is legible in the judgments recorded in the lectures themselves, and also in a family history that he composed late in life. The "Prefatory Remarks" to this genealogy reveal Walter's belief that history offered not only remnants of bygone eras to be enjoyed through their literary, political, or built remains, but riches for the modern, enlightened man. Believing that "It is only savages who disregard the past," Walter judged an awareness of history as an important characteristic of civilization itself, which could not progress without the acknowledgement of, and building upon, the work of prior generations. One passage of this document reveals with particular clarity Walter's searching, almost yearning, attitude towards history:

> The tendencies of civilization naturally incite in us a desire to know all that may be known of... history, as far, at least, as it concerns our own relations to the past. We instinctively seek to learn who were our progenitors, and what influences they exerted on the times in which they lived. We realize that they are connected with the fact of our own being; hence we have pleasure in perpetuating their memories; and we are incited by kindred impulses to transmit to posterity the records of our own existence.[17]

Walter esteemed history for the means by which he thought knowledge of it could shape the present and aid in the future progress of civilization worldwide. As a consequence of social refinement, history must be of interest to civilized people; certainly it would be a concern of those who believed in improvement. Walter deemed the recent increase in publishing, especially those books on historical subjects which were largely popular, as indicators of the civilized progress in his own age and country. He reveled in the fact that such a body of information was available for his use in Philadelphia, considering it a triumph of the modern period in which he lived.

A scholarly accomplishment, the range and character of the lectures are indebted to an extensive reading program which Walter began in his earliest days as an architecture student and was likely influenced by his mentors Strickland and Haviland, both of them authors and book collectors. The importance of books in Walter's architectural studies is revealed particularly well in two small notebooks that date to the early 1830s. In

---

[17] Walter, "Genealogical Sketches," PAT.

them Walter assembled sections from various sources, from engineering manuals to Renaissance treatises. Through the following decade he had not only found his way into the most extensive architectural libraries of his day, including the legendary one amassed by his colleague Ithiel Town, but, as recorded in diary entries and book sellers' receipts, was well on the way to amassing his own large collection which would number upwards of one thousand by mid-century.

The extent to which Walter indulged in book buying and reading is evident also in the numerous titles recorded within the text and marginalia of the lectures. Within the six lectures he refers to over seventy specific titles and writers, several of which are collections of multiple writers and essays, poems, historical figures and characters (see Appendix A). Walter's reading was extensive both chronologically and geographically, as demonstrated through his citations. The fifth-century Greek Herodotus, credited with inventing the discipline of history writing, appears in the same lecture as John Lloyd Stephens, whose pioneering excavations in Central America were chronicled in bestsellers published contemporaneously with Walter's

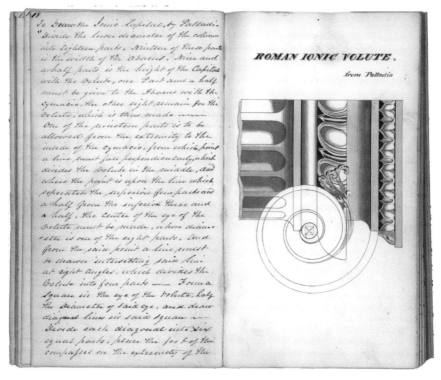

Thomas U. Walter. Architectural notebook illustrating "Roman Ionic Volute from Palladio,"
ca. 1831. The Athenæum of Philadelphia.

writing of the lectures. Walter benefited from the diversity of the available literature which familiarized him with such diverse locales as the well-known monuments of Athens, Rome, Paris and London, to the lesser-known, and more recently-explored, Elephanta, Copan, Nineveh, and Nankin.

The availability, and Walter's use, of this material made his lectures the most inclusive architectural history written by an American to date, even as such publications increased dramatically in number during the 1830s and 1840s. As an evaluation of architectural development from antiquity to the present, Walter's lectures reflect an expanding awareness of global cultures which also fueled his profession's captivation with historical architectural forms.

Walter's inclusiveness departed markedly from those few Americans who had earlier lectured or published on architecture. Those rare earlier works which took account of historical references did so in a cursory manner, either preceding or amending the real business of the book: setting forth directions for delineating tasteful architectural designs and patterns. Compared with Walter's study, their content is slight, usually confined to the classical tradition, sometimes skimming Egypt and the Middle Ages as footnotes, largely ignoring all other cultures.

For example, the Connecticut-born Asher Benjamin was not only America's first published author on architecture, but one of the most prolific, assembling a list of seven titles which were published as a total of forty-seven editions. The content of his books reflects the changing relevance of history as a matter of architectural knowledge through the first half of the nineteenth century. His first book, *The Country Builder's Assistant* (1797), is a series of drawing lessons which increase in complexity through the sections of the book. They have no preamble of any sort, historical or otherwise. By 1814 Benjamin felt compelled to include some historical commentary in *The Rudiments of Architecture*, which provides a short comparative consideration of Greek and Roman approaches to the design of details and a tale of the origins of buildings which draws from Vitruvius and the Bible. Yet this commentary is not integral to the matter of the book, which is again focused on practical geometry, definitions and drawing lessons. With the passage of three decades Benjamin became more responsive toward the growing importance of historical awareness in architectural practice, including in The Elements of Architecture (1843) a "cursory view of the ancient architecture of Egypt, Greece, and Rome."[18] Benjamin's capsule is more a descriptive chronology than a history. Egyptian temples are noted for their "colossal dimensions, solidity of construction, boldness and originality of design" whose designer-priests "employed architectural grandeur, with all

---

[18] Asher Benjamin, The Elements of Architecture, 1843 (New York: Da Capo Press, 1974), 147.

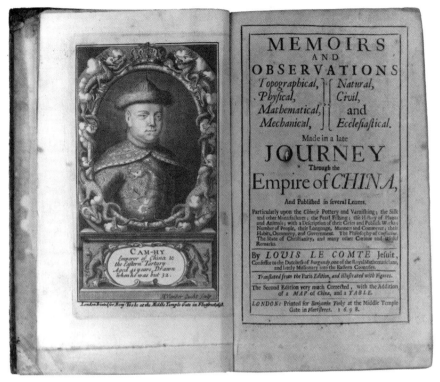

Louis-Daniel Le Comte, Journey through the Empire of China *(London: 1697).*
Courtesy, the Winterthur Library: Printed Book and Periodical Collection.

its accessories, to influence the minds of the people; although he recognizes that Roman amphitheatres prompted "sublime sensations," Benjamin does not linger on such theoretical notions, and hurries to a description of the building form and the numbers of spectators who were comfortably seated within it.[19] Although bending to the growing interest and expectations of historical knowledge, Benjamin seems most comfortable with the pragmatic leanings that characterized his earliest books. Indeed, he concludes his historical survey with five pages of dates and building data in a fixed chart: architectural history in a tabulated form.

Foremost among early writers who approached architectural history from a more critical point of view than Benjamin's is the English-born and German-educated Latrobe, who presented an *Anniversary Oration* before the Society of Artists of the United States in 1810. Not a historical account of architecture, Latrobe's comments used history as part of an apologia for the enjoyment of art and architecture in America, stressing their

---

[19] Benjamin, *Elements of Architecture*, 148, 179.

compatibility with democracies—a concept which was doubted by many who saw the arts as the luxurious indulgences of aristocrats. Citing the example of ancient Greece, Latrobe argued that art strengthened national morals and was indicative of liberty rather than a threat to it. The key to the accomplishments of Greek art was that it was made when Greece was free. Like other apologists, Latrobe focused on the social connection of the arts and the encouragement of public and government patronage, with which he predicted that "the days of Greece may be revived in the woods of America, and Philadelphia become the Athens of the Western world."[20] Rather than contributing to the collapse of the American democratic experiment, Latrobe promised that the arts would embellish domestic happiness, charm leisure, grace generosity, and honor patriotism.

Latrobe's handling of history was certainly among the more profound in early American architectural writings, but made no claims to be an inclusive history. One of the earliest writers to attempt such a task was Latrobe's pupil (and Walter's teacher), William Strickland, who presented a series of eight lectures in late 1824 and early 1825 before the Franklin Institute.[21] Strickland devoted the greater portion of his talks to the subject of Greek architecture, which he acknowledged as the reigning high style, its symbolism appropriate to America's youthful democracy. Assuming that this knowledge was shared by his audience, Strickland's lectures were rife with formal details that would have been of use to the aspiring architect, discerning builder, or connoisseur. The theoretical content of the addresses was sparse and derivative of European sources; his history, beyond the Greek installment, thin. Strickland ran through a breezy architectural account of eastern lands, in fewer than a dozen pages dispensing with India, Persia, and Egypt. Outside of a brief discussion of the "corrupted taste" of the Saxons and Normans and remarks on just two monumental buildings in Philadelphia (Latrobe's Bank of Pennsylvania and his own Second Bank of the United States), the remainder of his series would focus on the Classical tradition. The main thrust was on the Classical Orders, each of which was the focus of a separate lecture considering its derivation, history, and articulation as described by Palladio, Scamozzi, Wren, Chambers, and other canonical treatise-writers. Strickland's brief digressions considered Egyptian influence in Greek columnar architecture and Roman "corruptions" of the pure Greek system. His history was a setting for the further exaltation of Greek architecture, promoting the inherited, codified theory of taste, without critiquing its relevance or applicability: it was an

---

[20] Benjamin Henry Latrobe, *Anniversary Oration, Pronounced before the Society of Artists of the United States* (Philadelphia: 1811), 17.

[21] A partial record of Strickland's lectures was created by Reuben Haines III, who copied detailed text and careful drawings from Strickland's manuscript. See Reuben Haines III, "Notes on William Strickland's Architectural Lectures at the Franklin Institute, 1824-25." Wyck Papers, APS.

aesthetic fact, analyzed by Strickland only in terms of its proportioning systems.

Walter's other teacher, John Haviland, also focused on transmitting methods to correctly draw and detail the orders in his *Practical Builders' Assistant* (1818). His history lesson extends as far as relating the derivation of the Orders as recorded by Vitruvius, establishing the idea of proportional relationships and the primacy of Greek art. While paying some attention to Roman designs, he, like Strickland, focused on Greek remains as the best "models of imitation and confessed standards of excellence."[22] Thus they are the pedagogical centerpiece in Haviland's book, the majority of which comprises scores of specialized vocabulary definitions and clear instructions to correctly and precisely draw the orders.

A close contemporary of Walter's, Minard Lafever (1798-1854), wrote a series of popular books on architecture starting in the 1830s, in which the relevance of history became more apparent with subsequent editions. Years after its original publication in 1835, Lafever admitted in a later edition of *The Beauties of Modern Architecture* that he first deemed them "unimportant," but that a "more mature consideration" prompted his belief that "historical matters" could be useful to a builder by "giving him more magnified and pleasing ideas of his profession, as well as to discover that architecture is more than a mere mechanical art or profession."[23] Although Lafever made strides in offering a history that was broader and more inclusive than that of his predecessors, it offered no new insights or interpretations; it was also highly redundant across his several publications, and borrowed heavily — often employing lengthy verbatim extracts — from other sources, especially Elmes' 1821 *Lectures on Architecture*.

Walter had as little patience for authors who copied from other books as he did with architects who slavishly imitated historical precedents. It was probably *The Beauties of Modern Architecture* that prompted Walter to record his disappointment in a diary entry, complaining

> Don't like bookmaking while we have so many more good books than we read — don't think I'll ever make a book, was I ever to attempt it I might give every man an opportunity of buying for a few dollars, all the brains I've got — told Mr. Lafever so, he says he must 'go ahead.'[24]

While Walter disparaged the practice of equipping nonprofessionals

[22] John Haviland, *The Practical Builders' Assistant*, 3 vols., 1818-21 (Baltimore: Fielding Luca, 1830), 1:4.
[23] Minard Lafever, *The Beauties of Modern Architecture*, 1835 (New York Da Capo Press, 1968), 65.
[24] Walter, Diary, 16 January 1835, PAT.

with patterns and designs that were the product of the architect's mind — especially when they were the product of other architects' minds — his own desire to publish his lectures reveal that he thought he had produced something novel, original, and worthy of public attention.[25]

However, the distinction of publishing the first pure stand-alone architectural history in America belongs to Louisa Tuthill, whose *A History of Architecture from the Earliest Times* appeared in 1848, seven years after Walter bound and dated his lectures.[26] The book has a number of similarities with Walter's lectures, including the scope, ordering, organization, building examples discussed, and even some poetic excerpts and specific literary sources. Part of this resemblance can be explained by the fact that even while the numbers of architectural publications were on the rise, there still existed a certain set of books considered foundational studies. More than their familiarity with the increasingly established canon of architectural studies, both Walter and Tuthill depended on the resources available in Ithiel Town's library. It is clear from the three illustrations of Walter buildings in Tuthill's book (Girard College is its frontispiece) that Tuthill was an admirer of Walter's works. This raises an enticing notion that the two perhaps met and discussed the matters face to face, which would offer the soundest reason for the resemblances. While Tuthill's accomplishment, aimed at a popular audience,[27] should not be diminished, Walter's lectures offer a similarly ennobling view of architecture from the point of view of one of the country's most respected practitioners in essays that are distinguished by their professional aims and theoretical content.

Walter's historical study focuses on the cultural characteristics associated with the buildings that he selected for critical scrutiny. Part of his aim in writing and presenting the lectures was to encourage his audience to enjoy an opportunity to learn for the sake of intellectual exercise: to absorb history's lessons as a means toward improvement and as evidence of their own progress. Such could be accomplished with the application of architectural knowledge in a very specific way. While judging their merits as aesthetic objects, Walter embellished his descriptions of select buildings with narrative accounts of specific events, activating the monuments with the memory and associated values of people who once populated them. Thus, in what Walter called his "metaphysical" approach to architecture, taste did not turn solely on aesthetic matters, but rather on the values and

---

[25] Walter to A. Harthill, 24 Jan. 1860, Letterbooks, PAT.

[26] Tuthill's work began as early as the commencement of Walter's lecturing. See Sarah Allaback, "Louisa Tuthill, Ithiel Town, and the Beginnings of Architectural History Writing in America" in *American Architects and their Books to 1848*, ed. Kenneth Hafertepe and James F. O'Gorman (Amherst: University of Massachusetts Press, 2001), 199.

[27] In its introduction Tuthill expresses her hope that the book will become "an acceptable addition to every family library." Tuthill, ix.

Thomas Ustick Walter, Matthew Newkirk Mansion. Louis C. Tuthill, History of Architecture, from the Earliest Times; its Present Condition in Europe and the United States (Philadelphia, 1848). The Athenæum of Philadelphia.

ideals of patrons, designers and builders.

Such theoretical content is implicit through the first five lectures, but comes to a greatest clarification in the final one, "Architecture Considered as a Fine Art." That memories and sentiments could be associated with architectural forms had been forwarded as the theory of associationism in Archibald Alison's Essay on the Nature and Principles of Taste, published in 1790.[28] In the first pages of the Essay, Alison explains the workings of associationism:

> When any object, either of sublimity or beauty, is presented to the mind, I believe every man is conscious of a train of thought being immediately awakened in his imagination, analogous to the character or expression of the original object. The simple perception of the object, we frequently find, is insufficient to excite these emotions, unless it is accompanied with this operation of mind, unless, according to common expression, our imagination is seized, and our fancy busied in the pursuit of all those trains of thought, which are allied to this character or expression.[29]

It followed that people with similar "trains of thought" could be prompted to similar "emotions." Associationism offered the possibility that the speaker

[28] Alison's book was excerpted in the Architectural Magazine published by John Claudius Loudon between 1834-39, and to which Walter subscribed and repeatedly refers in the course of his architectural writings.

[29] Archibald Alison, Essays on the Nature and Principles of Taste (Edinburgh: Bell and Bradfute, 1790), 2,126.

and his audience might share a common understanding of architectural expressions. More importantly, associationism opened the possibility that the architect and his public could communicate through built form that triggered shared memories.

Selecting the appropriate formal cues was the modern architect's challenge; this discernment defined the increasingly cerebral work expected of the new professional. At the apex of cultural progression to date, the nineteenth-century architect saw himself with greater opportunities and challenges due to his historical awareness which had opened the whole range of architectural options to him; the greater number of options demanded greater discretion. Even the generations just previous to Walter and his teachers were constrained by the expense and difficulty of travel and availability of published subjects. The view of his forebears was thus largely circumscribed by the particular region and era in which they lived. The increased availability of books led to an explosion of stylistic variety in the early nineteenth century and offered new options to the modern architect who could pick and choose among "styles" which allowed him a method of communication through architecture. Such a notion was prominent in the buildings that rose in Philadelphia during Walter's youth, including Greek banks designed to suggest the ancient roots of the new republic that oversaw the federal banking system until the 1840s and Gothic churches meant to remind modern American citizens of the religious fervor of the Middle Ages.

Because a building could trigger mental associations, for Walter the act of design was as intellectual a pursuit as writing a book. Both were conditioned by the ability of an established language to communicate ideas. Historical precedents offered Walter a means by which he could suggest ideas to those who could be stocked with certain vignettes, values, and historical insights. He believed that a person who was open to such recollections would find that "his thoughts have been ennobled and enlarged by association with magnificent scenery, or that they have become degraded and contracted by association with mean and inharmonious objects."[30] Obviously Walter's aim was for the former, and he steered the course of the lectures to equip his audience with the tools that would allow them to seek and benefit from aesthetically pleasing environments.

Alison had underscored the necessity of education and experience for one to understand and appreciate architecture fully. He believed that while every person has some response to formal objects, it was a learned elite, stratified according to the level of their experience, who could best comprehend, and thus fully enjoy, architectural design.[31] Such was reflected in a publication to which Walter subscribed, the *Architectural*

---

[30] Walter, Lecture VI: 4.
[31] Alison describes the increasing levels of understanding historical precedents in the peasant, man of letters, connoisseur, and architect. Alison, 25, 369.

Magazine, whose editor, John Claudius Loudon, pronounced that superior enjoyment would be experienced by a person "who had treasured up many [sentiments] in his memory."[32] The very first words that Walter spoke to his audience address the cerebral focus required to fully comprehend the building art:

> Architecture is an art that must be understood to be enjoyed. The pleasures arising from a just perception of its beauties, can only be experienced by those who have obtained some knowledge of its principles, and its historical associations. An architectural object may, it is true, affect to a limited extent, almost every observer; but the refining and ennobling influences to which its peculiar imagery is addressed, are realized by those only who have cultivated a taste for its enjoyment.[33]

Walter departed from Alison's hierarchy in his belief that all Americans could achieve a "cultivated taste" since, according to his own experience, freedom of opportunity and education were equally available to all. Whereas Alison's taste was the privilege of the upper echelons of society, through popular education Walter meant to democratize taste, making it available to a greater number of Americans through public education, which he stove to provide in his lectures, and which he encouraged educators to adopt in the relatively new system of public education.[34]

Walter recognized the usefulness of associationism as a tool for architectural critique. As a method of connoisseurship it could be taught, and thus it appealed to his egalitarian efforts to raise the level of architectural appreciation among all Americans. When he argued that architecture was an art that must be "understood to be enjoyed," Walter had some notion of the principles of art in mind, and such concepts as unity, variety, and intricacy are discussed in Lecture VI, "On Architecture Considered as a Fine Art." But historical associations were potentially a more effective means by which to help his audience "understand" architecture, and thus they appear in each of the first five lectures. Because associationism was a direct link between physical objects and mental reflections, comprehending historical triggers could potentially lead to improvement. Walter believed that the intellectual exercise of recalling past memories and lessons

---

[32] John Claudius Loudon, "Architecture Considered as an Art of Imagination," *Architectural Magazine* 1, no. 4 (June 1834), 146.
[33] Walter, Lecture 1:1+.
[34] A remarkable proposal, considering that the first public high school had been open in Philadelphia only since 1838.

associated with good architecture would "excite in the mind agreeable emotions of taste, and thus afford a source of intellectual enjoyment."[35] Thus, in addition to providing shelter, well-designed buildings would ultimately and ideally contribute to the sense of civic improvement.

Walter's lectures sought to stock the collective mind of the audience with particular scenes for their recall. One of his more creative applications of associationism appears in Lecture II. Promoting his favored mode, Grecian architecture, Walter describes a scene in which "the traveler of the present day" walks among monuments raised by Phidias, Ictinus and Callicrates. Walter's narrative goes far beyond approval of general Greek aesthetics, or even popular claims that the style expresses the ideals of republican democracy.

> At every step some rich developments of transcendent genius meets [the traveler's] eye, and carries him far back into the distant past. — Here Eschylus strung the tragic lyre, — here Socrates and Plato reasoned on the immortality of the soul, — here Demosthenes poured forth the thunders of his eloquence against the Macedonian king; — here too, the great apostle of the gentiles proclaimed the sublime mysteries of Redemption.[36]

Walter selected each of the figures in this brief account for his specific relevance to the audience. Aeschylus, the fifth-century Greek dramatist, wrote the earliest surviving Greek tragedies, which express high religious and civic purposes. The fourth-century Demosthenes was the greatest orator of ancient Athens, and a stubborn foe of the Macedonian expansion that threatened Greek freedom. In addition to these lines first written for an audience in Philadelphia, a city with an inarguable significance to the story of America's independence, Walter's portrayal of Plato and Aristotle is also revealing. Of the innumerable subjects recorded in the philosophy of these two sages, Walter chose one which could direct their interests, and by extension the learning of the Greeks, into a confluence with a central concern of modern Christian thought: the immortality of the soul. To further underscore the Christian relevance of Greek architecture, Walter reminded his audience that some of the greatest sermons in the New Testament were sounded in Athens during the Apostle Paul's missionary journeys through Greece in the first century. In this Greek vignette Walter located suitable direction for the most important signposts of his life: philosophy, democracy, and Christianity, all three of which he hoped

---

[35] Walter, Lecture I: 3+.
[36] Walter, Lecture II: 4+.

would blossom in Philadelphia, which Latrobe had suggested could be the "Athens of the Western world."[37]
While the superiority of Greek architecture was based on historical, philosophical, and perhaps even religious associations, it was also preeminent for its purely formal qualities. Walter concentrated his discussion of architectural principles and aesthetic standards in the final discourse. Lecture VI departs from the historical commentary of the first five lectures in its thematic approach. Alternately entitled "Architecture Considered as a Fine Art" and "Philosophy of Architecture," it expresses Walter's approach to abstract aesthetic principles which he clearly enjoyed pondering; in a letter to a friend he described this lecture as "the best, because it is the most intellectual."[38]

In Lecture VI Walter draws from a number of traditions of aesthetic theory to explain both the "sources" and "effects" of architectural beauty, the most appropriate member of the Vitruvian triad of durability, utility and beauty for his audience to study. Walter reasoned that the other two "entirely practical" matters, structural soundness and functional convenience, should be of no concern to the public as long as they had been of sufficient concern to the architect. (Also, these "technical" interests were perhaps best left for the future architects to glean from practical experience in a professional office.)

Walter explained that the sources of beauty arose from a number of principles, among which rank the "unity of the whole" and a "contiguity of the parts" which are best suited to communicate one single clear idea to the mind. At the same time, he notes that a preoccupation with these principles, and their related concepts of symmetry, uniformity, and regularity, might lead to dull, monotonous designs. Without using the word, Walter was describing aspects of picturesque theory as espoused in Uvedale Price's *Essay on the Picturesque, as Compared with the Sublime and Beautiful* (1794). In contrast to the regularity of the beautiful, whose principles communicated a clear, single sensation to the mind, the picturesque embraced sudden variation, roughness, intricacy, and variety, vehicles to "excite and nourish curiosity."[39] Such activation of the spectator's mind was essential, as Walter strove to trigger mental associations. He spoke of the "pleasing impressions" prompted by intricacy and harmony, and their ability to "impel the spectator to think."[40] An adequately intricate building could engage a person for a length of time to reflect on the overall beauty of a building, allowing the time necessary to process associations. The architect's challenge was to handle all aesthetic principles in such a way as to compose buildings which

---

[37] Latrobe, *Anniversary Oration*, 17.
[38] Walter to Rev. E. L. Magoon, 16 September 1853, Letterbooks, PAT.
[39] Uvedale Price, *An Essay on the Picturesque, as Compared with the Sublime and Beautiful* (London, 1794), 69-70.
[40] Walter, Lecture VI: 17.

THE

ARCHITECTURAL MAGAZINE,

AND

JOURNAL

OF IMPROVEMENT IN

ARCHITECTURE, BUILDING, AND FURNISHING,

AND IN THE VARIOUS ARTS AND TRADES
CONNECTED THEREWITH.

CONDUCTED BY J. C. LOUDON, F.L.S. G.S. &c.

AUTHOR OF THE ENCYCLOPÆDIA OF COTTAGE, FARM, AND VILLA ARCHITECTURE
AND FURNITURE.

VOL. I.

LONDON:

LONGMAN, REES, ORME, BROWN, GREEN, & LONGMAN,

PATERNOSTER-ROW.

1834.

John Claudius Loudon, ed. The Architectural Magazine, *vol. I (1834).*
The Athenæum of Philadelphia.

were beautiful, for beauty was the means to the highest goal to which an architect might aspire. At this point Walter's theory turned to theology.

The final outcome of the aesthetic experience was determined not only by the quality of the design and the architect's intent. The viewer's preparedness would determine to what extent the experience was visual, historical, and spiritual. Beauty could communicate a unified, clear idea that would color the thoughts of those people who could contemplate it properly. Such a cultivated audience would "find that their ideas become purified, raised or expanded, according as they are surrounded with that which is beautiful." Their very souls had the chance of being similarly cleansed. As a person's thoughts attained "a pure and lofty tone," he would find his thoughts turning to that which is most pure, as Walter wrote, toward "the wisdom and power of GOD."[41]

By this connection Walter perceived the means by which beauty could trigger an intellectual response to aesthetic delight in the mind, but also actually touch the very soul and lead to moral improvement. Thus Walter discovered a means by which he could fulfill his Christian calling through architectural design. His thinking was founded on the Enlightenment ideal of the mind as the essential part of man which perceives and absorbs data from the external world. He elaborated on the dualism of philosophers like René Descartes, who distinguished the immaterial mind (also referred to as the *consciousness* or *spirit*) as distinct from the material body, the two together comprising the essence of humanity. Walter came to terms with a particular relationship between soul and mind within the body that links Enlightenment thought with his own Christian beliefs. Walter believed in a trichotomist view that dates to the early church, and was becoming increasingly important in the work of nineteenth-century English and German theologians whose work was read by conservative Protestants.[42] This view posited that man comprised three elements: mind, body, and soul. While men, plants and animals all have physical natures, or bodies, man is distinguished by possessing a psychological element, the basis of reason and emotion. Animals are thought to have a version of this element, although their rudimentary mind is better described as an instinctual nature. Man is further characterized by the third element in the trichotomist constitution: the soul, a religious element that facilitates man's perception of and response to spiritual matters, which actually resides in the mind. Each of these three elements is necessary to explain how Walter believed

---

[41] Walter, Lecture VI: 4-5.
[42] I am indebted to my colleague at Judson College, Dr. Brad Seeman, for guidance in locating sources on this subject. See Millard J. Erickson, *Christian Theology* (Grand Rapids, MI: 1985). See also John Beloff, *The Existence of Mind* (New York: Citadel Press, 1964), 22.

that physical objects could matter to man's spiritual essence. They were seen by him as nested shells, the innermost of which was the spiritual and eternal; the external was mortal and sensory; the middle the intermediary. The external shell, the mortal body, provided the sense organs — especially those of sight —which are fundamental for the gathering of information from the outside world. It encapsulates the mind, and passes sensory information to it. Walter's awareness of this connection prompted him to write a letter encouraging the faculty at the Baptist-founded Lewisburg College to complete their building: "I hope you will one day be able to fresco your entire building; its influence on the tastes of the students would be good;—colleges are too often neglected in everything that pertains to the eye, while that is quite as important an avenue to the mind as the ear."[43] The mind, itself not subject to time and thus eternal like its tenant, the soul, translates this information into abstract ideas which have a direct effect on the soul. Walter trusted that the stock of the mind—ideas—"may therefore be called the atmosphere, as well as the food of the soul, upon the quality and purity of which, depend its healthfulness and vigour."[44] Lodged within the undying mind and a mortal body, the soul was thus subject to the condition of its surroundings during an earthly life, which in turn was shaped by the aesthetic quality of objects like buildings.

This association between body, mind, and soul was the ultimate reason why architecture was of such solemn consequence. Ill-formed buildings would have a negative impact on the soul by filling the mind with ugly ideas, and, taking Walter's theory to the extreme, potentially contributing to the loss of eternal salvation. Walter explained that beautiful buildings, on the other hand, could

> excite in us the purest sentiments of infinity; by which our minds are realized to the contemplation of "beauties of eternal duration." The soul here takes an upward flight; it soars from the visible to the invisible, and finds itself in the unbounded fields of intellectual enjoyment; — it looks through nature up to nature's GOD."[45]

In Walter's estimation the architect held a grave responsibility in the exercise of his duties, more important than devising functional plans and sturdy structures, or serving the general calls for societal improvement. Architecture could directly influence the eternal status of a person who chose to surround himself with demeaning or dignified objects, including buildings.

[43] Walter to Rev. A. K. Bell, 17 January 1857, Letterbooks, PAT.
[44] Walter, Lecture VI: 6. Walter discovered this particular notion in J. Dowson, "Essay on the Metaphysics of Architecture," *Architectural Magazine* 2, no. 15 (May 1835), 245-49.
[45] Walter, Lecture VI: 27.

The confluence of aesthetic speculation, Christian theology, and trichotomist philosophy in Walter's thinking make his lectures the first formal architectural theory written by an American. They are a distinct accomplishment when judged against the content of his few contemporaries who also wrote on architecture and largely focused on pragmatic issues of drawing the orders and building methods, as noted earlier. These early works are not devoid of opportunities for theorizing, but rather transmit accepted notions without any critical examination. In 1830, Benjamin suggested the application of sublime theory in *The Practical House Carpenter*, explaining that churches could "produce in the beholder serious and devotional feelings" through the use of "large, bold angular outlines... and [by] giving all the decorations, either of mouldings or sculpture, a large and grave appearance, excluding all ornaments composed of slender, curved, or winding outlines, which are expressive of lightness and gaiety."[46] Yet this builders' guide explains neither the mental nor emotional workings by which such forms will prompt the intended response. Nor does Benjamin, or any other American architect, justify aesthetic preferences. The superiority of Greece is a common topic, yet commonly taken for granted. Strickland would go no further than to admit the canonical Athenian monuments were the models "educated men have in all ages agreed to admire."[47] Even those books which claim to distinguish themselves by a new context avoid theoretical critique. Had Lafever addressed the modernity of the works in his 1835 title *The Beauties of Modern Architecture* he would have offered a rare glimpse of the means by which a prominent architect understood his contemporary role while practicing in traditional architectural styles.

One American author who, like Walter, took a philosophical approach to architecture was Andrew Jackson Downing, whose *Treatise on the Theory and Practice of Landscape Gardening, adapted to North America... with Remarks on Rural Architecture* (1841) remained in Walter's library until his death. Published at the same time that Walter began lecturing, Downing's book included discussions of associationism and the application of a variety of historical styles. With Downing, Walter found a rare fellow laborer interested in producing the "treasures of the mind" while their peers largely fulfilled Tocqueville's predictions.

While Downing has enjoyed a deservedly central position in studies of American architecture, the richness of Walter's theory has been lost until recently. The ephemeral format of his lectures prohibited them from having the broad and lasting impact that Downing's several publications did (the *Treatise on the Theory and Practice of Landscape Gardening* alone remained in print until 1921 when its 10th edition was published).

The subtleties that blend Walter's religious beliefs and professional

---

[46] Asher Benjamin, *Practical House Carpenter* (Boston: for the author, 1830), 95-96.
[47] Haines, "William Strickland's Architectural Lectures," APS.

agenda are clearest in the lectures, and it is here that he best expressed the means by which architectural designs could capture a viewer's eye and engender thoughts which would turn the heart toward God, ultimately making a positive impact on society as tools of evangelism. While this function occurred most importantly on an exclusive basis, bringing the individual soul closer to God and salvation, when multiplied across an entire population the theory had the potential to impact the entire city, county, state, or country for the better. This was not just the hyperbole of an eager practitioner, but explains how the practice of architecture was an evangelistic exercise for this Christian architect.

Walter positioned the architect's work as having the potential to affect the behavior of society as a whole by reflecting, and therefore emphasizing, the noblest of commonly-held values. While focused on enhancing the way his listeners would appreciate architecture, and thus be improved by it, Walter's lectures affirmed professional architects in their essential role as the practitioners with the privilege and responsibility to order the environment. After explaining the workings by which architectural design could have an impact on the soul of man, Walter expressed the gravity of the architect's work:

> If then, such is the influence of external objects upon our intellect, it becomes a matter of great moment, that we should so regulate the order and appearance of things that are within our power, as to cause them to produce a favourable impression upon our minds.[48]

But such control could not be left to the governmental agencies normally considered in charge of "regulating" the public environment. In Lecture V Walter indicated their ineffectualness through citing examples of European town planning where restrictive design legislation met "but seldom with a desirable effect."[49]

The safeguard was instead an educated citizenry of patrons who could demand excellence, endorse skilled architects and abolish incompetent pretenders. Walter expected that the public would be willing partners in this effort, with faith that "The public mind is very susceptible to impressions in regard to beauty in Architecture."[50] Walter endeavored to persuade his audiences that only the properly-trained professional architect could negotiate the multitude of formal possibilities available and make prudent selections in the design process. Their mutual scrutiny would hold design professionals accountable, and make it possible for the professional architect to be recognized for his special talents, education, training and

---

[48] Walter, Lecture VI: 6.
[49] Walter, Lecture V: 51-53.
[50] Walter to Richard Morris Hunt, 23 March 1866, Letterbooks, PAT.

Fig. 1.

Minard Lafever, The Beauties of Modern Architecture, *1835 (New York: 1855),*
The Athenæum of Philadelphia.

contributions to the community.

Walter was certain of his lectures' potential benefit to the profession of architecture. Persistently distracted by financial troubles, he rarely missed an opportunity to collect professional fees. And yet he often lectured without remuneration and planned to publish his lectures with no expectation of financial gain; his incentive was to accomplish what would be "most promotive of the public taste."[51] Walter's role in the founding of his profession was part of a larger construction of professional America, one that promised the improvement of society by providing the nation with experts to address issues within their discrete fields of specialty. In the same period in which he wrote the lectures Walter was working with other architects to found American Institute of Architects (first fruitlessly in 1836, then successfully in 1857). Like his work on behalf of the AIA, the lectures were a consequence of Walter's social context, which inspired his ambition to distinguish the architect as an intellectual, a specialist whose work could elevate society by communicating the noblest values of ancient and modern civilizations through widely understood historical forms. Presented within lectures on the history of the world that themselves were evidence of his own learning, and intimating that the crucial role of architecture in a society must be handled by a competent, well-trained professional, Walter's lectures underscored the intellectual character of the architect in a day when any man armed with a pattern book could identify himself as an architect. The lectures reflected Walter's belief that history was an important means by which the rising professional could distinguish himself as an authority and as a man of letters. This was especially critical during the decades when the profession was being formed, a time that coincided with the continued consolidation of the relatively new nation. Walter wrote the Lectures on Architecture as a means to equip his fellow citizens and their architects to improve America's social environment and the character of its individual citizens as well.

---

[51] Walter to A. Harthill, 24 Jan. 1860, Letterbooks, PAT. In another letter Walter reflected that even though he received no fee for one series of lectures that "the reputation of our profession demands that I should make a good job of it." Walter to Richard Morris Hunt, 12 Jan. 1860, Letterbooks, PAT.

On Ancient Architecture.

Thos. U. Walter
Philad.r Oct. 12. 1841

Delivered Nov. 11. 1841

Interior of the Temple of Apollinopolis at Edfu (Intérieur du Temple d'Apollinopolis à Etfoù).
Dominique Vivant Denon, Voyage Dans Le Basse Et Le Haute Egypte *(Paris, 1802).*
Courtesy, the Winterthur Library: Printed Book and Periodical Collection.

LECTURE I
ON ANCIENT ARCHITECTURE

Introduction to Architecture and the Lectures

[1+] Architecture is an art that must be understood to be enjoyed. The pleasures arising from a just perception of its beauties, can only be experienced by those who have obtained some knowledge of its principles, and its historical associations. An architectural object may, it is true, affect to a limited extent, almost every observer; but the refining and ennobling influences to which its peculiar imagery is addressed, are realized by those only who have cultivated a taste for its enjoyment. Hence, it is of no small importance that an art, so prolific of intellectual pleasures, should be generally understood and appreciated.

An impression that the study of Architecture belongs exclusively to Architects, has, no doubt, done much to retard the progress of the art, and to limit its humanizing and elevating influences on [2+] the public mind. — Such an impression, however, is erroneous. — It is undoubtedly desirable that every one should acquire some knowledge of the elementary principles of Architecture, of its historical associations, and of the general laws that govern it, as a fine art: — such a preparation of mind will enable any one to realize the beautifying effects to which architectural composition may be addressed, while the knowledge necessary to <u>produce</u> such a composition could only have been acquired by years of study.

It is proposed, in the present lectures, to treat the subject in as popular a manner as its technical character will admit. We shall glance cursorily at its history, make a brief examination of its elementary principles, and conclude with a discourse on its Philosophy.

[3+] It should be remarked that Architecture possesses a twofold character. — As far as it relates to our physical comforts it is simply a <u>useful</u>

art; — in this relation it is usually so designated; but in its <u>adornments</u> it is, in an eminent degree, an imaginative art; — in this relation it is called a <u>fine</u> art. As a <u>useful</u> art it employs material forms to throw around us a shelter from the weather, adapted to our physical wants; — as a <u>fine</u> art, it so moulds, embellishes, and disposes those forms, as to produce gracefulness and beauty, exciting in the mind agreeable emotions of taste, and thus affording a source of intellectual enjoyment. Its developments being, generally, of a durable character, it bears a faithful record of ancient times; handing down, from age to age, through the revolutions of a changing world, the spirit of departed [4+] generations. This fact is attested by remnants of the past, speaking from every land where man has made his home.

On the shores of the fertalizing Nile, the father-land of science and the arts, are still to be found stupendous mementoes of a people long since passed away. These splendid productions of Egyptian power and skill, described by Herodotus some three-and-twenty centuries ago, are seen today, triumphing over the desolating powers of time, and standing in solemn grandeur, as witnesses to the truth of what the venerable father of history has told us.

[3] On the plains and promontories of Attica
> Where "many a sculptured pile
> Still o'er the dust of heroes lifts its head"

the lovely remnants of a tasteful people stand in time-worn splendor corroborating Pausanias, the famous historian of Greece.

And Rome — the city of the seven hills — "she who was called eternal," still abounds in monuments of by-gone ages, which serve [4] as guiding stars in penetrating the mist of traditionary fable, popular legend, and doubtful history which surrounds the story of that ancient nation, and which would otherwise have involved it in profound obscurity.

Our subject on the present occasion will be confined to a few remarks on the rise and progress of Architecture; a brief examination of its firm foundations laid by the descendants of Ham on the shores of the prolific Nile; and a glance at the principal styles which were originated anterior to the establishment of the arts in Greece.

The Origins of Architecture

Architecture, considered simply as a useful art, undoubtedly derived its origin from the first wants of our race. — Man could not have existed long without a place for repose, and protection from the weather; his earliest occupation must therefore have been to convert the simple elements of nature around him into a dwelling, the type of which he probably found in the fabrics of the brute creation. But unlike all other beings of earth he possesses a ray of [5+] immortality—a principle which enables him to unite with action the heaven-born power of thought. While the beaver has continued to build his dam, and the bird his nest, as they were built in the beginning of time, the course of man has been onward in improvement, until the primeval cave has been transformed into a temple, the hut into a mansion, and the cabin into a palace.

Architecture of the Ancient Near East

So rapidly did the art of building advance, in the early ages of the world that Cain, its third inhabitant, is said by Moses to have "build a city which he called after his son Enoch." We also read that Tubal-Cain was "an instructor of every artificer in iron and brass" and of Jabel, that he was the father of such as dwelt in tents and have cattle, plainly indicating that this city of Enoch consisted of permanent houses, as they [6+] who followed pastoral occupations had moveable tents for the convenience of attending their flocks.

We can however come to no certain conclusions respecting the Architecture of this long lived race;—none of their works are known to have survived the flood. Lamartine conjectures that some of the massy foundations of the Temples at Balbec are of antedeluvian origin, but there are no grounds for the supposition. The only historian of the race that lived before the flood was Moses, and he was led, for some wise purpose, to omit every thing that would tend to gratify mere curiosity. In his discription of the ark we have, however, conclusive evidence that the antedeluvian builders were no mean artificers. The mechanical skill which must necessarily have been developed in the construction [7+] of so gigantic and strong a vessel could only have been possessed by a people who had made the art of building their study.

The sacred historian informs us that after the waters were abated from off the earth, and it began again to be peopled, "the posterity of Noah journeyed from the east, and finding a plain in the land of Shinar, they dwelt there" and built a City, and a Tower, whose top they purposed to make to reach the heavens; but they were stopped in their work; their language was confounded, and they were scattered throughout the earth.

The descendants of Cush remained in the neighbourhood of Babel. Nimrod, his son known in profane history as Belus, is said to have founded there the kingdom of Assyria; the words of the Bible are, "and the beginning [8+] of his kingdom was Babel, and Erech, and Accad, and Calneh, in the land of Shinar."

This Bable is undoubtedly the Babylon subsequently known in history; but it is not to be supposed that it was the original city which surrounded the Tower of that name. The confounding of the language of the builders of that edifice, no doubt, gave them quite enough of that locality; the bible says, "they left off to build the city;"[1] besides, it is not to be supposed that GOD would permit a work he had so signally stopped, to be afterwards prosecuted, and completed; hence we infer that what was afterwards known as Babylon was built on another site in Shinar.

The Babylon described by Herodotus, and the Tower that stood in its midst were, no doubt, commenced by Belus, and it is that Babylon [9+] which is afterwards referred to so freely in the Bible, the remains of which are, in our own day attracting so much notice.

The Tower, the ruins of which are now known as the <u>Birs-Nimrod</u> is discribed by Herodotus as being 650 feet square at the base, and Strabo makes it 650 feet high; this gives it the proportion of the Egyptian pyramids. — It consisted of <u>eight</u> steps or stories, which were build in inclined planes so as to admit of persons walking around it until they reached the top, upon which was an observatory for astronomical purposes. There were numerous chapels in different parts of the Tower for idolatrous worship — chiefly for the god Baal.

It is generally supposed that this was the original Tower of Babel; — Rollin, and others favor this opinion, but it is not at all probable.

[10] The early inhabitants of the Post deluvian world could scarcely have had skill enough to have made such a structure. Besides, it was evidently built from the bottom for idolatrous worship, which was unknown until after the dispersion, Belus himself, being the first idol god ever worshipped, and that did not take place until after his death, — his son Ninus deifyed him, and it was not long before he was transformed by fable into the son of the Egyptian <u>Osiris</u>, and a statue consecrated to his memory.

The city of Babylon, according to Herodotus was 15 miles square, surrounded by a wall 87 feet thick and 350 feet high. It was entered by 100 gates of brass — 25 on each side. From all of these gates were streets 150 feet wide crossing each other at right angles, thus making [10+] 50 streets each 15 miles long, which together with the avenues which extended around the city against the walls, made, in the aggregate 810 miles of streets.

The river Euphrates run through the city and Strabo tells us of one bridge over it that was 650 feet long.

There was also an extraordinary structure called the <u>pensile</u>, or hanging gardens, but which were in reality <u>tower</u> gardens; they consisted of a tower of 400 feet square and 350 feet high built in regular stories with stairways and rooms throughout; and on the top was a covering of flat

---
[1] Genesis 11:8.

stones 16 feet long and 4 feet wide; on this was placed a layer of reeds mixed with bitumen on the top of which was a covering of lead. On this the soil was laid, of sufficient thickness to sustain the largest forest trees. By these means a garden [11+] was made at an elevation equal to the walls of the city, so as to be seen from the surrounding country.

The discriptions of Babylon by Herodotus are very circumstantial, and were written on the spot but a century after it was taken by Cyrus. Further developements of the existing ruins will no doubt authenticate that venerable father of history.

The sovreign who is said to have contributed most to the Architectural improvement of Babylon, and the strengthening of its walls and [8] bulwarks was the famous queen Semiramis, the first female who ever occupied a throne.

Babylon continued to flourish until 538 years before the Christian era, when it was taken by Cyrus, and its walls subsequently destroyed by Darius; after which it gradually wasted away, until even the geographical position of it became a problem. — Thus are fulfilled the predictions of Isaiah respecting this ill-fated city. — The prophet denominates it "the glory of kingdoms," and "the beauty of the Chaldees' excellency," and then declares that it "shall be as when GOD overthrew Sodom and Gomorrah;" — that "it shall never be inhabited, neither shall it be dwelt in from generation to generation; — neither shall the Arabian pitch his tent there; — neither shall shepherds make their fold there; — but wild beasts of the deserts shall lie there; — and their houses shall be full of doleful creatures; and owls shall dwell there; and satyrs shall dance there. And the wild beasts of the islands shall cry in their desolate houses, and dragons in their pleasant palaces; — and her time is [9] near to come, and her days shall not be prolonged."*

Thus did the Prophet denounce Babylon when in the zenith of her glory, and in every particular have his predictions been accurately fulfilled. — The Late M[r]. Rich, in his narative of a journey to the site of Babylon in 1811 describes the ruins as consisting chiefly of "mounds of earth formed by the decomposition of buildings, channeled and furrowed by the weather, and strewed with pieces of brick, bitumen, and pottery."[†] — In an excavation made during the visit of that intelligent traveller, a colossal lion, composed of coarse granite rudely sculptured, was uncovered; and in many places walls were exposed built of bricks laid in a lime-cement which had become so hard as to render them inseparable.

Other walls have been discovered consisting of <u>burnt</u> bricks with a thin bed of reeds and bitumen between each layer; — many of the bricks have inscriptions on them, engraven in [12+] unknown characters.

---

* Isaiah [See Isaiah 13:19-22. The Chaldees were part of the Babylonian Empire. *Ed.*]
† Rich

Nineveh, another city of Assyria, is also said to have attained to great magnificence. It was founded about 200 years after the flood and became the capital of the Assyrian Empire. According to Diodorus of Sicily, it covered an area of 50 miles in circumference. The prophet Jonah tells us that it was "an exceeding great city of three days' journey;"* by which, he probably meant that it required three days to walk around it.

It was destroyed in the year 606 B.C. Its latest monuments, therefore, date back not less than five-and-twenty centuries, while the foundation of its earliest is lost in an unknown antiquity. When the "ten thousand" greeks marched over this plain under Xenophon, in their celebrated retreat, about 400 years before Christ, the name of Nineveh was already forgotten on its site. Even [13+] at that time its pondrous walls and ramparts had perished, and mounds covering its palaces alone remained, much as they do in the present day.

But Nineveh now appears again to testify to her own long lost splendor. The celebrated Layard has penetrated the great mound of Nimroud, and by indefatigable exertion, and untiring industry has had the satisfaction to bring to light the most interesting relics of departed ages, that have ever yet been discovered.

It is not a little remarkable that an empire so renowned for power and civilization as Assyria undoubtedly was, should have been so completely overthrown, as to render, even the site of its once magnificent capitol, a doubtful question. And it is no less remarkable that the discoveries recently made should have so suddenly opened [14+] to us the architecture and the records of that ancient people sculptured in imperishable characters. We have here the "temple-palaces" of a forgotten race, "disentombed from the sepulcher of ages" — "the metropolis of a powerful nation recovered from a long night of oblivion."

I propose, at some future day, to devote an entire lecture to the recent discoveries in Assyria.

Egyptian Architecture

About the same time that Nineveh was founded Dardanus built Troy, and Mizraim, the son of Ham led a colony into Egypt, where he founded a kingdom which lasted nearly 1700 years. There architecture was first reduced to a science, and there we find the first authentic source of the arts of civilized life.

[10] The numerous memorials of that ancient people even now surpass in grandeur and extent the works of every other nation in the annals of the human race. Their gigantic pyramids and ponderous tombs which

---
* 3 [Jonah 3: 3. *Ed.*]

Entrance to the Temple at Luxor (Entrée de Loùqssor). Dominique Vivant Denon, Voyage Dans Le Basse Et Le Haute Egypte *(Paris, 1802). Courtesy, the Winterthur Library: Printed Book and Periodical Collection.*

have long outlived the memory of the tyrant Kings whose [11] ashes they contain; their stupendous temples, their towering obelisks, their long avenues of sphinxes extending as far as they eye can reach, their magnificent porticoes, courts, and halls, embellished with innumerable statues, all glow with the spirit of departed ages, and afford the student of architecture a prolific field of thought and research.

The Egyptians were undoubtedly the first nation who promoted general science; their wisdom in the philosophy of government, as well as in the pursuit of the arts excited the admiration of surrounding nations, and eventually constituted their country a school of politics of science and of the arts. — Luke, the Evangelist, in describing the good qualities of Moses says that "he was learned in all the wisdom of the Egyptians, and was mighty in words and deeds;" thus corroborating the testimony of Herodotus and others that the land of the Pharoes was a land of learning.

The most illustrious men of Greece were sensible of the wisdom of the Egyptians; Homer, Plato, Pythagoras, Lycurgus, Solon, and many others equally celebrated, repaired to the cities of the Nile to complete their studies: — and [12] to that ancient nation most of the arts and laws of Greece may be traced.

But not withstanding the wisdom and learning of the Egyptians, they abandoned themselves to the grosest, and most ridiculous superstitions: — they deified vile and loathsome animals placing them in temples, and honoring them with devoted religious worship; — those who happened to kill any of the sacred brutes were punished with death, while the murdered animals were embalmed, and deposited with great solemnity in tombs provided at the Public expense. "You enter (says Lucian) into a magnificent temple, every part of which glitters with gold and silver: you there look attentively for a god, and are cheated with a stork, an ape, or a cat."*

The gods Osiris, and Isis, supposed to be the Sun and Moon† were worshiped throughout all Egypt, in addition to which most of the cities had their own tutelar deities, as the dog, the wolf, the hawk, the crockodile, the ibis, or stork, the bull apis, and the cat, with many others quite as ungodlike: — and indeed some [13] of the Egyptians carried their superstitions so far as to ascribe a divinity to leeks and onions, and in necessitous times, the protection of these vegetable gods was most devoutly invoked, and their succour confidently looked for, and depended upon with a faith not to be shaken by disappointment.

The golden calf made by the Israelites during the stay of Moses on Mount Sinai, was, no doubt intended as an imitation of the god Apis, with the worship of which they became familiar during their residence in

---

* Rolin, v 1, p. 20
† Clas. Dic.

Egypt. — "They made a calf in Horeb (says the Psalmist) and worshiped the molten image. Thus they changed their glory into the similitude of an Ox that eateth grass."*

The satirist Juvenal reproaches this ridiculous idolatry of the Egyptians in the following racy language

"Who knows not that infatuate Egypt finds
Gods to adore in brutes of basest kinds?
This at the crocodile's resentment quakes,
While that adores the Ibis, gorged with Snakes!
And where the radiant beam of morning rings
On shattered Memnon's still harmonious strings, [14]
And Thebes to ruin all her gates resigns,
Of huge baboon the golden image shines!
To mongrel curs infatuate cities bow,
And cats, and fishes share the frequent vow!
There, leeks are sacred, there 'tis crime, in sooth,
To wound an onion with unholy tooth!"
"Ye pious nations, in whose gardens rise
A constant crop of earth-sprung deities."†

The absurdity of the superstitions of Egypt, and her acknowledged wisdom in politics and the arts of civilization, are facts that we, at this distance of time, find it difficult to reconcile.

The chief glory of the Egyptians seems to have been to raise monuments to astound posterity, and defy the dilapidating influences of time, while time shall last: — already have the magnificent ruins of their massy structures endured the storms and wars of thirty centuries; and another period of like duration would probably make but little change in their appearance.

The degree of excellence to which this powerfull race attained in Architectural science, [15] although truly astonishing was confined to but few principles: — these however were characterized by a boldness of form, and a solidity of construction which has rendered their works imperishable.

In some instances the chambers of their temples are roofed with solid slabs of granite reaching from wall to wall: in others they are formed by projecting several courses of stones equally over each other, from the opposite walls until they reach the centre.

One of the most striking peculiarities of Egyptian Architecture consists in the buildings being made larger at the base than at the top; thus giving an inclination to the walls, by which strength as well as beauty is obtained. The cornices, or crowning feature of the walls were all very similar in

---

* Ps 106/ 19,20 [Psalms 106:19-20. *Ed.*]
† Sat. xv [*The Satires. Ed.*]

form, differing only in size and decoration. — They consist simply of a large cavetto resting on [16] a bead, and crowned with a fillet; — the bead is, in most instances enriched with transverse and diagonal bands, and extends down each external corner. (Explain on elevation of Temple).[1]

The spaces between the columns were generally closed to about half their height with ornamental walls, so disposed as to show a small portion of each column: — a winged globe was usually sculptured on the cornice over the centre intercolumniation, and often on many other parts of the building, especially over the doors.

The principal features of Egyptian Architecture are exhibited on the drawing before you, which represents the front of the Temple of Isis at Dendera.

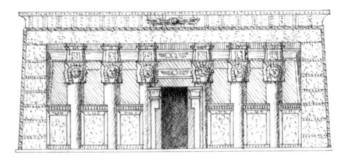

The capitals of Egyptian columns vary in form with every temple, and in some examples [17] we even find them widely different in the same portico. — All Egyptian capitals admit, however, of being divided into three general classes, the distinctive characters of which are as decidedly marked as those of the Greek or Roman orders; and, when taken in connection with their respective columns and entablatures, might with propriety be called Egyptian orders.

These classes or Orders are exhibited by the three examples before you; the first of which is from a small temple on the Île d'Elephantine on the river Nile, the second from the temple of Isis at Dendera, and the third from the grand temple at Karnak.[2]

---

[1] Written in pencil, this parenthetical comment is in an unusually careless hand and probably refers to the lost watercolor rendering of the Temple of Isis at Dendera. See Appendix B.

[2] Walter's sketch at the bottom page 17 of three finely-drawn Egyptian Orders includes numerical proportional notations. From left to right, the first (what he calls the "Robust" Order) reads: "Four diameters, 1 dia. 28 min;" the second ("Isis" Order) reads: "Six diameters, 1 dia 31 min;" the third ("Foliated") reads: "Seven diameters; 98 min."

[18] The first example is the most robust, and agrees in its superior strength and dignity with the massy Doric of the Greeks;—the second exhibits a medium between the heaviest and the lightest, thus occupying the same middle ground as it regards proportions as the Greek Ionic;—and the third corresponds with the Corinthian, both in its superior lightness over the other orders, and in its capital being always composed of foliage placed against a bell-shaped ground.

The Column of the Robust order, in the example represented on the drawing is precisely four times its diameter in height, which seems to indicate that the diameter of the column was taken as a modulus in proportioning the orders even at that remote period.—An example of this order, in Thebes has columns as high as five and a half diameters;—there

The Temple at Dendera (Vue géométrale du Portique du Temple de Tentyris). Dominique Vivant Denon, Voyage Dans Le Basse Et Le Haute Égypte *(Paris, 1802). Courtesy, the Winterthur Library: Printed Book and Periodical Collection.*

are however but few specimens in Egypt which exceed five. — In some examples the columns and capitals are perfectly smooth, being neither reeded, banded, nor sculptured; a specimen [19] of this description exists in the palace of Abydus, one of the cities of the Thebaid. — An example is found at Karnak, in which the capital is carved similar to the one represented on the drawing, while the shaft is left entirely plain; — every specimen, however, of this class of columns presents the same general outline.

The second grade or order is of lighter proportions than the first, the columns being six diameters in height. — The capital is quadrangular, having on each of the four sides a head of the goddess Isis with cows ears, boldly sculptured, and surmounted with a temple in miniature; — it might therefore be called with propriety, the Isis order.

The third class is that in which the capitals of the columns are made in the form of an inverted bell, and embellished with foliage; hence the most natural appellation we can give it is the foliated order. — The height of the column in the [20] example before you is seven diameters.

It is curious to notice the mathematical process by which this ancient people arrived at their architectural forms — (explain plan of capital).[1]

The proportions of columns with foliated capitals are however in many instances no lighter than those of the other orders, and indeed there are some examples as massy as any column in Egypt: — in the temple at Medamoud, on the confines of the desert, in the Thebaid, the robust order of column is used with the foliated order, of similar proportions in the same portico; — this however may be considered as an exception to the general rule. — At Ombos, the columns of the foliated order are but five and a quarter diameters in height; at the Memnonium in Thebes they are five and a half; at Latopolis five and three quarters; and in the grand temple at Apollinopolis they reach nearly to seven.

Several examples are found in Egypt in which foliated and isis capitals are united on the [21] same column, thus making a compound order. — From this combination the Romans no doubt derived the idea of a composite order.

This species of composition is found on the Île de Philæ, at Dendera, at Karnak, and at Apollinopolis.

There are very few good specimens of Egyptian Architecture to be found in modern buildings. The best that has yet been executed in any part of the world is the building called the Toombs, or city prison, in New York — that is a magnificent structure, true in every particular to the principles of Egyptian art, and its proportions are on so grand a scale as to carry the mind back to the days of the Pharoes — It was built by the late M[r].

---

[1] This brief paragraph was added on the page facing [20] and probably refers to a lost rendering. See Appendix B.

Haviland of Philad[a].

The Prisons at Newark and at Trenton in New Jersey, and the Female Apartment of the Philad[a.] Prison, are likewise in this style, and are all stone structures. (Remark on the errors of the present day in reference to this style).[1]

Of the Domestic Architecture of Egypt we can know but little, as all traces of it have long since been obliterated;—there can be no doubt however, that it reached considerable perfection.—A people as well skilled in the art of building as the Egyptians were, would not be likely to content themselves with mean and uncomfortable dwellings. We have it from Diodorus that the private residences in Thebes were four and five stories in height, which indicates considerable proficiency in Domestic Architecture.

But the noblest remains of this astonishing people are their Temples, of which those at Dendera, [22] Karnak, and Apollinopolis are the most celebrated.

The temple of Isis at Dendera, a representation of which is before you, was so extensive that the Arabs built a village on its roof, the ruins of which are still to be seen.—The enormous masses of stone employed in the construction of this gigantic edifice, its majestic appearance, the variety of its ornaments, and the solemn grandeur that pervades the whole, excite the wonder and astonishment of every beholder;—Belzoni confessed himself lost in admiration while seated before it; Denon looked upon it as the sanctuary of the arts and sciences, and other travellers have been equally enthusiastic in their descriptions of its grandeur and beauties.

Another species of the Architecture of this ancient people is their Obelisks; all parts of Egypt abounded with them;—their form was invariably the same, being always composed of a single block of granite, square on the plan and slightly tapering to the top, which was terminated in a sharp point, hence they are often [23] called needles.—Rollin says "they were for the most part cut out of the quarries of Upper Egypt where some are now to be seen half finished."—M[r]. Stephens remarks, in his entertaining "Incidents of travel" that "these quarries stand about half an hour's walk from the river, in the bosom of a long range of granite mountains, stretching off into the desert of Arabia. Time and exposure have not touched the freshness of the stone, and the whole of the immense

---

[1] Walter added the two preceding paragraphs on the page facing [21]. They replace and expand upon an edited section, cut from the text, which reads:

M[r]. *Haviland has employed this order* [the "Robust Order"] *on a magnificent scale in the Halls of Justice in New York, and in the Newark Prison in New Jersey; he has also used it, though of much lighter proportions in the façade of the Pennsylvania Insurance office in Walnut Street.*

The identification of "the late Mr. Haviland" in this rewrite establishes the date of the additions following Haviland's death in 1852. On page 19 Walter deleted the following similar commentary, again speaking of the "Robust Order:"

This order has been beautifully adapted to Modern Architecture by M[r] Haviland in the Penitentiary of New Jersey at Trenton. — A specimen of it is also exhibited in the facade of the Debtor's apartment adjoining the Philadelphia Country Prison.

Nineteenth-century decorum prohibited Walter from naming himself as the architect of the latter.

quarry looks as if it was but yesterday that the Egyptian left it. You could imagine that the workman had just gone to his noon day meal; and as you look at the mighty obelisk lying rude and unfinished at your feet, you feel disposed to linger till the Egyptian shall come to resume his work, to carve his mysterious characters upon it, and make it a fit portal for some mighty temple."*

Pliny tells us that the Kings of Egypt cut these immense blocks in emulation of each other, out of a quarry at Syene, in the Thebaid.—They are supposed by Diodorus to have been [24] erected about 250 years before the founding of Rome or a thousand years before the Christian era; but other authors give them a much higher antiquity.—They were certainly erected before the Persian Conquest, as Egypt was undoubtedly too much enervated after that period to have produced works of such immense labor and difficulty; and indeed we have it from Strabo that some of the obelisks in Heliopolis bore marks in his day of the fires with which the armies of Cambyses surrounded them during the mad career of that infatuated monarch in Egypt.

Notwithstanding the vast dimensions and immense weight of the Egyptian obelisks, several of them were removed to Rome by her ambitious rulers, where they were reared to grace "the seven hills" and serve as trophies of the gigantic power of the Roman empire.—Publius Victor mentions forty two which were conveyed to Rome between the reigns of Augustus and Constantine, some ten or twelve of which are still standing. [25] Augustus was the first who attempted the hazardous experiment of transporting them, and the success that attended the undertaking emboldened Caligula, Constantine and others to follow the example. And now these majestic links in the chain of ages, are seen rearing their lofty tops amid the fallen and mutilated grandeur of the "Imperial City."—In a visit to Rome a few years ago I met with nothing that produced a more lasting impression on my mind than these obelisks;—standing in the midst of the ruins of ancient splendor, the relics of a still more ancient race were before me;—relics which antiquity herself had treasured up as time-worn mementoes of another—a more distant age.[1]

The obelisk that Augustus brought to Rome was first placed in the Campus Martius, but has since been removed to the Piazza di Monte;—it was originally erected in Heliopolis by Sesostris.

There is also one standing in front of the Trinita de'Monti, which was brought [26] from the gardens of Sallust, and is forty eight feet in height above its pedestal.

Another stands near the fountain of the Piazza del Popolo, of seventy four feet high, and one in front of S.t Peter's of seventy eight feet.

* v 1, p 99

[1] The original text reads "In a recent visit to Rome," referring to Walter's 1838 travel to Europe.

The French removed one measuring seventy six feet in height by eight feet in width from the temple at Luxor, and raised it in the Place de la Concorde in Paris in 1836. — The weight of this immense stone is estimated at 350 tons.

Pliny says that the vessel which conveyed the one in front of S^t. Peter's to Rome equaled in length nearly all the port of Ostia; he relates that forty six cranes, six hundred men, and forty horses were employed in removing it, and that the timber, ropes, and iron, which were used in the operation cost 20,000 crowns.

We shall now proceed to notice the Pyramids: — these architectural monsters possess however but little to interest us beyond their magnitude, and antiquity.

[27] Of the three Pyramids near Cairo, the largest is 660 feet square at the base, and 500 feet in height. [*It therefore covers an area considerably larger than either of our Public squares and its elevation is equal to twice and a half the height of Christ Church Steeple. — This immense pile is at present terminated by a platform of about seventeen feet square.*][1]

The whole of this Pyramid is constructed of stones of vast dimensions, some of which are four feet in height, and three feet in thickness, and it is said that none are less than thirty feet in length. Herodotus relates that a hundred thousand workmen were employed at the same time in building it; and that ten years were occupied in hewing and conveying the stones, and twenty years more in finishing the structure.

Historians differ both as to the origin of these Pyramids, and the purposes to which they were applied; — Belzoni has however made some recent discoveries which prove then to be the tombs of their founders.

As to the manner in which these [28] prodigious structures were erected, Diodorus and Pliny both say that the process of construction was carried on by means of terraces disposed in the manner of inclined planes, and Herodotus tells us that when the first range of stones was laid, the workmen raised other stones upon them by means of short engines of wood, and thus continued with the several ranges or courses to the top.

It is generally supposed that the whole of these colossal piles were faced with marble, and some are of the opinion that they were once crowned with obelisks; and although it is not improbable that such was the finish intended by their ostentatious projectors, it is very doubtful that such a design was ever accomplished. — Their present termination seems to call for something on the top, but had they ever been crowned by obelisks some indications of them would certainly have remained.

At a short distance from the Pyramids stands another curious relic

---

[1] The Franklin Institute audience could have clearly envisioned the two-hundred foot high steeple of the church just blocks from their lecture hall as well as the dimensions of Philadelphia's five great squares.

called the Sphinx of Ghiza:—this singular object consists of an [29] immense figure representing the face of a woman and the body of a lion; its length is about one hundred feet, and its breadth forty; and the whole of it is composed of a single stone.—The head, according to Doctor Pocock is twenty six feet high, thirty five feet in circumference, and fifteen feet from the ear to the chin:—nearly the whole figure was buried in sand until the time of the invasion of Egypt by the French; it was then partially uncovered, and was afterwards entirely cleared.

Captain Cabillia, who visited Egypt a short time before Belzoni uncovered its entire front;—he found a large tablet on the breast adorned with figures and hieroglyphics, and a small temple between the paws;—this traveller makes the length of the legs fifty seven feet, and the height of the paws eight feet.—M^r. Stephens who saw it in 1835 reports it as being again partly covered with sand:—he remarks that "its head, neck, shoulders, and breast are still uncovered; its face, though worn and broken, is mild, amiable, and intelligent, [30] seeming, among the tombs around it, like a divinity guarding the dead."[*]

One of the richest and most complicated works of the Egyptians was the famous Labyrinth near the Lake Mœris, the ruins of which are still to be seen;—ancient writers describe it as the most beautiful work the Egyptians ever executed. Herodotus attributes its construction to the twelve kings of Egypt who reigned simultaneously about 680 years before Christ; he describes the works as one of astonishing magnitude and grandeur, having within its walls twelve magnificent palaces containing three thousand chambers some of which possessed great beauty. The turns and windings through the halls and chambers were so intricate, says our author, that without an experienced guide it would be impossible to escape wandering.

All the walls and ceilings were of white marble, and exhibited a profusion of sculpture; and the galleries in the halls were supported by columns of the same material.

The Egyptians never could have [31] constructed the stupendous monuments which still adorn the vallies of the Nile without a far greater degree of knowledge in the Mechanic arts than is usually attributed to them.—While the nobler efforts of their skill have withstood the powers of time, the lighter—frailer evidences of genius have perished; and most of their arts have been buried in oblivion, or passed to the credit of other nations.—It is known that they possessed the art of tempering copper tools so as to cut the hardest granite;—they had also artificial causways, graded and formed with grooves similar in principle to the railroads of our day;—and indeed it is said that remnants of iron have lately been found in the grooves. Arago goes so far as to contend that they possessed

---

[*] p 51

a knowledge of steam power, and its application to the purposes of propelling machinary.

But it is to their astonishing productions in Architecture that we must turn for evidences of their former greatness,—in these inanimate material forms, still living with the impress of creative minds,—we have the work of human hands [32] that have reposed for thirty centuries forgotten in the grave,—landmarks of ages far back in the history of the world,—telegraphs, by which the distant past is borne onward from generation to generation, through the present to succeeding ages.

Hindu Architecture

Another interesting species of Architecture is presented in the remains of the ancient Hindûs.—The productions of this extraordinary people consist chiefly of excavations in solid rocks, supposed by some to have been executed anterior to the construction of the oldest temples in Egypt.— Monsieur d'Ancarville, who has examined the subject with great attention thinks they were made at least 2000 years before the Christian era.

A remarkable specimen of this description of Architecture is found at Elephanta, a small island in the harbour of Bombay. It consists of a cave of 15 feet in height 135 feet in depth, and 135 feet in width, excavated in the side of a stone mountain; the ceiling being supported by portions of the rock left standing in regular rows like columns.

[33] The sides of this subterraneous temple are decorated with about fifty colossal statues, from twelve to fifteen feet in height; some of which have four hands, and others six, holding sceptres, shields, symbols of justice and religion, warlike weapons, and trophies of peace: some have an expression of horror, while others exhibit an aspect of benignity.

The largest and most extraordinary specimen of sculpture belonging to this cave is an immense bust, the face of which measures five feet, and the width across the shoulders twenty feet.

There are four doors of entrance to the cave at each of which are two gigantic statues of thirteen and a half feet in height, bearing but little resemblance to the human form; according to Neibuhr, their execution is remarkably good.

On the Island of Salsette, which is also situated near Bombay, there is another subterraneous temple yet more magnificent than that of Elephanta: —Linschotten, who visited it in 1759 represents it as being as extensive as a [34] town; he describes the front as hewn out of the rock in four stories or galleries, in which there are three hundred apartments, each of which has an interior recess, or sanctuary, and a tank for ablution.

The ceiling of this cave is supported by 35 pillars, of an octagonal form,

about five feet in diameter;—their bases and capitals are composed of
Elephants, Horses, and Tigers.—There are said to be not less than six
hundred figures of idols within its precincts.

Other excavations of a similar kind are found at Elora. A range of
temples is here to be seen occupying more than one and a quarter miles
in extent, all of which have been carved out of the mountain, and adorned
with elaborate sculpture. "The so much boasted pyramids of Egypt are
trivial monuments (says Sonnerat) compared with the pagodas of Salsette,
and Elora. The figures in bas relief, and the thousands of columns with
which they are embellished, cut out of the solid rock indicate at least a
thousand years of consecutive labor, and the injuries of time show at least

Temple at Elephanta. Louisa C. Tuthill, History of Architecture, from the Earliest Times; its Present
Condition in Europe and the United States *(Philadelphia, 1848). The Athenæum of Philadelphia.*

three thousand years duration."[1]

In more modern times Hindoo Architecture has assumed a very different character. — In Benares, usually called the "holy city," many of the houses are extremely rich and grand; some of them are as much as six stories in height, with fronts composed of large stones jointed [35] and fitted with the most scrupulous accuracy, and embellished with horizontal bands of elaborate sculpture.

The public buildings of Benares consist of numerous Hindoo temples, a spacious Mosque, and an observatory; all of which are famous for their magnificence.

In the City of Agra, are also many interesting specimens of Hindoo Architecture, the most remarkable of which is a tomb, erected by the Emperor Shah Jehan in the year 1642, at an expense equal to three and a half millions of dollars; the whole of the structure is composed of white marble richly ornamented; it is said to be the finest piece of Oriental Architecture ever executed under Mahomedan rulers.

Some of the buildings at Old Delhi, are also very splendid; one in particular is described in the Asiatic Researches as a structure of incomparable richness; and though stripped and plundered by various invaders, it still presents an object of uncommon interest. — The roof is supported by numerous columns of fine [36] white marble, all of which were once richly adorned with inlaid flower work of beautiful stones, and the cornices and friezes are crowded with sculpture.

The ceiling was formerly incrusted with rich foliage composed of silver, but which it need scarcely be said has all disappeared. — The inlaying of the compartments of the walls is said to be an exquisite piece of work. — The barbarous outrages which are continually perpetrated on this luxuriant structure, must, however, soon make an end of it.

Another description of Hindoo architecture is found in the metropolis of Dacca, a city of Bengal, situated on the banks of the Ganges. — The ruins of this city differ in taste and style from any other buildings in this part of the World: — the most striking peculiarities of its architecture are lightness and elegance, and the lofty octangular minarets which rise above its walls and cornices produce a richness of light and shade — a brilliancy of effect which renders the distant view of it particularly beautiful.

[37] One of the best examples of this species of Architecture, is the celebrated Pagoda of Seringham, which covers an area of nearly four miles in circumference.[2]

The Brahmins maintained in this vast establishment, by the liberality of superstition, formerly composed, including their families, a multitude of not less than forty thousand souls, living in "a subordination which knows

[1] This paragraph was added on the page facing [34], with a note indicating that detailed descriptions of the excavations at Elora were found in the *Asiatic Researches*.
[2] This paragraph was added on the page facing [37].

no resistance, and a voluptuousness which knows no wants."

Persian Architecture

We shall now proceed to consider briefly the Architecture of Persia.

The only edifice of any importance left by this great and luxurious people, to represent them to posterity, is the palace at Persipolis.

This structure, according to Le Brun, originally consisted of 205 columns of seventy feet in height; forty of which are supposed to have been standing at the time the Mahomedans invaded this part of Persia, from the circumstance that the natives call the place "Kilmanar," or the forty columns: — the number has since been reduced to nineteen.

From the slender proportions of these columns, and from the fact that no fragment of architrave, cornice, or roof, has been discovered amongst the ruins, it is thought, by some, that the [38] palace never had a roof. One writer supposes that it was only a summer residence, and that a temporary covering, composed of wood, or silken drapery, was placed upon the columns: — there can however be little doubt that it had a permanent roof; and that the material of which it was composed was wood. — Marble columns of seventy feet in height would never have been erected to support an awning; and on the other hand had stone been used for the Entablature and roof, there would certainly have been enough of it remaining, at least, to settle the question.

The palace of Solomon, which must have been built somewhat in the same style of Architecture had, as we are expressly informed in the sacred writings, a wooden Entablature as well as a wooden roof, and we may fairly infer that the same material was used for similar purposes at Persipolis.

Solomon's palace is called in the book of Kings, the house of the forest of Lebanon, and in the account there given of it, we read that it was built of "hewn stones and cedars" above; and [39] that it was covered with cedar above upon the beams that lay on the forty five pillars, fifteen in a row." Here then is an example of the use of wood in the most celebrated building of the age, and there can be no doubt that it was used at that time in many of the best structures of the east for the architraves, or in the language of scripture, for "the beams that lay on the pillars."[1]

Sir Robert Ker Porter, in the account he gives of his travels in Persia says, that "nothing can be more striking than the view of the ruins of Persipolis; — so vast and magnificent, — so fallen, mutilated, and silent; — the court of Cyrus, and the scene of his bounties; — the pavilion of Alexander's triumph, and the awful memorial of the wantonness of his power"; all is

---

[1] Walter's information on the construction of the Palace of Solomon comes from 1 Kings 7.

The Ruins of Persepolis. P. V. N. Meyers, Remains of Lost Empires *(New York, 1875).*
The Athenæum of Philadelphia.

"beautiful as desolate."

The upper platform of this palace is 350 feet by 380, the greatest part of which is covered with broken capitals, shafts of columns, and countless fragments of the [40] building, some of which are richly ornamented with sculpture.

The columns are upwards of five feet in diameter, and the shaft is fluted in fifty two divisions, being more than double the number used in any other species of Architecture. — The base is formed of a square plinth, on which rests a bell shaped moulding surrounded with lotus leaves, and surmounted by a torus, or bead. — The capitals consists of a double demi-bull, many of which are in a good state of preservation. (See drawing)

The ruins of this palace afford striking evidence of the former splendor and luxury of the court of Cyrus. — It was wantonly devoted to destruction by Alexander during a fit of intoxication, in which he indulged after the taking of the city of Persipolis.

This event occurred 329 years before Christ, and we have no account of any means having ever been taken to rebuild it.

The style of Architecture displayed in the palaces of Persipolis differs very materially [41] both from the Egyptian and the Hindoo, being distinctly marked with features which characterise a separate school of Architecture; — some remains it is true, have been found in the province, which exhibit an Egyptian origin, but which were no doubt introduced by Cambyses at the time of his conquest over Egypt.

The fondness of the Persians for sculpture appears to have been excessive, and their taste in its design particularly grotesque; they usually represented triumphal processions; — offerings of horses to the sun, and oxen to the moon; — figures bearing a sort of umbrella; — others armed with the lance, in conflict with the lion; — some carried hammers in their hands, others shields, and not unfrequently the representation of a lotus flower was borne by each of the figures in the procession.

Phœnician Architecture

The Phœnicians are another nation who probably had a style of architecture peculiar to themselves; we have however no accurate delineations of existing ruins to assist us in coming to any certain conclusions respecting it.

[42] This ancient people inhabited the coast of Asia, eastward of Egypt, extending from the Deserts of Arabia to the Mediterranean Sea: they are generally supposed to be that part of the family of Noah who settled on the coast of Palestine, and are the same people who are called in the Scriptures

the Canaanites.

Their first settlements were in the Isles of Cyprus and Rhodes, and they passed successively into Greece, Sicily, and Sardinia; — afterwards into Gaul, and still advancing discovered the southern and western coasts of Spain, and eventually reached Britain.

Sidon, the eldest son of Canaan founded their Capital, which bore his name; and which was afterwards eclipsed by Tyre, a city which attained to great magnificence, and which is poetically described in the 27th and 28th chapters of Ezekiel. — The prophet calls it the "renowned city," and speaks of it as being "in the midst of the seas," perfected in beauty by its builders, and immensely rich in all the elegancies and luxuries of life.

[43] Herodotus mentions a splendid temple of Hercules at Tyre; and Hiram, King of Tyre and Sidon, is celebrated as the founder of many magnificent works.

A further proof that the Phœnicians were far advanced in the arts, is found in the fact that Phœnician Architects were employed by Solomon, in the construction of the temple at Jerusalem; a circumstance, sufficient of itself to show the high estimation in which they were held. — Strabo, speaking of Tyrus and Aradus, says that they had temples resembling those of the Phœnicians, which implies that the Phœnician style of Architecture had peculiarities which distinguished it from others. — There is little doubt, however, that their buildings were chiefly composed of wood, that material being abundantly supplied from Mount Libanus.

The Phœnicians have been celebrated as the inventors of Navigation, Arithmetic and writing. — They appear also to have been distinguished for [44] their excellence in manufactures, and in all works of taste; and their commerce is represented as having been very extensive.

Israelite Architecture

The style of Architecture practiced by the Israelites after their conquest of Palestine was probably similar to that of the Phœnicians, but unfortunately we are left without a vestage of any of their works.

The buildings erected in the reign of Solomon, and the Tabernacle constructed in the wilderness under Moses, are described in the Old Testament, but the sacred writers have not told us enough about their architectural proportions and embellishments to lead to any definite idea as to the particular style of any of them; nor have other writers done any thing towards illucidating the subject.

During a residence of more than two hundred years in Egypt, the Israelites could not have failed to become well grounded in the system of Egyptian Architecture. The greater part of the mechanical labor of the nation was probably performed by that enslaved people, for we are told by Moses, that the Egyptians [45] "made their lives bitter with hard bondage, in morter, and in brick, and in all manner of service in the field."[1] – Many of the obelisks, the Pyramids, and the stupendous temples of Egypt, which to this day astonish the world, were doubtless wrought by Jewish hands; and there, at this moment they stand, memorials of the Hebrew captives, and the folly of tyrant kings.

But notwithstanding the Jews were held in abject slavery by their idolatrous masters they managed to preserve their national peculiarities, and to retain, through all their years of servitude, a respect, at least, for the worship of the GOD of their Fathers; – it is therefore probable that, while the style of Architecture practiced by them after their Exodus had of necessity some resemblance to that of Egypt; yet the prejudices they naturally entertained against their cruel opressors led them to impart to their buildings an effect as different as possible from that of the land of their hardships and misery.

During the forty years they wandered [46] in the wilderness, it was impossible for them to have any stationary place for religious worship, they were therefore directed to construct the portable temple called in scripture the Tabernacle. This movable building measured 75 feet in width by 150 feet in length; it was surrounded by fifty six columns, ten being placed on each end, and twenty on each side. – In this we have a style of building differing materially from any thing in Egypt; the columns being made to extend all around, similar to a Greek temple, while the Egyptians never had so much as a projecting portico; all their columns being placed in recesses.

This temporary edifice was used by the Jews some time after their establishment in Palestine: – about 470 years from the time of its construction, preparations were made under David for building the celebrated temple on Mount Moriah, which was finished and dedicated in the reign of his son Solomon.[2] [*This magnificent structure occupied the summit of the mountain; its aspect must* [47] *therefore have been particularly imposing.*

The principal front consisted of the ulam, probably a grand portico; the ceiling was composed of cedar, – the roof was flat, and covered with plates of gold, and the interior was richly decorated. – The main edifice contained two courts; the first, and largest, was for the assembly of the people; and the second, which was called the priests' court, was the Temple.

Before the ulam were two columns of brass of seven feet in diameter, and forty two feet in height. – The capitals were executed in bronze, and are said in scripture to have represented "lilly work;" the "lilly" having probably been used in the same manner as the lotus flower in Egyptian capitals.

These columns were no doubt placed before the Temple simply as a decoration,

[1] Exodus 1:14
[2] Walter originally stated the length of time to be 600 years.

in the same manner that obelisks were placed before Egyptian temples.]

We are told by the sacred writer that Solomon wrote to Hiram, King of Tyre for the timber required to construct the Temple, and [48] for artists to direct the work, we may therefore infer that the Architecture was chiefly in the Phœnician style, whatever that may have been.

All we know of this building is derived from the Old testament accounts of it, which are too well known to require repetition here.[1]

Chinese Architecture

We shall notice briefly, in the next place the Architecture of the Chinese: —the works of this extraordinary people exhibit a peculiarity of style, which separates them in Architecture, as decidedly as they are separated in their habits and pursuits of life from all other nations.

Tents and pavilions appear to have been their original models for every description of building, and these forms have never been so much varied from, as to conceal the primitive idea.

Architecture with the Chinese is a matter of police arrangement, depending in a very small degree either on theory or good taste. The sizes of the various grades of building are prescribed by laws of ancient origin; — the number [49] of the courts, — the size of the terraces, — the dimensions of the rooms, and the elevation of the roofs are all accurately laid down by progressive rules of increase; — first, from the simple citizen to the man of letters; — second from the man of letters to the Mandarine; — third from the mandarine to the Prince; — and fourth from the Prince to the Emperor.

The common houses are mere one-story huts, with no opening but a door in front, windows being prohibited except when the establishment is designed for a shop. — The roofs are all finished with a curve rising from the centre to the corners, which produces an effect similar to the looping up of the corners of a tent; — these corners are frequently terminated with golden dragons, having bells suspended from their mouths. — The figure of a dragon being an imperial emblem, its use is common in the decoration of Chinese works of every description.

Columns were used in the better houses to support the roofs, as well as to form a veranda, which, in some instances extends entirely [50] around the building; — the bases are usually composed of stone, and the shafts of wood, without capitals.

The Palaces are alike celebrated for vastness of dimensions, and a total absence of every thing like good Architectural taste.

The Pagodas, and lofty towers have more pretentions to beauty than the

---

[1] This sentence was added to the original text when Walter removed the italicized Old Testament account on manuscript page [47].

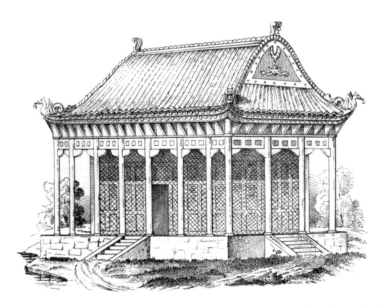

Chinese dwelling. Louisa C. Tuthill, History of Architecture, from the Earliest Times; its Present Condition in Europe and the United States *(Philadelphia, 1848). The Athenæum of Philadelphia.*

dwellings. In some provinces every town, even to the most inconsiderable hamlet has its Tower; — the most celebrated, is the "porcelain tower" or pagoda in the City of Nankin: — La Comte describes this structure as being two hundred feet in height, of an octagonal form, divided into nine stories, the base resting on a massy foundation of brickwork raised ten feet from the ground, and surrounded by a flight of twelve steps: — the lowest story is one hundred and twenty feet in circumference, and the others are of smaller dimensions decreasing in diameter as they ascend: — the building is terminated by a large pole surrounded by an immense iron hoop disposed in convolutions which present the appearance from a distance of [51] rings diminishing in the form of a cone: this pole extends about thirty feet above the roof, and the apex is crowned with a gilded ball. — Each story has projecting roofs covered with green tiles, and the walls are faced with coarse porcelain slabs: — the interior apartments are all crowded with gilded idols, and a staircase of one hundred and ninety steps leads from the bottom to the top, through every room.

All the towers of China are alike in general design, differing only in height and embellishments.

Another species of Architecture which this singular people have practiced to a considerable extent is their Triumphal arches; their annals mention no less than three thousand three hundred and thirty six celebrated persons to whose memory such structures have been erected.

But the most marvelous work the Chinese have ever executed is their celebrated wall, by which they have endeavoured to shut themselves up from the rest of the world. — It was commenced about 200 years before the [52] Christian era, and was probably projected with a view to prevent the incursions of the Tartars of the Desert; the length of it is upwards of 1500 miles, the height forty five feet, the thickness eighteen feet, and the number of towers with which it is fortified about forty five thousand.

M^r. Barrow, who saw this immense work in company with Lord Macartney, about the close of the last century made some calculations as to the quantity of materials it contains, and found that all the buildings then in England and Scotland were bearly equivalent to the wall alone; and that the towers themselves, independent of the wall contained as much masonry and brickwork, as the whole city of London did at that time.

The imperial canal has also been frequently referred to as a great work of art; but from the descriptions of recent travellers it has doubtless been overrated; we are told by M^r. Abel, in his journal of the embassy to China in 1816 and '17 that this canal, in every part of its course, passes through alluvial soil, readily penetrated by the [53] impliments of the workmen, and is intersected by numerous streams. — "It would be difficult (says M^r. Abel) to find any part of it carried through twenty miles of country unaided by tributary rivers;" its course is neither through mountains or over vallies, and the sluices which keep its necessary level are of the rudest construction.

The Chinese have likewise been celebrated by some writers for their skill in bridge-building; but in this department of Architecture they are quite as superficial and as tasteless as in any other; — and indeed, from all the information we have, in relation to the progress of civilization amongst them, it is very doubtful whether they ever excelled in any kind of building. Their seclusion from other nations, their manners, their laws, and their religion, all tend to retard the advancement of art, to suppress the soarings of intellect after knowledge, and to deepen the gloom of ignorance and superstition with which they have ever been enveloped.

Ancient American Architecture

The next, and last subject to which I shall invite your attention on the present occasion [54] is the ancient architecture of America.

The mutilated monuments of by-gone ages which still exist in the equinoxial regions of South America, in Central America, and in Mexico, exhibit the genius of a race whose only resources were their own energies, and whose only school of art was nature, in her wildest and most savage aspects.

In the works of this ancient people, a grade of intellect is developed, which seems to occupy an intermediary station between the civilization of ancient eastern nations, and the rudeness of uncultivated savages.

Notwithstanding the high-wrought descriptions of early Spanish writers in which the glories unveiled by Cortez—the magnificence of Montezuma's court, and the splendor of Peru at the time of the conquest, are set forth in glowing terms, we find nothing in the remains of the ancient Americans to warrant the belief that they ever were more than about half-civilized;—their conceptions were evidently those of a rude, [55] a semi-barbarous race:—their architecture, their sculpture, and their paintings are all stamped with ideas of the coarsest and most exaggerated character; while at the same time they exhibit an interesting spectacle of the natural progress of the human mind in a species of independent civilization, no where else to be found.

That the Ancient inhabitants of the old world had some knowledge of the Western hemisphere seems scarcely to admit of a doubt:—Plato, mentions an Island called Atlantis, which the Egyptian priests described to Solon, as exceeding in magnitude any of the eastern continents; Proclus, Porphyry, and others confirm the account, though some have considered it fabulous;—Diodorus mentions that the Carthaginians discovered a large island beyond the Pillars of Hercules, or the straits of Gibralter, which, for political reasons they would not suffer to become known to the Europeans.*—These, with many other allusions of a similar character made by ancient writers, evidently referred to another continent [56] beyond the sea.

The striking analogies which exist between the works of the ancient Americans, and the remains of eastern nations, such as their forms of idolatrous worship, their divisions of time, their mystic rights, and many of the ornaments of their Architecture, afford conclusive proof that some kind of intercourse existed in early time between the two hemispheres, though probably to a very limited extent.

"In the mythology of the Americans (says Baron Humbolt[†]) in the style of their paintings, in their languages, and in their external conformation we discover the descendents of a race of men, which, early separated from the rest of mankind, has followed for a lengthened series of ages a peculiar road in the unfolding of its intellectual faculties, and in its tendencies towards civilization."—The same author speaks of a very striking resemblance between the Mexican paintings, and the hieroglyphic writing on the roles of papyrus found in the swathings of Egyptian mummies,* at the same time

---

* Crabb
[†] v 1 p 200
* v. 1. 160

observing that [57] "the natives of America were very distant from that perfection to which the Egyptians had obtained."[†]

Del Rio, who visited Mexico in the year 1786 observes that in the fabulous superstitions of the ancient Americans as portrayed on their bas-reliefs we see a strong resemblance to the idolatry of the Phœnicians, the Greeks, the Romans, and other primitive nations white men with long beards and sanctity of manners had changed the religious and political system of nations; seem to indicate that Christianity had indeed been preached on the new continent.[‡]

In view of these facts there appears to be but little doubt that the inhabitants of the Western world had some means of communication in early time with the polished nations of the east; — but when, and how such communication took place will probably ever remain a mystery.

When the Spaniards first invaded America it was supposed that the only people who had made any progress in civilization were the inhabitants of the Equinoxial regions. Subsequent discoveries however prove that a partial civilization once extended throughout the whole of North America. — In Florida, in Kentucky, in Ohio, and even as far north as the plains of Upper Canada, innumerable relics have been found, bearing marks of a far more intellectual people than any of the Indian tribes of modern times. Weapons of brass, sculptured stones, urns [59] made of vitrified sand and flint, brass rings cut out of the solid in the form of a chain and engraved with characters not unlike the Chinese;[§] and a thousand other evidences of civilization have been discovered in almost every section of country north of the Equator.

Many of the vast tumulli and ancient fortifications which still exist in the regions of the west, and which are usually attributed to the present race of Indians, seem also, to be the work of a better people.

Some of the most interesting remains of American architecture are the Pyramidal edifices of Mexico. — These structures consist of truncated Pyramids crowned with temples. — They were called by the natives teocallis, or houses of the gods.

Each teocalli was built in the midst of an enclosed square containing gardens, fountains, and dwellings for the priests.[**] The chapel on the summit contained a colossal idol, and the inside of the structure constituted the mausoleum of the Mexican kings. Here, as in every place where man has fixed his habitation, we find the alter, the temple and the tomb.

A group of these pyramidal buildings still [60] exists on a plain about 24

[†] v. 1. 160
[‡] Hum 1. 196
[§] Priest 89
[**] Hum v. 1. p 81

miles from the city of Mexico.—Baron Humbolt* describes it as consisting of one dedicated to the Sun measuring 180 feet in height; another to the Moon of 145 feet; with several hundred smaller ones varying from 30 to 35 feet; all of which are disposed in lines so as to form streets running from north to south.—On the summit of the two large ones, colossal statues personifying the Sun and the Moon were erected of stone, and covered with plates of gold; of which they were stripped by the soldiers of Cortez.

Another was discovered about 60 years ago, on the east of this group built entirely of hewn stone of extraordinary size, beautifully and regularly shaped and joined;—its height is about 60 feet, and the steps are covered with hieroglyphic sculpture.[†]

A similar structure is found in the city of Cholula, in Mexico, which is supposed to possess a much higher antiquity than either of the others;—its perpendicular height is 164 feet, and its summit is reached by one hundred and twenty steps.

When the race called the Aztecks, took [61] possession of the equinoxial region of New Spain, about the year 1190, these pyramids were then standing, and were attributed by the conquerors to a powerful nation called the Toltecks, who inhabited Mexico some 500 years before.—But we can come to no certain conclusion as to the time when any of these structures were erected.—The annals of the Mexicans appear to go as far back as the sixth century of our era:[‡] beyond that period their history becomes lost in the mysterious legend of a heroic age.

The Architectural works of Peru possess an interest fully equal to those of Mexico.—The Peruvians were a race of mountaineers, whose wants scarcely reached beyond the actual necessaries of life; their Architecture was consequently limited to but few principles.—The most of their buildings bear the same;—from which he concludes that some of them pursued their conquests even to this country, where they probably remained long enough to enable the aborigines to imitate their ideas, and adopt in a rude manner many of their arts.

Some contend that the nations of the east held communication with the Americans even since the commencement of the Christian era:—the cosmogony of the Mexicans; their tradition of the mother of mankind having fallen from her first state of happiness and innocence; the idea of a great inundation, in which a single family escaped on a raft; the history of a pyramidal edifice raised by the pride of men, and destroyed by the anger of the gods; the confession [58] of sins by the penitent; the universal belief that general character, having but little exterior decoration, and exhibiting marks of a people innured to hardship and toil.

A character of solidity is imprinted even on their most inconsiderable

* v 1. 85 [the temples of the Sun and Moon are in Teotihuacan. *Ed.*]
† Hum 87
‡ Hum 1.28

structures. — In the edifices of Cuzco, and the surrounding country, stones [62] were used of enormous magnitude, some of which measure six feet thick, eighteen feet broad, and nearly forty feet in length.

In some of the smaller buildings, the stone work is executed with a beauty and an accuracy which indicate a high degree of mechanical knowledge: — the face of each stone is formed with a slight convexity, and the corners are slanted off so as to produce an effect similar to the angular rusticated work of the Romans; — were it not for these indentations the perfection of the joints would render them almost imperceptable.

After the conquest of the kingdom of Quito by the Peruvians, they opened a communication between Cuzco, (their capital), and their new possessions in the north, by the construction of a permanent roads of free stone, along the ridge of the Cordilleras; — portions of this road yet remain, and it is said to equal the finest ancient causways of Rome.

Between Cuzco, and Quito,* a distance of 12 or 1300 miles, station houses, or inns were built, at regular distances, for the accommodation of the Prince and his attendants.† — These houses were [63] called the palaces of the Incas, or princes of Peru; — they were all built on the same general plan, and probably about the same time. Each house had a door in front of 6 or 8 feet in height, the top of which was made narrower than the bottom; — the walls of the building were about 17 feet in height.

From the striking similarity which exists in all the works of the Peruvians, it appears as though they either aimed at a severe nationality or held in great reverence some consecrated prototype.

The cement used in the construction of the ancient buildings of Peru, is found to consist, in some instances, of an argillaceous marl, which effervesces with acids, and forms a true morter; and in others, of an asphaltum cement, similar to that found in the remains of remote antiquity on the banks of the Tigres, and the Euphrates.

Del Rio mentions in his description of the ruins near Palenque, a morter made of lime, but which was probably the marly composition alluded to.

Baron Humbolt supposes that the Peruvians executed all their works with tools made of [64] copper hardened with tin; — a chissel composed of these materials was found in a silver mine near Cuzco, worked in the time of the Incas; it consists of 94 parts copper, and 6 parts tin. This composition was used by almost every nation of the Old world, and was even preferred to iron long after the latter material had become common.‡

Ruins of a most extraordinary character exist also in Central America; some of which have been examined and described by modern travellers, while many others no doubt remain buried in impenetrable thickets,

---

* Hum 1.242
† v 2 p 1
‡ 261

sharing a common oblivion with the long lost race who built them.

The most important ruins which have yet been discovered in that country are descried by M^r. Stephens in his entertaining "Incidents of travel in Central America, Chiapas and Yucatan;" — as we shall not have time on the present occasion to pursue the subject, I take pleasure in referring you to that interesting work.

Conclusion

Having now completed a hasty glance at the various modes and styles of building [65] which had their origin in the rudeness of remote antiquity, I propose to direct your attention in the next lecture to the Architecture of ancient Greece — a land "where sovreign beauty dwells;" — where, trophies of immortal genius date up the lapse of time through more than twenty centuries, and gild the wreck of ages with a softened — an enchanting lustre; and where,

> "mingling in the dust,
> The column's graceful shaft, with weeds o'ergrown,
> The mouldering torso, the forgotten bust,
> The warrior's urn, the altar's mossy stone;
> Amidst the lonliness of shattered fanes,
> Still, matchless monuments of other years."*

---

* Hemans 160

Stone Idol. John Lloyd Stephens, Incidents Of Travel In Central America *(London, 1841). Courtesy, the Winterthur Library: Printed Book and Periodical Collection.*

Lecture 2nd

On the Architecture of Ancient Greece

Thos. U. Walter
Philad.ª Oct: 28. 1841

Delivered Nov. 18. 1841

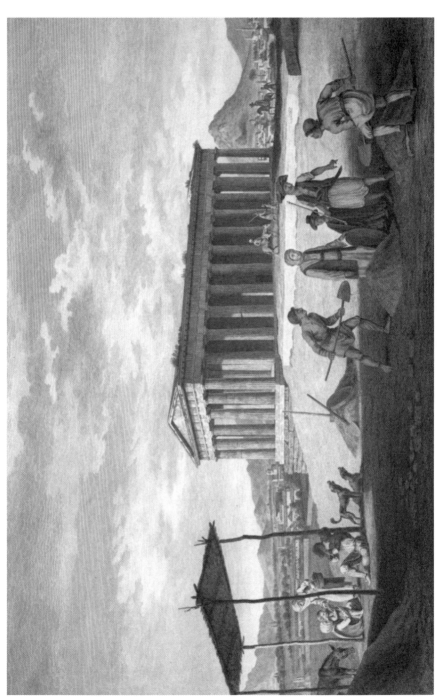

The Temple of Theseus (Theseum). James Stuart and Nicholas Revett, The Antiquities of Athens *(London, 1762-1816). Courtesy, Anne and Jerome Fisher Fine Arts Library, University of Pennsylvania.*

LECTURE II
ON THE ARCHITECTURE OF ANCIENT GREECE

Introduction: Greek Culture and Climate

[1+] The associations connected with the ancient Greeks, invest the remains of art, which still grace the plains and promontories of Attica, with an interest that imparts a lustre to every page of their eventful history.— While their poetry, their oratory, their philosophy, and their laws, exercise an imperishable influence on mankind, the magnificent relics of their taste and skill in Architecture, still bearing the impress of their own bright genius, reflect on every land, where the arts of peace are known, the spirit of a polished—an intellectual people.[1]

The geographical position of Greece, the mildness of its climate, and the purity of its atmosphere, all tended to the advancement of literature and the arts. Its situation with reference to surrounding nations, and the numerous bays and harbors which [2+] indent its coasts, combined to facilitate commercial enterprise, and to give it the mastery of the seas; while the extensive ranges of mountains, which formed the natural boundaries of its several states, separated the inhabitants into different provinces, the tendency of which, was to excite that spirit of emulation and rivalry—that love of glory and distinction which eventually characterized the nation.

Thus may we account for that heroic splendor, which imparts such life and vigor to the productions of the poet and the philosopher,—the orator and the historian:—and thus were the energies of a noble race, called out to adorn the country, and to teach the world

"How fair the works of mortal hand may be."

The geological formation of Greece [3+] conduced greatly to the advancement of the arts, particularly of architecture and sculpture.—Vast

---

[1] Although Walter rewrote the first seven pages of this lecture sometime after 1841 he did not substantially alter the lecture's content from the original text.

ranges of primitive limestone extend throughout the country; and an exhaustless abundance of marble, of incomparable beauty was found in the quarries of Paros, near Delos, Pentelicus and Hymettus, near Athens, and Marmarium, in Eubœa. [*From these sources the beautiful creations of human genius may be traced, by which the national taste of Greece was formed, the faith, as well as the valor of her sons inspired, and the story of her greatness perpetuated from age to age.*]

The associations inseparably connected with the tasteful relics of this classic nation enhance their intrinsic elegance, and heighten the pleasures they afford when considered simply as works of art. The temples to which Pericles, and Plato, and Socrates, and Aristides, and many others, whose names embellish grecian history, were accustomed to resort, still stand as memorials of these master minds—The traveller of the present day walks on the [4+] pavements that were trod by the sages and heroes of ancient Greece;—their works are still before him;—he looks with delight on the graceful conceptions of the inimitable Phidias or contemplates the beautiful productions of Ictinus and Callicrates, with emotions he can never describe;—at every step some rich developments of transcendent genius meets his eye, and carries him far back into the distant past.—Here Eschylus strung the tragic lyre,—here Socrates and Plato reasoned on the immortality of the soul,—here Demosthenes poured forth the thunders of his eloquence against the Macedonian king;—here too, the great apostle of the gentiles proclaimed the sublime mysteries of Redemption [*and to this spot were turned the eyes of those who fell on the plains of Marathon*].

Settlement and Colonization

Before proceeding to consider the full development of art in Greece, it will be proper [5+] to notice briefly its beginnings. The first inhabitants known to have occupied the country were rude barbarians consisting of a few thinly scattered tribes known by the names of the Pelasgi, and the Hellenes;—they dwelt in caves, and lived by hunting,—they were savages. [*Notwithstanding the barbarity of this people, several colonies of Egyptians and Phœnicians sought an asylum amongst them, and history records that these emigrants being kindly received, soon induced the ferocious natives to apply themselves to agriculture and the arts; while the minds of the adventurous strangers expanded under the influence of liberty, the sweets of which they had never before enjoyed, and which they found in the romantic wilds around them, in all its native purity.*]

A Colony, under Inacus emigrated to Greece about the year 1858 B.C. and founded the City of Argos. About 300 years afterwards the famous city of Athens was founded by Cecrops, a native of Sais, in Lower Egypt.* We are not, however, informed as to what progress these colonies made, in the way of Architecture, previous to the period assigned as the close of the Trojan war, which was about 375 years after the founding of Athens.

The earliest structures of Greece, no doubt [6+] partook of the Egyptian character;—the colonists were chiefly Egyptians, and would naturally follow the processes of art known to them in their own country [*and the aborigines knew as little of the arts of civilized life as the Indian tribes of our own country did in the days of Columbus*]; it is therefore probable that the Architecture, as well as the Laws and the Mythology of Egypt were transplanted by the Colonists into Greece.[1]

[*History furnishes no authentic information of the progress of Architecture in Greece previous to the Trojan war: — Homer, it is true, speaks of the court of Priam, but without giving us any idea whatever of the taste and style of the building; — he tells us that it was surrounded by stupendous columns of stone, well wrought; and that it embraced fifty rich pavilions, and twelve other apartments of great beauty; he also mentions the dwelling of Paris; but none of his remarks are descriptive of the Architecture.*][†]

Greek Architecture

[7] According to Herodotus the greatest part of the first gods that were adored in Greece came from Egypt,[‡] and the same author asserts that the Egyptians were regarded as the first of our race who paid a solemn and public devotion to the deity.[§] [*Diodorus speaks of the worship of Saturn, Jupiter, Ceres and others, Grecian deities as having been established from time immemorial.***] — Pliny says of the labyrinth at Thebes in Greece that the Architect Dœdalus closely imitated in that structure the celebrated Labyrinth in Egypt. Therefore we may reasonably infer that the first ideas of systematic Architecture entertained by the Greeks, were of Egyptian origin;—they seem to have, no doubt borrowed from Egypt the arts of civilization, and purified them in the alembics of their own genius, already realized under the refining and ennobling influences of climate and political freedom.

[8] One of the most ancient examples that remain of Grecian architecture, is the temple of Jupiter Panhellenius in Ægina;—this edifice is still almost

---

* Diod. Lib. 1. 33 p
† Iliad v 1 311
‡ Herod. L. 11.50
§ Her., lib. 11 n 4
** Dio. Lib 1.17

[1] The change in this sentence reflects the evolving nature of nineteenth-century understanding of the antiquities of Central and North America due to several new publications on the subject around mid-century.

entire; Pausanias says, that it was built considerably anterior to the Trojan war, which occurred 1184 years before Christ; this, however cannot be true, but it goes to show that this temple had outlived tradition of its origin[*] even as early as the times of Pausanias. — It is built in the Doric order, with six columns on each end, and twelve on each side; — its proportions are heavy, and indicate great antiquity: — twenty eight of the columns with their architraves are yet standing, but the rest of the Entablature has fallen, and the cell or body of the building is totally destroyed.

The Doric temple at Corinth, presents another example of Grecian architecture, of remote antiquity; — this edifice has also outlived its history;[†] — its remains consist of five columns supporting their respective architraves. [*At Syracuse in Sicily are the* [9] *remains of a temple to Minerva supposed to have been built as long ago as 700 years before Christ's era, but the history of the early settlement of Sicily affords no means of determining the age when any of the temples were erected.[‡]*]

The famous structures of Selinus are likewise of high antiquity, having been founded at least 500 years before the Christian era; — they consist of the ruins of six temples, which are said to be among the most surprising efforts of Grecian skill.[§] The appearance of these stupendous works, indicates that wealth and power existed in this ancient state; although its history comprises little more than the record of its foundation and its destruction.

The ruins of the splendid and costly temples of Agrigentum, also furnish strong evidence of the boldness and skill of the ancient Greeks. — The most important of these remains is the temple of Jupiter Olympius; — a structure which rivals in point of magnitude of proportion, every other effort they ever made in Architecture.

[10] Its dimensions were 369 feet in length, 182 feet in width, and 120 feet in height: — it was ornamented on the outside by 38 semi-columns of 13 feet in diameter, and 61 feet in height, supporting an entablature of 26 feet: — the columns are fluted, and each flute is large enough to receive the body of an ordinary sized man [— *the diameter of each capital is sixteen feet and its height eight feet three inches.*

We are informed by Diodorus of Sicily, that the porticoes are embellished with excellent sculpture; — on one front, the contest of the Giants was represented, and on the other, the siege of Troy.[**]]

The Temples of Agrigentum were commenced about 450 years before Christ, and were all the work of a single century.[††]

[*] Ionian Antiquities vol. 2 p 16
[†] Stuart Athens vol. 3. ch X
[‡] Wilkins Vit, Intro p 51
[§] Magna Grecca, p 4
[**] Dio. Sic. Lib. XIII
[††] Stuarts Athens v 4 ch 1

Classical Athens

Next in the order of time, are the peerless remains of Athens. — In these we find richness, and a grandeur, that surpasses every preceding or contemporary work; — here we pause on [11] "the full perfection of art." — The ruins of the Parthenon — that beautiful fane of Minerva, still crown the Citadel; — near to it are the remains of the Erectheum, the temple of Minerva Polias, and the Pandroseum; — at the entrance of the Acropolis stands the magnificent Propylæa, with the temple of Victory without wings on the right, and the picture gallery of Polygnotus on the left; — near the hill of the Areopagus, on the road to the Academy, is seen the chaste and beautiful temple of Theseus almost entire; — every part of Athens abounds with the most undoubted evidences of her former grandeur, wrought in the pure and snow-white marble of her surrounding mountains. — The temple on the Illisus, — the portico of the Agora, — the Choragic monument of Lysicrates, — the tower of Andronicus Cyrrhestes, — and some of the lofty columns of the temple of Jupiter Olympius, have been spared by [12] time to serve as landmarks in the story of Athenian greatness.

As Byron says:
"But one vast realm of wonder spreads around,
And all the Muse's tales seem truly told,
Till the sense aches with gazing to behold
The scenes our earliest dreams have dwelt upon."*

Of all the public buildings of Athens the Parthenon is unquestionably the most perfect in its proportions, and in every respect the most beautiful. — As a finished monument of classic taste it stands unrivalled, — the highest triumph of Grecian genius, — the master work of a master mind.

This majestic structure exhibits the Doric order in its fullest perfection: — it was commenced 448 years before the Christian era, and finished in 16 years: — its length is 227 feet, breadth 101 feet, and height 65 feet. — The whole mass was composed of marble from mount Pentellcus, of the purest and most dazzling whiteness, wrought with [13] the exquisite finish of a cameo. — The cell, or body of the building, was surrounded by 46 columns of 6 feet in diameter, and 34 feet in height. — Seventeen were placed on each side, and eight on each end, together with an inner row of six; thus making the end porticoes two ranges of columns in depth. (refer to the plan & elevation)

The Metopes, or spaces between the triglyphs, — the Pediments, and the friezes under the porticoes were all enriched with the most beautiful sculpture, embracing a length equal to eleven hundred feet, and comprising upwards of 600 figures, many of which were colossal.

---

* Childe Har. C. 11

The Parthenon. James Stuart and Nicholas Revett, The Antiquities of Athens *(London, 1762-1816). Courtesy, Anne and Jerome Fisher Fine Arts Library, University of Pennsylvania.*

The sculptures of the pediment on the western end present a group exhibiting the contest of Minerva with Neptune for the soil of Athens; and those on the eastern front commemorate the birth of the Athenian goddess. — The Metopes, which are each about four feet square, were adorned with representations in alto-relievo, of Centaurs and Lapithæ, and other mythological [14] subjects. — A continuous frieze extends around the whole outside of the cell, on which the Panathenaic procession was beautifully sculptured in basso-relievo.

This temple was used in the Venitian war as a powder magazine; and during the siege which took place in the year 1687,* a bomb was thrown by the Venitians, which ignited the powder,[†] and blew out the middle of the building,[‡] leaving the two ends standing.

Thirty nine of the columns still remain supporting the entablature, the most of which is very much mutilated. — The metopes have been robbed of their sculpture, and one of the Pediments had shared the same fate; many of the figures of the inner frieze, however, still remain; and one of the Pediments is sufficiently perfect to allow the imagination to fill up the outline of its original beauty.

[15] The position of this temple is every way worthy of its Architecture; — it occupies the summit of the Acropolis, and from whatever quarter the traveller approaches Athens, whether by land or sea, its majestic

---

* Stuarts Athens
† Fanelli
‡ Woods letters from Greece

remains meet his eye, and crown the picture. — The autumnal tinge which time has shed over it, blends the native whiteness of its marble into soft and sunny hues, which impart to it an overpowering charm.

"As traces left on earth's forsaken plains
By vanished beings of a nobler sphere!
Not all the old magnificence of Rome,
All that dominion there hath left to time,
Proud Coliseum, or commanding dome,
Triumphal arch, or obelisk sublime,
Can bid such reverence o'er the spirit steal."*

In this temple stood the famous statue of Minerva, the height of which according to Pliny was 37 feet 8 inches; it was composed of ivory and gold, and Pausanias describes it as having a helmet on, a Medusa's [15C] head on the breast, a spear in one hand, and a statue of Victory in the other, measuring nearly 6 feet in height. — Thucydides says, the gold about it weighed 40 talents, which, according to the value of gold at that time was worth at least $600.000.

This colossal and costly figure was the work of the inimitable Phidias;[†] and we are told that the Olympian statue executed by the same artists even exceeded this in magnificence; he also executed the Minerva Areïa at Platæa, and the statue of Jupiter at Megara. [*Winkleman records from ancient authors, upwards of a hundred figures of this costly and magnificent character; and considering the existing deficiency of historical information respecting a large portion of ancient Greece, it is probable there were numerous others of which we have no account.*]

Grecian Architecture reached the summit of perfection during the administration of Pericles. — This accomplished statesman took the deepest interest in the embellishment of his favorite city, which he [16] proudly predicted would triumph over the effects of time, and exist in splendor when the edifices of rival states would be mouldring in ruin. [*So he would have it, and in a qualified sense, so it is. — He was once charged before an Athenian assembly with wasting the public funds, to which he magnanimously replied, "then be it charged to my account, not yours;"[‡] demanding however, in return, the privilege of having his name inscribed on the new edifices instead of that of the people of Athens; but at this request their pride rebelled and they subsequently authorized him to use the public treasure with an unsparing hand, in carrying out his magnificent schemes for beautifying the city.*]

---

* Hemans. Greece v. 82
† Stuarts Athens, v 2 p 27
‡ Plut. V. 2. c. 1

Greek Principles; the Orders

In all the architectural efforts of the ancient Greeks, they arrived at a degree of perfection that could never have been attained without the aid of profound science; — they founded their [17] designs on fixed principles of art hence they never failed to awaken in the mind agreeable emotions of taste.

Their system of Architecture has been divided into three general classes, denominated Orders; — the first is called the Doric, the second the Ionic, and the third, the Corinthian; a representation of each is which is here exhibited. (see drawing) The Doric conveys an idea of great strength, — of stern and massy grandeur; — the Ionic is somewhat more adorned, though its character is that of chaste and simple majesty; — while the Corinthian displays the highest degree of ornament, and conveys an idea of sumptuousness.

Thomson speaking of these orders in his poem on Liberty says
"First unadorned
And nobly plain, the manly Doric rose;
Th' Ionic then, with decent matron grace
Her airy pillar heaved; — luxuriant last,
The rich Corinthian spread her wanton wreath. [18]
The whole so measured true, so lessened off
By fine proportion, that the marble pile,
Formed to repel the still or stormy waste
Of rolling ages, light as fabrics looked
That from the magic wand aërial rise.
These were the wonders that illumined Greece
From end to end."

These orders develope the same constituent principles as the columnar Architecture of the Egyptians; the three classes of Egyptian columns spoken of in the preceding lecture, correspond in general expression with the three Grecian examples before you: — thus affording further proof that Grecian architecture derived its origin from Egypt.

Vitruvius, the only ancient writer on Architecture, whose works have reached our times, has attempted to trace the origin of the orders to other sources: but his accounts are contradictory, inconsistent, and improbable. — He tells us that Dorus the son of [19] Hellenus built a temple to Juno in the City of Argos, which was found by chance to be in the manner we call Doric;* — This, we cannot, of course believe. — In another place he deduces this same order from a log-cabin; tracing with the utmost precision, all its details through the refinements of Carpentry; leaving nothing to chance;

---

* Vit liv. 1. c. 1 [Vitruvius, *De architectura* IV.1.3-6]

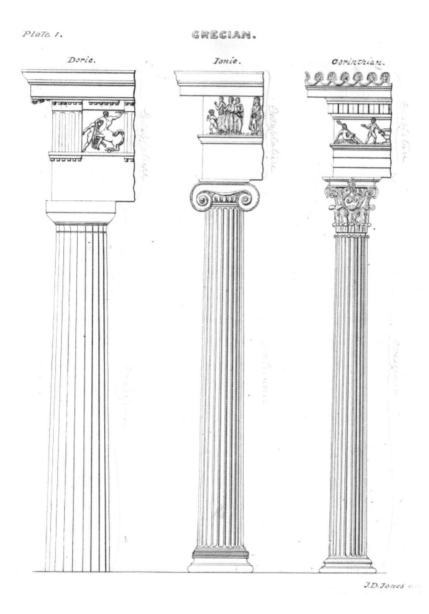

The Three Greek Orders. John D. Jones, "A Sketch on Architecture, by a Student" (1836).
Gift of Kenneth Miller. The Athenæum of Philadelphia.

this, to a limited extent was probably true.—He then asserts that the Doric column was modeled by the Grecian colonists in Asia Minor on the proportions of the male human figure; and that it was made six diameters in height, because a man was found to be six times the length of his foot;—"thus (he remarks) the Doric column was first adapted to edifices, having the proportions, strength and beauty of the body of a man." We doubt whether the Greeks ever thought of the proportions of the human body when they hit upon the design of their Doric Column. The details of the order were probably suggested by constructions in carpentry as all the features seem to have a meaning in that connexion (see diagram).[1]

[20] The account given by the same author of the origin of the Ionic order, is quite as fanciful as what he says about the Doric;—he tells us that this order is founded on the proportions of a female; the lower diameter of the column being one eighth part of its height; and that it might appear the more graceful, mouldings were added around its bases to represent the shoe, and volutes to the capitals to imitate the twisted braids of hair falling on each side.

Thus, says our author, were two species of orders invented;—one representing the strength and simplicity of man, the other the elegance and fine proportion [21] of woman; and this latter order was called Ionic, because it was invented by the Ionians.

The third order, which is called the Corinthian, is said by Vitruvius to have been made in imitation of the delicacy of shape, and slender proportions of a youthful female.—"At an early age" remarks this ancient writer, "the limbs are formed more slightly, and admit of more graceful decorations."[2]—He tells a very romantic story about the invention of the rich capital which crowns the column—"a young Corinthian female," he remarks, "being attacked with a fatal disorder, died; after she was interred her nurse selected a basket of such trinkets as pleased her when living, and placed them at her grave, covering it with a tile to protect its contents from the weather;—the basket being accidentally placed on a root of acanthus, depressed it in the middle, occasioning the leaves and stalks [22] which grew up in the spring to encircle and twine around the basket;—but being resisted by the projecting angles of the tile, they convolved at the extremities in the form of volutes;—this was seen by Callimachus, the sculptor, who, delighted with the novelty of its figure, and its delicate and appropriate form, encircled by the beautiful foliage, formed from its model, a new

---

[1] Here Walter made a significant change to his text. The original language (spanning pages 19-20) that he later deleted placed primacy on the precedents modeled by the Egyptian and Phoenician colonists:

> The origin of the Doric order is not to be found in the construction of edifices with the trunks of trees;—nor can its beauties be attributed either to the work of chance, or to the proportions of the human figure;—it came from Egypt; the mother of the arts; and there still exist even in the most ancient Egyptian structures, many forms from which the fertile imagination of a Greek would be likely to draw the idea of the proportions and arrangements of this order.

[2] Vitruvius, *De architectura* IV.1.8.

capital to some columns he had sculptured for Corinth; — thus composing this the most elegant of the orders."

We are wholly indebted to this fable at least for the <u>name</u> of the Corinthian order, as there is nothing either in ruins, or authentic record to prove that it was ever known in Corinth.* — The story of the Corinthian girl was probably invented by some Grecian poet, and related by Vitruvius as genuine.†

The antiquity of the writings of this author, and the almost universal currency his stories have obtained, seemed [23] to make it necessary thus to allude to them. — His want of historical correctness has probably arisen from the prejudices of the age in which he lived, — the Augustan age of Rome; and from the entire ignorance, or inattention of his country men to the spirit of Greek combinations.

Having spoken only of <u>three</u> orders, it will be proper to remark, that it has been usual to divide Architecture into <u>five</u>, adding the <u>Tuscan</u>, and <u>Composite</u>, to the <u>Doric</u>, <u>Ionic</u>, and <u>Corinthian</u>: — but neither the Tuscan nor the composite are entitled to the rank of separate orders. — The Tuscan is simply a modification of the Doric executed originally in Etruria, where it was undoubtedly used as the Doric order. — And the Composite is but a combination of the Ionic and the Corinthian: — it was complied by the Romans, and has been denominated by some the Roman order; — but these interpolations will come more properly under consideration [24] in the next lecture which will be on Roman architecture; and in which I shall compare the Greek and Roman orders, pointing out the peculiarities of each.

The Classical Orders and Modern Architecture

It is often asked by those who have never given much attention to the subject why Architects confine their practice in columnar architecture, to the ancient orders — and they are frequently reproached for not inventing new ones. — But if it be considered that the three Grecian orders embrace all the general expressions that can be given to the simple form of a column and entablature, the invention of a new order will no sooner be sought than the achievement of a perpetual motion, or the discovery of the Philosopher's stone. — We have in the Doric, — strength, robustness, and masculine vigor; and in the Corinthian, elegance, lightness and feminine delicacy; — while a medium between the two is found in the Ionic; — these orders are therefore the Alphabet of Classical Architecture, and we have no more need of a new one, than we have of additional letters in the formation of words [25] or a new note in the musical scale. — All the modes of building with columns

---

* Hoskins treatise p 11
† Elmes lectures p 170

that nature dictates, have been fully developed in these orders [—*in these we have the robust, the chaste, and the elegant*[1]]:—and any attempt to invent others can obviously result in nothing more than mere modifycations of the old ones:—it should therefore be remembered, that as the orator uses the Alphabet to produce the words he requires to convey his ideas;—and as the musician employs no other tones and semitones than those comprised in the musical scale, few and simple as they are;—so must the architect be content in the practise of columnar architecture, with the principles that nature dictates; all of which are fully developed in the three orders.

We have therefore no reason ever to expect the invention of an entirely new order, nor is such an event desirable, even though it were possible;—the Greeks have unquestionably perfected columnar architecture, and to attempt to improve perfection would not be more useless than unsuccessful

"To guard a title that was rich before,
To gild refined gold, to paint the lily,
To throw a perfume on the violet;
To smooth the ice, or add another hue
Unto the rainbow, or with taper light
To seek the beauteous eye of heaven to garnish,
Is wasteful and ridiculous excess"*

Many are under the impression that the Grecian orders are established upon arbitrary rules, and determinate calculation; [26] and that they constitute so may exact patterns, which the ancients have bequeathed to us, and which Architects must either copy line for line, or submit to the charge of ignorance or heresy;—such however is not the fact;—the rules which govern the modern practice of the orders are by no means arbitrary,—they were made to fit the ancient orders, and not the orders to conform to the rules;—the orders existed long before the rules.

The existing remains of grecian art show plainly, that the ancient greeks themselves, never adopted any fixed rules for proportioning the details of their orders;—in all their buildings we observe uniformity of principle, but no two examples are any where to be found in which the proportions are exactly similar:—the general expressions of the orders were always adhered to; but without imposing any fetters on genius other than the limits that nature herself has drawn.

If we refer to the monument of Lysicrates and the Tower of Andronicus Chyrrhestes [27] we shall find two examples of the Corinthian order no more alike than a rose and a lilac; but these beautiful productions of nature

---

* Quatremére de Quincy, by Kerch [Kuch?], 77 [Added to the facing page, these lines from *An Essay on... Imitation in the Fine Arts* (see Appendix A) originally derive from Shakespeare's *King John* (Act IV, scene II). Ed.]

[1] Walter discovered such qualities in his three "Egyptian Orders." See Lecture I:18.

are both flowers; so it is with these examples of the Corinthian order; they are both foliated; and in truth every foliated capital, — whether it be ancient or modern belongs to the same order: — unless the characteristic feature of one of the other orders should be introduced, which would change it into what the moderns have called the composite order.

If instead of using the nomenclature of Vitruvius in designating these orders, we were to adopt the terms which naturally belong to them, calling the Doric the Grecian order, par excellence, and its Ionic and Corinthian modifications, the voluted and the Foliated orders, there would undoubtedly be less misapprehension on the subject.

These observations are of course intended to apply exclusively to the art of building with [28] columns. — The Architect may produce the most elegant compositions without having any reference whatever to the orders; — he may invent new styles, and produce novel and beautiful forms, entirely without the aid of the ancient; — but whenever he finds it necessary to introduce columns into his compositions, he must turn to the principles developed by the greeks; let him think as the Greeks thought and he will never go astray.

Caryatids and Persians

There are some examples in Greece of a style of building in which representations of human figures are used instead of columns. — The first we hear of this kind of Architecture in the Grecian states, is found in an account given by Pausanias of the Persian portico at Sparta; which was erected shortly after the defeat of Xerxes; — the Architraves were upheld by sculptured figures habited in the loose drapery and flowing robes of the Asiatics; but of this edifice nothing now remains; [29] and indeed this bold and haughty race has left us no memorial of their skill in Architecture.

["In rugged grandeur frowning o'er mankind,
stern, and disdainful of each milder grace.
As to the sky some mighty rock may tower,
Whose front can brave the storm, but will not rear the flower."
— "their life a battle-day!
Their youth one lesson how" to fight and "die!"*]

The temple of Pandrosus at Athens furnishes a beautiful example of this kind of building — This structure is one of the richest and most highly finished edifices on the Acropolis: — the portico is composed of female figures elegantly sculptured, sustaining on their heads an entablature alike sumptuous and proportionate. [This building is joined to the temples of Erectheus and Minerva Polias, and these edifices were probably erected

* Mrs. Hemans Mod. Greece 54 x 55 v

The Corinthian Order from the Monument of Lysicrates. James Stuart and Nicholas Revett, The Antiquities of Athens *(London, 1762-1816). Courtesy, Anne and Jerome Fisher Fine Arts Library, University of Pennsylvania.*

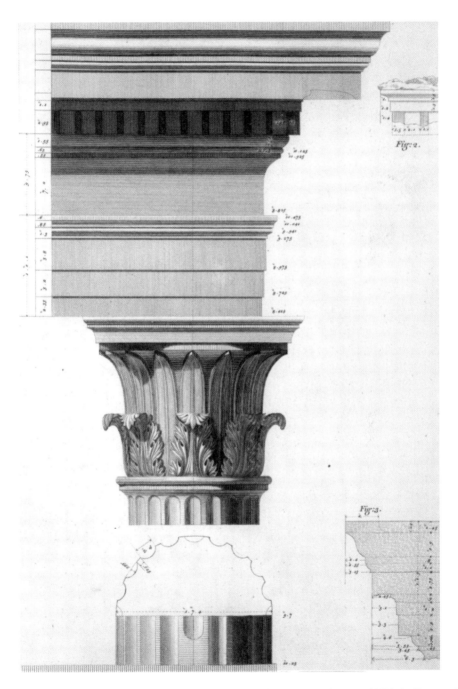

The Corinthian Order from the Tower of Andronicus Chyrrhestes. James Stuart and Nicholas Revett,
The Antiquities of Athens *(London, 1762-1816). Courtesy, Anne and Jerome Fisher Fine Arts
Library, University of Pennsylvania.*

conjointly; — they were commenced under the administration of Pericles, but in consequence [30] of his death, or the calamities and expenses of the Peloponnesian war, the work was suspended for twenty years, and resumed in the archonship of Diocles, in the four hundred and ninth year before Christ. *]

All Statues employed to support entablatures are termed Persians, and Caryatides; from an allusion made to them by Vitruvius: — he tells us that after the Greeks had defeated the Persians, and destroyed the city of Carya, their Architects employed female figures in constructing the Public buildings to perpetuate the ignominy of those who deserted the cause of liberty and their country:[†] — male figures are called Persians, and females Carians, or Caryatides.

We must however differ from Vitruvius in opinion as to the origin of this description of building also; — it is doubtless of the remotest antiquity; — in Egypt there are yet numerous remains of it, and also in the cave of Elephanta near Bombay, — a work of art yet more ancient. — It is [31] therefore certain that this style of building was invented long before the Persian conquest.[‡]

In the Choragic Monument of Thrasyllus at Athens, we find another variation from the established taste of the Athenians; — in this structure the entablature is supported by square blocks of stone, used in the same manner as attached columns.

This edifice is composed of several features of the Doric order, and presents a pleasing combination of Grecian forms; — the square columns are imitations of the antæ usually placed on the corners of the cell, in Doric buildings; — the entablature is lighter than that of the Doric order, — the frieze is ornamented with wreaths sculptured in the stone in basso-relievo, — and guttæ, or drops extend along the top of the architrave in a continuous line across the whole front. This building was constructed about 320 years before the Christian era.[§] (Refer to Patent Office — north front)[1]

The System of Greek Architecture; Terminology

The whole system of [32] Grecian Architecture is embraced in the three Orders with the modifications alluded to; and that of the Romans being entirely borrowed from Greece is founded on the same principles;

---

* Stuarts Athens v. ii c 1. 65

† Vit. Lib. 1 ch 1. [Vitruvius, *De architectura* I.1.5. *Ed.*]

‡ Gwilt on the Origin of Cary.

§ Stuarts Athens, v. 2 ch 4. p. 87

[1] This parenthetical note on the facing page identifies the addition to Walter's Washington years; the Patent Office project started in 1850.

consequently the term <u>orders</u>, is applicable both to Grecian and Roman Architecture;—but all other systems of building are known by the name of <u>styles</u>; which are designated according to the countries whence they proceed. [*As the Egyptian the Persipolitan, the Chinese, the Norman &c. none of which are reducible to the proportions of an order, except the Egyptian; and the discoveries in that country are of so recent a date that no one has yet produced a classification of its Architecture.*]

By an Order of Architecture we understand one or more columns supporting an Entablature, all the parts of which are proportionate to each other.

The Column comprises the <u>Base</u>, the <u>shaft</u>, and the <u>Capital</u>;—and the Entablature includes all that part of the [33] order which rests on the columns.[1]

The <u>Base</u> consists of horizontal moudings encircling the bottom of the shaft:—this feature is peculiar to the Ionic and the Corinthian orders, the Doric column having no such finish.

The <u>Shaft</u> is that part of the column included between the base and the capital; and which is usually ornamented with vertical flutes, and

The <u>Capital</u> forms the crowning member of the column.

The <u>Entablature</u> is divided into the <u>Architrave</u>, the <u>frieze</u>, and the <u>Cornice</u>.

The <u>Architrave</u> is the beam or stone which rests immediately on the columns.

The <u>Frieze</u> is the part comprised between the architrave and the cornice; it is frequently ornamented with sculpture and rests on a moulding which divides it from the Architrave.

The <u>Cornice</u> is the upper division of the Entablature, and consists of an assemblage of projecting horizontal moudings.

[34] All the orders admit of these primary divisions, but their proportions, and the form of their separate members differ in each of them respectively.

It is usual to measure the several parts of an order by the lower diameter of the shaft of the column, one half of which is called a module, from the Latin <u>modulus</u>, a measure:—each module or semi-diameter is divided into thirty parts which are denominated minutes:—this scale therefore, unlike the standard measure of an inch, a foot, or a yard, is as various as the diameters of the column.

The Doric Order

The Doric Order being the most ancient will first claim our attention. This <u>drawing</u> presents a representation of it as executed in the Temple of

---

[1] A marginal note in pencil here reads "Exemplify the following remarks by the drawings of the three orders."

Theseus at Athens. The columns of this order differ as before remarked from those of the Ionic and Corinthian in having no base: — the shaft is usually ornamented with twenty flutes which are much shallower than those of the other orders, and which are formed without fillets between them.

There are some Grecian examples [35] of the Doric order in which the fluting of the columns has been omitted; — but in most of these the flutes have been commenced at the top, and the bottom, with the evident intention of continuing them through the shaft, but which was probably prevented either by a change of administration or the death of some ruler.

The reeded columns of the Egyptians no doubt suggested the first idea of flutes to the Architects of Greece; — some however contend that fluting was originally invented for the purpose of enabling those who frequented the temples to lean their spears against the columns without their being in danger of falling down — this conjecture is founded on a passage in Homer, in which Minerva on entering the hall of Ulysses, is said "to place her spear by the tall column within the polished spear holder, in which there were many others:"* — but this quotation may allude to some repository which contained the weapons of the Prince, and in which Minerva placed hers also.

The Capital of the Doric column is [36] composed of a large convex moulding surmounted by a square tablet: — the moulding consists of a segment of a parabola, or a hyperbola; but in no instance in Grecian Architecture of the segment of a circle.

This simple combination of surfaces presents the charms of reflected light in beautiful perfection; — the sparkling and brilliant portions softened down into deep and decided shadows impart a richness to the whole composition.

The Architrave of the Doric order is never ornamented, but always presents a plain unbroken surface.

[37] The frieze is embellished with triglyphs, which constitute its distinguishing feature. — These ornaments consist of projecting blocks regularly disposed throughout the whole extent of the front; thus — one triglyph is usually placed over each column, and one over each intercolumniation: — sometimes however the centre intercolumniation is made wide enough to admit of two, as in the Doric Portico, and the Propylæa at Athens: — the corner triglyphs are always placed, in Greek architecture, on the angles of the frieze, as here represented, making the end intercolumniations less than either of the intermediate ones; — but in Roman architecture, they are generally placed over the centre of the corner columns, so as to make the intercolumniations equal.

---

* Homer Od. 1.127

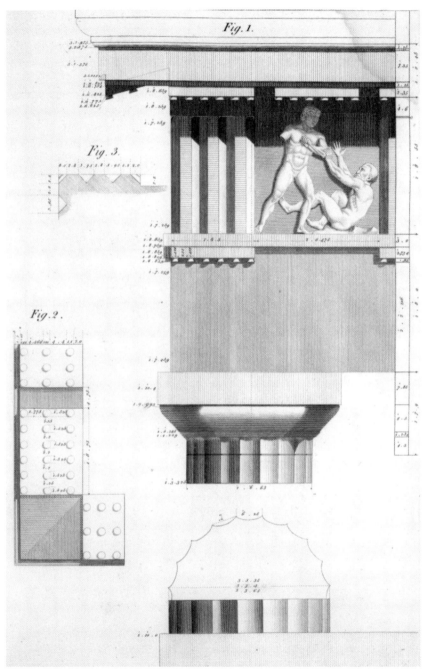

The Doric Order from the Temple of Theseus. James Stuart and Nicholas Revett, The Antiquities of Athens *(London, 1762-1816). Courtesy, Anne and Jerome Fisher Fine Arts Library, University of Pennsylvania.*

The spaces between the triglyphs are called Metopes; (see drawing) in some buildings they are enriched with sculpture, and in others they are left plain: — in the earliest examples of the order they were probably [38] left open; and indeed we find some remarks in Euripides which seem to afford conclusive evidence that such was the original finish: — in his "Ephigenia in Tauris" Pylades in councelling Orestes about entering the Temple of Diana, calls his attention to "the open space between the triglyphs," as affording sufficient room "to admit them to descend and purloin the image."

The Cornice of this order consists of an assemblage of mouldings projecting about a half a diameter or one module from the face of the frieze; thus — the under side of it is ornamented with rectangular blocks called mutules, one of which is placed over each triglyph, and one over each metope; — pendant drops of a conical or cylindrical form are suspended from the under side of the mutules; also under each triglyph: — the crowning member of the cornice consists of an ovolo and fillet similar in form to the capital of the column.

In greek temples where the ends of the Naos or cell are left open, the walls are [39] terminated with square pillars called antæ. In some examples these antæ are placed on the corners instead of corner columns, and the side walls of the building continued out until it joins them, thus making a recessed portico; the edifice is then said to be a temple in antis. — These antæ are never diminished, nor fluted; — their capitals consist of a congeries of small mouldings entirely different from the capitals of the columns.

Although the Architects of greece have rigidly maintained the Doric character in all the edifices they constructed of that order, yet they varied their proportions in every example; — they pursued a general system, but never produced two buildings exactly alike: — the hypatheral temple at Pæstum, is as truly doric as the portico of the Agora at Athens; yet the columns of the former are but four diameters in height, while those of the latter are more than six.

The Doric order exhibits contrast, [40] variety and uniformity, harmoniously blended into a perfect unity of effect. — The column is enriched with its flutings, and the diversified lights and shades of its capital; and the frieze is no less elegant in the distribution of its triglyphs and sculptured Metopes; while the broad unbroken surface of the Architrave separates these richer parts and gives to each additional value. — And again, the splendid ordonnance of the portico relieved by the plain wall of the cell and rendered distinct by the deep shadows produced by its projection, throws over the whole

"The harmony of grace, the beauty of repose."

An eloquent writer in speaking of the Doric order observes, "could the very foundations of the earth assume a harmonious form and rear themselves into symmetry, it seems as if they must create this order."[*]

---

[*] North American review, Oct 1836 [Walter added this comment to the page facing [40]. Ed.]

Among the ancient Doric remains of this order are the ruins of the three temples at Pæstum; the temples of Concord and Juno at Agrigentum; the temple of Minerva at Syracuse; the temple of Apollo and the portico of Philip at Delos; the Parthenon, the Propylæa, the temple of Theseus, and the Portico of the Agora at Athens, the temple of Minerva on the promontory of Sunium, the [41] temple of Jupiter Nemeus, between Argos and Corinth; the temple of Jupiter Panhelleneus on the Island of Ægina; two temples at Selinus, and one at Ægesta.

[*The Custom House in Chestnut Street is an excellent modern adaptation of this order; another has been made by M*^r. *Strickland in the United States Bank, the porticoes of which are proportioned from the temple of Minerva Parthenon at Athens.*]

The best example of the Grecian Doric order in the United States, and probably in the world is the Custom house at New York; — the porticoes of this structure are exact copies of the Parthenon, and its dimensions are nearly equal to those of its famous prototype. (Speak of ceilings of porticoes) (Refer to Patent office Washington)[1]

[*There are many other specimens of the Doric order in Philadelphia, as the Church of the Epiphany in Chestnut Street, the Reformed Dutch Church at the corner of Tenth and Filbert Streets, the Unitarian Church &*^c.; — *but none are on so grand a scale, as the Porticoes of the Bank of the United States.*[2] *The appearance of the south front of this edifice by the soft and silver light of the Moon is so enchanting that I have often wondered while musing alone on its beauties that crowds were not seen flocking to enjoy the scene.*]

The Ionic Order

We now proceed to the <u>Ionic</u> Order. This system of building follows the Doric in the order of time as well as in the extent to which it admits of embellishment. — It presents, as [42] before remarked, an admirable medium between the grandeur of the Doric and the luxuriance of the Corinthian. This drawing presents an example of it from the Temple on the Illisus at Athens.[3] The Architects of Athens applied the Ionic order chiefly to small buildings; its proportions being too light to produce the bold and massy effect they sought to impart to their larger edifices. — Its embellishments are rather suited to please from their gracefulness and richness, than to awaken the sublime sentiments to which the Doric order is so peculiarly addressed; — where the dimensions of buildings would not admit of producing an effect of grandeur. The Athenian Architects always

---

[1] This paragraph was added to the original text at an unspecified time and cites the Custom House in New York (Town & Davis, 1833-42) and the Patent Office in Washington (1850).
[2] All three churches are Walter designs; the bank is Strickland's.
[3] This sentence referring to the rendering was added to the original manuscript at some point after 1841.

sought to awaken agreeable emotions of taste by substituting a character of elegance and beauty.

The proportions of the Ionic order are much lighter than those of the Doric in every respect; the height of the column including its base and capital is from eight to nine times its diameter, while the best examples of the Doric are only from five to six.

In all the grecian remains of this order [43] the shafts of the columns are ornamented with twenty four flutes separated by fillets.

The Capital of the column, which has the same general form in every example; constitutes the distinguishing feature of the order; — it consists of volutes formed of an assemblage of spiral lines, falling like a scroll, on each side of the upper diameter of the shaft thus. — The spiral lines composing these volutes are joined in the front of the capital, forming a curve, which rests upon a moulding sculptured in the form of eggs with tongues between them.

In the temples of Erectheus and Minerva Polias at Athens the upper part of the shafts of the columns are ornamented with honeysuckles, and the "egg and tongue" moulding is surmounted by a large torus with cross bands cut upon it, so as to present something of the appearance of rope: technically called a guilloche.

The corner capitals of Grecian Ionic porticoes were formed differently from [44] those on the intermediate columns; instead of their two faces being parallel to each other as in the rest of the Capitals, they were made contiguous, so as to present one face to the front, and the other to the flank; thus making it necessary to project out the corner volutes diagonally: — this however is at best but an awkward expedient, and should never be resorted to except where the portico is returned on the sides of the building.

The base of the Ionic column consists of a large convex moulding called a torus supporting a concave moulding denominated a scotia, and surmounted by another Torus embellished with horizontal channels: — these mouldings are separated by small fillets and in some cases the upper torus is enriched with the guilloche. — The lower torus rests on the floor of the portico without a plinth; and [45] the upper one is joined to the column by a cove called an apophyge.

The ancients never executed this order without some kind of a base; — the heavy projections of the volutes, and the richness of the whole capital require ornament, as well as projection at the bottom of the column.

In the richest examples of the Ionic order, the architrave is divided into three equal parts called faciæ; but in the simpler specimens we find this feature entirely plain as in the Doric order.

The Frieze is also plain in many examples, but sometimes it is ornamented with Sculpture.

The Ionic Order from the Temple on the Illisus. James Stuart and Nicholas Revett, The Antiquities of
Athens *(London, 1762-1816). Courtesy, Anne and Jerome Fisher Fine Arts Library,
University of Pennsylvania.*

The cornice usually consists of a large projecting member called a corona, supported by a plain bed moulding[1] and crowned with another moulding called the Cymatium from its wave-like form — thus — In some examples dentels or teeth are introduced under the corona, and the cymatium is enriched with honeysuckles.

[46] The most beautiful ancient specimen of this order is the small Ionic temple on the River Illisus at Athens; — the breadth and harmony of its component parts, and their judicious arrangement, — the graceful contour of the volutes, — the massy and effective mouldings of the cornice, — the spaciousness of the Frieze, so well adapted to the sculpture with which it is decorated, — and the plain but proportionate architrave, render this one of the most delightful examples of ancient art: — its unity of effect, and justness of proportion recommend it as one of the canons of the order.

The temples of Minerva Polias and Erectheus, on the Acropolis of Athens, called by Pausanias the double temple, present a much richer example of this order: — the volutes of the capitals are composed of a greater number of spiral lines, than those of the temple on the Illisus; the height of the capital is greater, and the neck is richly ornamented [47]: — the architrave is cut in faciæ, and all the mouldings of the entablature are enriched.

The temple of Minerva Polias at Priene, in Ionia, of which Pytheus was the Architect, is also a good specimen of this order. [*The Cymatium, or upper member of moulding of the cornice is remarkably high, and richly ornamented; — dentels are introduced under the corona of the cornice with beautiful effect; and the whole entablature is an admirable composition, upon the purest principles of the art. — The capital is similar in form to those of the little temple on the Illisus, but its enrichments are more elaborate: — the eyes of the volutes are deeply sunk for the purpose of affixing festoons of flowers, as was the custom of the Greeks on days of public festivity.*[*]]

The temple of Bacchus at Teos, of which Hermogenes was the Architect, and the temple of Apollo Dedymæus, near Miletus may also be referred to as standard [48] specimens of the Ionic order. [*Several of the best public buildings of Philadelphia are composed in this order; amongst which are the much admired porticoes of the bank of Pennsylvania, by the late M[r]. Latrobe; — the porticoes of the United States Mint, and the United States Naval Asylum by M[r]. Strickland; — and the Porticos of the First Presbyterian Church and S[t]. Andrews Church by Mr. Haviland; and the mansion of Mathew Newkirk Esq., in Arch S[t].*] The Treasury building in this city is an example of this order (— refer to the old and the new portions).[2]

---

[*] Chandler Ionian An., p 17

[1] Likely a misspelling for "bead moulding."
[2] This sentence was added for a Washington audience and replaces references to Philadelphia.

The Corinthian Order

Having examined the Doric and Ionic orders, it remains for us to consider the Corinthian.

The origin, as well as the reputed origin of this order has been related before; — it is the richest and most embellished of them all, and may be considered as the highest triumph of art in architecture. (this drawing exhibits an example of it as executed in the Monument of Lysicrates at Athens.)

[49] The proportions of this order are much lighter than either of the others, the height of the column being never less than nine times its diameter, and sometimes it is even more than ten: — the entablature is also lighter and its ornaments and mouldings are more delicate.

The Capital consists of the representation of foliage, finished on top with an abacus or tablet; — the leaves are so disposed as to bring an annular row around the lower part of the capital, springing as it were from the top of the shaft of the column; — from behind these leaves another annular row arises, adhereing to the body of the capital and extending about half way up to the abacus; — from between these upper leaves stalks grow out, and extend upwards to each corner of the abacus, under which they terminate in volutes; — from these stalks, helices or tendrils spring out, convolving in the [50] middle of each of the four faces of the capital.

Although this description embraces almost every example of the Corinthian Capital, yet no two examples are exactly similar; — in some the leaves are higher than in others, and the formation of the helices and volutes differ in every ancient specimen; — we also find variety in the character of the foliage; in some the acanthus is imitated, in others the olive, the parsley, or the water leaf. (refer to tobacco, corn &ᶜ.)

The shaft of the column of this order is usually ornamented with twenty-four flutes, in the same manner as those of the Ionic order.

The best existing example of grecian Corinthian architecture is the Choragic monument of Lysicrates at Athens; — notwithstanding this little building is but eight feet in diameter it presents a most interesting specimen of refinement and elegance in art.

[51] The Capital of the Column is particularly excellent; — the rich and sparkling foliage contrasted with the simple form of the water-leaf, — the graceful and flowing lines of the volutes and helices; — the beautiful contour of the abacus, and the ingenious and admirable termination of the flues of the shaft, form a combination of parts perfectly harmonious and graceful. [Mʳ. Strickland has made an excellent adaptation of this example in the Philadelphia Exchange, he has also used it in the front of the Mechanics Bank

and again in the Philadelphia Bank. – The order of the Girard College is likewise composed from the same specimen.]

We have no example of the grecian Corinthian order in Washington.

The exterior of the capitol is designed in grecian taste, but its leading features are drawn from Roman examples but we will speak more particularly of this when we come to discus <u>Roman</u> Architecture. – The Girard College in Philad^a. is in the grecian Corinthian order, and that order has never been executed on so grand a scale in any other building in the world either in ancient or in modern times. [1]

The door pieces of the Tower of Andronicus Cyrrhestes at Athens furnish another example of the Corinthian order; but which, from its extreme simplicity may be considered as an exception to the general principles upon which the ancients composed [52] this order. – The Capital of the column is bell-shaped, and its embellishments consist simply of an annular row of <u>olive</u> leaves, which encircle the lower half; and a row of water leaves around the upper half: – the abacus or crowning member is moulded on its edges and square on its plan.

This specimen has never been very highly esteemed; – it forms, however, a pleasing variety in architectural composition. [*It has been used in porticoes over front doors in several instances in this city, and an excellent application of its capital has been made by M^r. Strickland in the front of the Chestnut Street Theatre.*]

Temple Forms

Having examined the three orders of columnar Architecture as practiced by the Greeks, we proceed to consider briefly, the general form of their <u>temples</u>.

All greek temples are embraced in the seven orders represented on the [53] diagram before you. [2]

The <u>first</u> is that in which the front of the building is formed by terminating the side walls with antæ, and placing two columns between them, – thus. – This order is called <u>Temple in antis</u>; that is, its columns are by, or with antæ.

The <u>second</u> has a portico across the whole of <u>one</u> end of the edifice, thus; – it is denominated <u>Prostyle</u>, or columns <u>before</u> the building.

The <u>third</u> order embraces such buildings as have porticoes at both ends; – it is called <u>Amphiprostyle</u>; or columns before both the front and the back of the edifice.

---

[1] Walter added both this paragraph and the sentence above it to the page facing [51]. The necessity to place Girard College in Philadelphia clearly dates the change to his Washington years.

[2] The term "orders" here refers to the classification of temples by their plans as occurs in Vitruvius.

The <u>fourth</u> order is called Peripteral; a term which signifies winged, or aisled on <u>every</u> side; — it embraces such buildings as have a single row of columns surrounding the whole edifice, thus. — The term Peripteral is also applied to circular temples, where the columns are placed around a cell: [54+] — but where there is no cell, and the columns simply support a circular roof, the structure is called Monopteral or a single aisle or canopy.

The <u>fifth</u> order is temple surrounded with a <u>double</u> row of columns — it is called <u>Dipteral</u>, or double aisled.

The <u>sixth</u> order has the same exterior finish as the fifth; and its only difference consists in omitting the inner row of columns; it is called <u>Pseudo-Dipteral</u>, or false dipteral; from the fact that it conveys from a distance the same idea as a dipteral temple.

The <u>seventh</u> and last order embraces such temples as are left open or unroofed in the centre; — they are called <u>Hypæthral</u>; a term derived from a greek word signifying, open to the sky; — the space between the inner columns being left without a roof, while the rest of the building is covered.

[54] The Greeks also paid great attention to the manner in which they distributed their columns; — they considered the proportions of the spaces, or intervals between them as of much importance as the proportions of the columns themselves. — These spaces or intervals are denominated intercolumniations; they are divided into five classes or styles; — the first is called Pycnostyle, or columns thickly set; the spaces between the columns being each but one and a half diameters.

The second is called systyle, and has two diameters between the columns.

[55] The third is denominated Eustyle or, as the term indicates, the most graceful manner of intercolumniation; — by this mode the columns are placed two and a quarter diameters apart.

The fourth is called Diastyle, and has three diameters of the column for its intercolumniation.

The fifth is denominated Areostyle, or columns thinly set; this mode has its intercolumniations equal to four time the diameter of the column.

Besides these orders or styles, porticoes are also named from the number of columns of which they are composed; as tetrastyle, hexastyle, and octastyle, according as they may have four, six, or eight columns in front.

Hence we find temples designated first by the order of their columns, as Doric, Ionic, or Corinthian, — secondly by the manner of placing them in relation to the cella, and Prostyle, Peripteral, &c., thirdly by the manner of intercolumniation [56] as Systyle, Eustyle &c., and fourthly by the number of columns in front, as hexastyle, Octastyle, Decastyle &c.

The Greeks usually disposed the columns of their temples so as to have one more than twice as many on the sides, as they had on the ends;—if, for example they placed eight on the ends, they would make seventeen on the sides, as in the Parthenon at Athens;—or if the end porticoes were six columns in width, then there would be but thirteen on the sides, as in the Temple of Theseus.

One of the most beautiful features in a Greek temple is the Pediment, or triangular elevation formed at each end of the building by the inclination of the roof;—the Greeks were particularly happy in proportioning this part of their structures;—they generally made the elevation from twelve to sixteen degrees; according to the width of the front, taking care in all cases to have the Pediment about equal in height to the Entablature. The spaces between the cornices were usually decorated with elaborate sculpture. So much was this feature of Architecture admired [57] in ancient times that Cicero foolishly says, "if there were to be erected a Capitol in heaven where it never rains, it would be finished with Pediments and a roof."

Greek Science

All the works of the ancient Greeks show a profound knowledge of every branch of science connected with Architecture.—We learn of their preeminence in the cultivation of all the arts of peace from Homer, Hesiod, Herodotus, Strabo, Diodorus, Pliny, Senaca and many others,—and the testimony of these authors is fully corroborated by the beautiful relics of this tasteful people.—Their knowledge of Geometry, perspective, and Anatomy is incontrovertible;—they studied height, distance, and picturesque effect with the greatest accuracy;—columns of a great height were made to diminish less than those that were shorter,—and what shows a still greater knowledge of optical effect, the corner columns of their temples were made thicker than intermediate ones, so as to counteract the apparent reduction in [58] their diameter, caused by their insulated position.(—Refer to plan, and speak of Girard College.)

Vitruvius tells us, in the preface to his seventh book, that when Eschylus wrote his tragedies, (which was about 500 years before Christ), "Agarthacus made scenes, and left a treatise upon them;" and that "after him Democritus, and Anaxagorus went still farther in that way, showing the power of imitating nature, by making all the lines to vanish to one point, as to a centre, when viewed at a fixed distance, by which means they were enabled to represent in their scenes the images of real buildings, as they usually appear to the eye."*

This quotation clearly shows that the principles of perspective were

---

* Elmes lec 4 p 185

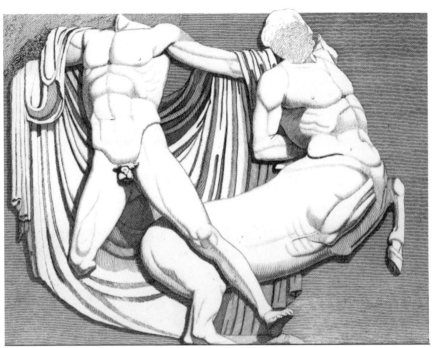

Metope from the Parthenon. James Stuart and Nicholas Revett, The Antiquities of Athens (London, 1762-1816). Courtesy, Anne and Jerome Fisher Fine Arts Library, University of Pennsylvania.

understood by the Greeks, long before the building of their best edifices.

Those who deny to this polished people the praise that belongs to them have contended [59] that they could not have understood even the <u>simplest</u> principles of Geometry, because Euclid, the earliest author in that science, whose works have reached our time, lived considerably after the best age of grecian architecture;—but we want nothing better than their works to prove, not only that they understood Geometry, but that they attained great <u>proficiency</u> in it, long before Euclid produced the profound and ingenious demonstrations which have reflected such lustre upon his memory.

Their knowledge of <u>Anatomy</u> must also have been very considerable;— the beautiful remains of sculpture which yet adorn many of their edifices prove their skill in this science beyond a doubt.—It has been gravely asserted that they never attempted to dissect, because laws are on record which prohibited dissection;—but to borrow a maxim from "<u>the law</u>," "<u>the exception proves the rule</u>;"—there could have been no necessity for enacting laws <u>against</u> dissection, if it had [60] never existed.—The splendid sculptures of the Parthenon, the Theseum, and many other grecian remains, exhibit a perfection in the art, that never could have been reached without the most thorough knowledge of <u>some</u> parts, at least, of Anatomy;—in some figures we find a delicate hinting at muscles which are so deeply seated as not to be visible except in the peculiar action in which they are represented.[*]—M[r]. Elmes says, in speaking of the marbles of the Elgin collection, which were taken from the temple on the Illisus and the Theseum, "they looked palpably like flesh;" "they appeared as heroic forms of heavenly proportions, held by the magic wand of a Prospero in temporary inaction;—they seemed like petrefactions of heroic nature, and yet they were but dusty fragments of Grecian taste."[†]

> "O conquering genius! That could'st thus detain
> The subtle graces, fading as they rise,
> Eternalize expression's fleeting reign,
> Arrest warm life in all its energies,
> And fix them on the stone."[‡]

Ruins

[61] But "Greece is changed in all that could be changed by time;"—the spirit of her lofty sons, who "thus impressed their mighty image on the years to be," is gone!—and desolation now reigns triumphant over all the proud and peerless memorials of her former greatness.

The mutilated remnants of her mighty genius, "girt solemnly with all the imploring beauty of decay," are surrounded by the rudest and most unsightly fabrics barbarian hands could raise.—Her richest trophies of surpassing taste, wrought in the snow-white marbles of Paros and Pentelicus, of Hymettus and Marmarium, and which stood, while Greece was free, in all the majesty of perfected art, have been torn from their places, and broken up to construct the roughest masonry of modern times;—while the reckless Elgin, and other barbarous despoilers from foreign lands, have contributed in no small degree to consummate the desolation that now broods over the lovely remnants of this [62] polished people:—in the language of the Giaour

> "'Tis Greece, but living Greece no more!
> So coldly sweet, so deadly fair,
> We start, for soul is wanting there.
> Hers is the loveliness in death,
> That parts not quite with parting breath;
> But beauty with that fearful bloom,

---

[*] Haydon on the Elgin marbles
[†] Elmes: lectures p 183
[‡] Mrs. Hemans Mod. Greece p. 94

That hue which haunts it to the tomb,
Expression's last receeding ray,
A gilded halo hovering round decay,
The farewell beam of feeling passed away!
Spark of that flame, perchance of heavenly birth,
Which gleams, but warms no more its cherished earth
Clime of the unforgotten brave!
Whose land from plain to mountain-cave
Was freedom's home or Glory's grave!
Shrine of the mighty!"*

The influences of Greece on architecture have passed away—her Classic forms have yielded to more ornate conceptions and the elements of beauty in building are no longer sought among the antiquities of a long forgotten age.[1]

---

* Byron's Giaour

[1] These lines constitute one of the more significant mid-century changes to the Lectures. The lines, in pencil and on the facing page, reveal Walter's acknowledgement that his favored mode, the Grecian style, had failed to win popularity and was being overcome by the "mongrel" post-bellum styles that he abhorred. The addition changes the format of the Lectures as well, since originally all five historical essays ended with quotations from poetry.

Lecture 3rd

On the Architecture of Ancient Rome

Thos. U. Walter
Philad.ª Nov. 24, 1841

Delivered Nov. 25. 1841

The Colosseum. George Ledwell Taylor and Edward Cresy, The Architectural Antiquities of Ancient Rome *(London, 1821-22). Courtesy, Anne and Jerome Fisher Fine Arts Library, University of Pennsylvania.*

LECTURE III
ON THE ARCHITECTURE OF ANCIENT ROME

Introduction: The Settlement of Italy and Founding of Rome

[1+] The Architecture of the early ages of Rome, cannot be traced, with any degree of certainty, to a higher antiquity than that which its existing remains authenticate. — The history of the heroic age, which is said to date back to the siege of Troy, rests almost exclusively on mysterious legend, traditionary fable, and scattered fragments of mythology. We shall therefore advert but briefly to the story of the early days of the Empire, and limit our investigations chiefly to the principles of Roman Architecture, as we find them developed in the monuments of Roman genius that still embellish "the city of the seven hills."

[2] History tells us that a Trojan Prince named Æneas, emigrated with about 600 of his countrymen into Italy, immediately after the destruction of Troy, which is said to have occurred 1184 years before the Christian era; and that they landed on a small territory called the Latium, on the east side of the river Tiber, where they founded a city, and entered into a treaty with Latinus, the King of the country, by which treaty they eventually became possessed of the entire kingdom.

They carried with them the statue denominated the Palladium, and established the ancient religion of Troy throughout the country. — This statue became the tutelar deity of Lavinium, and afterwards of the whole Roman empire. — Ovid speaks of it as representing the goddess Pallas, whence it is supposed to have derived its name.

Dionysius says that Æneas took with him into Italy, together with the Palladium, the statues of many other gods which were honoured in Greece; — and it is generally supposed that most of the manners [3] and customs of the Greeks were introduced into Italy by this colony.

About 400 years after Æneas, the government fell into the hands of Romulus, who is reputed to have been the founder of the Roman Capitol, which he is said to have called Rome, in allusion to his own name.

Chronologists differ as to the precise period when the city was founded, but the best historians have fixed it in the third year of the sixth Olympiad, which is 431 years after the destruction of Troy, and 753 years before the beginning of the Christian era.

Greek Influence on Etruscan and Early Roman Architecture

The earliest buildings of Rome are represented as having been extremely rude and unsightly; [*the inhabitants are said to have paid no regard either to the beauty of the houses or the regularity of the streets; — every man built according to his own fancy, and*] the whole town is said to have consisted, previous to its destruction by the Gauls, of a vast group of miserable huts, without upper stories, and totally destitute of every thing like [4] ornament.[1] — The palace of the Kings, which was probably one of the best buildings in Rome at that time, was made of rushes and roofed with straw: "such were the beginnings of the capitol of the world."[*]

The earliest inhabitants of Rome were principally emigrants, from countries where architectural science had been more or less cultivated; we may therefore infer that the principles of art were not wholly neglected, even in their rudest structures.

It is not however probable that the style of building which prevailed in Rome previous to the subjugation of Greece, bore much resemblance to the system which was afterwards practiced. — Had the Romans been entirely free from local prejudices on the subject of architectural forms and proportions, they would have received Grecian art in all its elegance and purity; — but the previous knowledge they possessed, and an unbounded thirst for superiority, which has always characterized the nation, [5] seems to have led them to consider the perfect forms of the Grecian models, as a mere ground work, upon which to build their own national reputation: — hence ensued the peculiar manner of building ever since known under the name of Roman Architecture.

The state of the arts among the Romans at the time of their invasion of Greece may be inferred from Plutarch; — he relates that Marcellus being called to Rome after a campaign in Greece, "carried with him the most valuable of the statues and paintings in Syracuse, that they might embellish his triumph, and be an ornament to the metropolis; for, before this time

---

[*] Hook's Rome p 45 v 1

[1] The Gallic sack of Rome occurred in 390.

that city neither had, nor knew any curiosities of the kind, being a stranger to the charms of taste and elegance:" — "thus did Marcellus," continues our author, "become acceptable to the people, having adorned the city with a variety of beautiful curiosities in the Grecian taste."

Many of the Romans however censured the proceedings of [6] the consul, first for having as they said led not only <u>men</u> but the very <u>gods</u> in triumph; and secondly, because he had spoiled a people inured to agriculture and war, and who were previously, as Euripides says

"In vice untaught, but skill'd where glory led
To arduous enterprise."

But notwithstanding the censures of the people, Marcellus prided himself on being the first who taught the Romans to esteem, and to admire the exquisite performances of Greece, which had hitherto been unknown to them.

The whole temple of Jupiter Capitolinus in Rome is said to have been composed of the materials of an Athenian edifice; — and, in the words of Plutarch, "the columns were cut and repolished after their arrival in Rome, in order to produce a greater degree of elegance and lightness; but what they obtained in this quality," remarks that author, "they lost in grandeur and symmetrical proportion." [*The Roman system of Architecture can therefore be considered as very little more than a grand spoliation of Grecian art, perpetrated by* [7] *an unskillfull, inexperienced, and comparatively barbarous hand and a barbarous people.*]

Grecian artists, it is true were imported by the Romans, and employed upon many of their works, but the purity, and correctness of Grecian taste not being appreciated in Rome, they were not permitted to think, and act for themselves: — their imagination was gradually reduced to the standard of Roman genius; and they found out by experience that "<u>they who live in Rome must do as Rome does.</u>"

Development of Roman Architectural Character

Had the disposition and pursuits of the Romans favored the advancement of the arts, the transition of architecture from Greece to Rome would have constituted the brightest era in architectural history; — but such was not the case; — Rome was inhabited by a warlike, a ferocious people, whose only steps to power and greatness were oratory, and war; and among whom few things were cultivated but eloquence and the sword; — their architecture was therefore chiefly directed to pamper the vanity of their [8] leaders, — to embellish their triumphs, or to perpetuate the success of their arms. — Temples were raised in honor of those, who, by military prowess extended the dominion of the empire, and priests, and pontiffs were employed to pay them impious homage. — Triumphal arches were erected to commemorate the achievements of aspiring potentates, — and ponderous columns reared to record the success of the Roman sword.

The frequent conquests made by the Roman army afforded abundant means, as well as opportunities for architectural display; and had the taste of the people been previously softened and refined, and their sensibilities humanized by the influence of the peaceful arts, [*and their character elevated and established by that true religion which flows from the eternal throne,*] their works would have come down to us invested with all the purity and dignity of perfect proportion.[1] But unfortunately for art, — unfortunately for mankind, Rome afforded to architecture but a dubious road through the lapse of ages she called her own. The scenes of [9] blood with which the imperial city was polluted from day to day, blunted the feelings of the people, seared their consciences, and suppressed all the delicate and tender emotions on which depend the enjoyments of intellectual refinement: — [9] their holidays were emphatically "<u>festivals of blood</u>;" — around the arena of the great Colosseum — "that imperial slaughter house of Rome" they found their highest pleasures: — the ferocious populace daily assembled in eager crowds impatient to behold the sports of death; — barbarian gladiators were here brought forth, and, "butchered to make a Roman holiday."

"And here, where buzzing nations choked the ways,
And roar'd or murmur'd like a mountain stream
Dashing or winding as its torrent strays. —
Here, where the Roman millions' blame or praise,
Was death or life, the playthings of a crowd."*

Thus were the finer feelings of the Roman people destroyed, and thus was a passion for the showy and wonderful engendered [*to the entire exclusion of all the delicate and chastened emotions of mind, which are* [10] *ever awakened in the mind by harmony and proportion.*] Hence we find the Architecture of the Romans far more colossal, gorgeous and expensive than the chaster monuments of Greece. — Their passion for pomp and splendor led them into a redundancy of ornament, — an exhuberance of embellishment that rendered them totally unfit for the enjoyment of the more intellectual charms of gracefulness and harmony.

Imperial Patronage

But however spiritless and insipid the <u>taste</u> of the Roman Architects may have been, it is evident from the monuments they have left behind,

---

* Byron Childe Har., p 179 64 v 142

[1] The phrase "all the purity and dignity of perfect proportion" replaces the original and more spiritual language "all the sweetness of heavenly proportion, and living beauty."

that the patronage they received was boundless; — the best blood of Rome seems always to have been enlisted in the cause of art, and the public purse was open for any expenditure that would tend to bring honor on the national character.

The reign of Julius Cæsar, the first Roman Emperor, is said to have been particularly favorable to the advancement of Architecture; — that monarch embellished Rome with many very considerable structures, and he is represented [11] as having been passionately fond of the arts. In the language of the bard of Avon, —

"This was the noblest Roman of them all;"
"His life was gentle; and the elements
So mix'd in him, that Nature might stand up,
And say to all the world, <u>This was a man!</u>"*

Architecture was also patronized to a great extent under Augustus, who, as we are informed by his biographer, boasted on his death-bed that he found Rome composed of bricks, and left it a city of Marble. — The works erected under the peaceful reign of this Emperor, were more numerous, and in better taste, than those of any previous or subsequent administration.

Caligula, Nero, Claudius, Vespasian, Titus, Domitian and Nerva were all famous for their zeal in promoting architectural science; and Trajan, in whose reign the Roman empire florished most, embellished the Capitol with many very important works. — He built the celebrated Forum, the Trajan Column, and the Triumphal arch that bears his name.

[12] In short, architecture continued to florish among the Romans, though with abated lustre, until the seat of empire was removed to Byzantium by Constantine the great, in the 328th year of our religion. — Many temples, and expensive Christian churches were built by this Emperor both in Rome, and in Byzantium (then called Constantinopolis, or the city of Constantine, subsequently by the Europeans Constantinople, and now by the Turks Stamboul) but all the works of this monarch afford incontestable evidence of the vitiated taste of the times.

Architecture had now ceased to exert any influence over the people, and as a consequence, many of the noblest monuments of by-gone ages were torn to pieces to make new buildings, of the most monstrous forms, or carried to Constantinople to grace the new Capitol. — Thus did some of the best edifices of Rome perish by the hands of her own sons, — and thus was prostrated most of the monuments of art which had been accumulating in the "city of the seven hills" for more than two thousand years.†

---

* Shakespeare, Julius Cæsar
† Neibhur

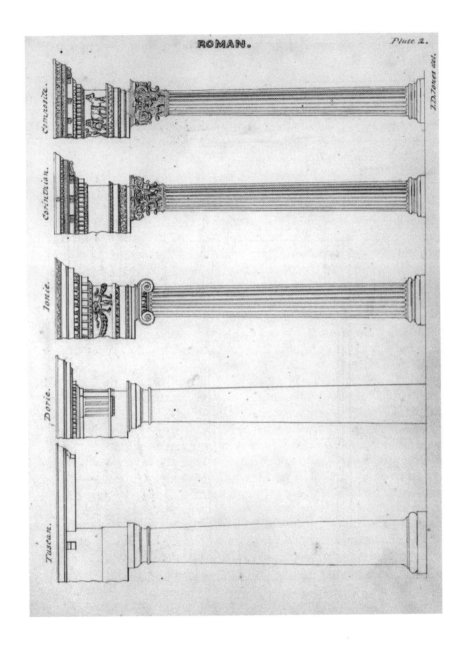

The Five Roman Orders. John D. Jones, "A Sketch on Architecture, by a Student" (1836). PAT, Gift of Kenneth Miller.

Elements and Principles of Roman Architecture: The Orders

[13] Having glanced at the causes which produced the Roman system of Architecture, we proceed to consider briefly its elements, or constituent principles.

The columnar architecture of the Romans is usually divided into five orders denominated Tuscan,—Doric,—Ionic,—Corinthian, and Composite.—(see diagrams) The Tuscan and the Composite are not however entitled to the rank of separate orders; the Tuscan being simply a modification of the Doric, and the Composite a union of the Ionic and the Corinthian; they therefore embrace no principles which are not included in the others. The dignified appellation of orders has been given to them by writers of comparatively modern [14] date, without either reason, or authority to warrant it;—Vitruvius, who wrote in the days of Augustus, during whose reign Roman Architecture attained its zenith would unquestionably have spoken of new orders, had there been any;—he mentions, Tuscan temples, and various kinds of Capitals employed in Corinthian structures, but nowhere alludes to them as forming separate orders; and we have no reason to suppose that even the Roman Architects themselves ever considered columnar architecture as being divisible into more than the three orders Doric, Ionic and Corinthian, all of which were derived from Greece.

And again, if we admit that the difference between the Tuscan and the Doric, or the Corinthian and the Composite, is sufficient to sanction the custom of calling them separate orders, then might every Architect claim the credit of having invented new orders; [15] as there are probably but few who have not found it necessary, in adapting examples from the antique to particular situations, to vary from the originals as much as the orders in question differ from each other.—The ancients themselves differed more in the execution of the same order than the Tuscan varies from the Doric, or the composite from the Corinthian;—hence we might give the name of a separate order to almost every building of antiquity, with as much propriety as to apply such a term either to the Tuscan or the Composite.

All the forms of Roman, as well as Grecian architecture are included in the three orders, which represent respectively the robust, the chaste, and the elegant;—the simple, the voluted and the foliated:[1]—these, (as remarked on a previous occasion) embody all the principles of columnar construction which nature dictates; their number can therefore never be increased:—hence the orders called Tuscan and Composite should be considered as belonging to the Doric, and the Corinthian, their constituent element being the [16] same.

---

[1] Walter used these terms to describe the three "general classes" or "distinctive characters" of the orders as they developed in Egypt and Greece. See I:17 ff and II:17 ff.

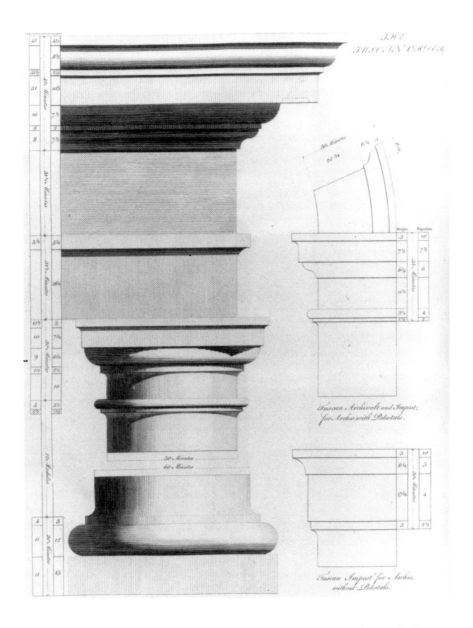

The Tuscan Order. William Chambers, A Treatise On Civil Architecture *(London, 1759). Courtesy, the Winterthur Library: Printed Book and Periodical Collection.*

The division of the columnar architecture of the Romans into five orders having however met with an almost universal reception, the necessity seems to be imposed upon us of adopting the same nomenclature; we shall therefore consider the Roman Orders under the respective names which modern writers have given them.

The Tuscan is the most simple, and massy of all the Orders; its agreement with the Doric, and its relative proportions will be better understood by comparing the drawing of the Tuscan with that of the Doric.

The shaft of the Tuscan column is never fluted, and the base which is about half of a diameter in height, consists of a single torus, a fillet joined to the shaft by an apophyge, and a plinth, which is sometimes circular on its plan and sometimes square.

The capital, which also occupies half a diameter, is divided into three equal parts, one of which is given to the abacus, or square member on top, one to the ovolo under it, and [17] the third to the neck. — The height of the entire column is usually about seven diameters, and the entablature one and three quarters.

Vitruvius has given to the cornice a projection equal to about one fourth the height of the column, while other authors confine it to about one tenth.

The proportions of this order are unauthenticated by any existing remains, and almost every writer on Roman architecture has made one to suit his own fancy. — Serlio, Scamozzi, De l'orme, Vignola, and Sir William Chambers have all tried their skill at it with but little success; none of them having ever been able to separate it from the Doric, so far as to give it the least title to the distinctive appellation of an order.

Palladio has manufactured his Tuscan from fragments of an ancient temple he found in Italy, which he considers as full proof of its genuineness; but the ruins he speaks of were probably nothing more than some barbarism of the Doric. — The best example is that given [18] by Sir William Chambers, which is the one here represented.

[*A specimen of this order according to Vitruvius may be seen in the Porticoes on the ends of the Callowhill Street market, fronting on Crown and on Sixth Streets. Unfortunately however they are entirely composed of wood, and their beauty has been shockingly marred by painting the columns a rusty black probably to make them dirt-proof.*

*M*ʳ*. Haviland has given us a modification of the Doric in his Asylum for the Deaf and Dumb on Broad Street, which may be considered as belonging to the Tuscan order, and which is unquestionably far superior to any example that ever came out of the Italian School.*]

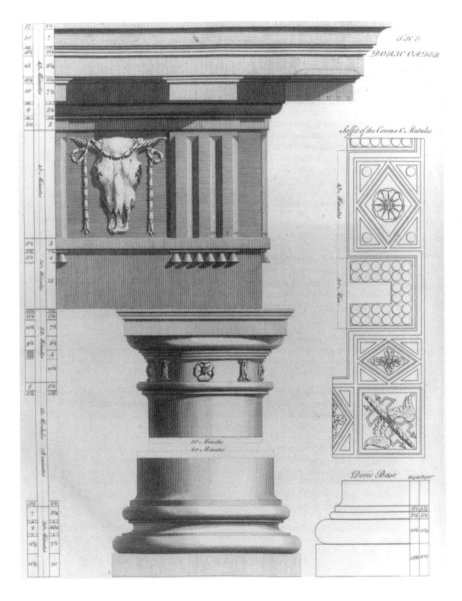

The Doric Order. William Chambers, A Treatise On Civil Architecture *(London, 1759). Courtesy, the Winterthur Library: Printed Book and Periodical Collection.*

The next order in the Roman system is called <u>Doric</u>; the distinguishing features of which correspond in general form with the [19] Doric order of the Greeks, although in spirit they widely disagree.

By comparing the Grecian and Roman examples of this order before you it will be observed that while all the general features of the Grecian model have been preserved in the copy, the graceful and poetic expression of the prototype has been entirely overlooked. — The whole order, according to the Roman School is a mere coarse and vulgar adaptation of the greek original. — The column is reduced in thickness to about one eighth of its height; the echinus of the capital is converted into a quadrant; the simplicity of the abacus is destroyed by the addition of a useless moulding on its upper edge; the sparkling and brilliant effect produced by the pendant guttæ or drops, is entirely lost by sinking them into the mutules; a base is added to the shaft except in a very few of the most ancient examples, and fillets are placed between the flutes; — the mouldings of the cornice are all harsh and incongruous; and the gracefulness [20] and harmony of the frieze is materially lessened by the arrangement of the triglyphs. — In all <u>Grecian</u> temples, the corner triglyphs are placed on the angles of the building, which brings them outside of the centre of the corner columns; but in every Roman example they are placed directly over the <u>centre</u> of the columns leaving a small space beyond them; — this gives an unfinished appearance to the frieze, and produces the effect of weakness at the corners; — this interpolation was no doubt made by the Romans for the purpose of equalizing the intercolumniations; but even the attainment of <u>that</u> object is not desirable when an idea of great strength is intended to be conveyed, as in the Tuscan or Doric orders. [*The only correct Roman Doric specimen on a large scale in the neighborhood of Philadelphia, is the centre Portico of the Entrance to the Laurel Hill Cemetery, the proportions of which are according to Sir William Chambers.*]

The <u>third</u> order of Roman architecture is called Ionic. — The characteristic features [21] of this order are more positively determined than those of any other; hence we find the same general form in every example, whether Greek or Roman. — You will however observe by comparing the two specimens of this order before you that the same spiritless and meagre effect which pervades the other Roman orders is manifest in this also; — the graceful curves and flowing lines so beautifully combined in the Capital of the column in the Greek example have no parallel whatever in any attempts the Romans ever made to imitate this order.

The base of the column, which is an imitation of the Attic base of the Greeks is also sadly deformed; — the scotia is girted in until it seems to weaken, rather than strengthen the structure; and a plinth, as unsightly as it is inconvenient has been superadded.

The Ionic Order from the Temple of Fortuna Virilis. George Ledwell Taylor and Edward Cresy, The Architectural Antiquities of Ancient Rome *(London, 1821-22). Courtesy, Anne and Jerome Fisher Fine Arts Library, University of Pennsylvania.*

The proportions of the Entablature have likewise been changed, and its original simplicity and chasteness lost in the mass of clumsy mouldings of which it is composed.

The columns of the Roman Ionic order are usually about nine diameters high, [22] and the entablature about two and a quarter.

The principal specimens of this order are to be found in the Temple of Fortuna Virilis, the theatre of Marcellus, and the Baths of Diocletian.

The next order according to Roman nomenclature is called Corinthian. — This system of building was also the subject of considerable change in its transition from Greece to Rome; but, unlike the innovations which were made upon the other orders, many of the alterations that were effected on this, were evidently for the better.

The foliated capital (which is always the distinctive feature of the Corinthian order), was seldom used by the Greeks, while the luxurience of its effect rendered it a desirable feature in the more showy and ostentatious displays of the Romans; it was therefore more frequently employed, and consequently better understood in Rome than in Greece. It should however be remembered, that in the formation of the Corinthian capital alone, can the credit be conceded to the Romans of having improved upon the Architecture of the [23] Greeks; every thing else that they attempted to make better lost its grace and elegance in their hands; and even in this order, notwithstanding the <u>capitals</u> in some of their specimens are exquisitely beautiful, the redundancy of modillions, dentils, and heavy carved mouldings with which their entablatures are charged, destroy the effect which would otherwise be produced by the gracefulness of the Capitals.

Roman Corinthian columns are usually about ten diameters high, and the entablature they sustain, about two and a half.

The most beautiful ancient example of this order is the three remaining columns of the Temple of Jupiter Stator in the Campo Vicino, the Capitals of which are richer and more perfectly proportioned than any other specimen of Roman art. — Among other ancient examples of this order are the Temple of Jupiter the Thunderer, the portico of the Pantheon, the Forum of Nerva, the Temple of Antoninus and Faustina, and the temple of Mars the Avenger.

[24] This drawing exhibits the Corinthian order from the temple of Jupiter Stator, and the one below it, the same order from the monument of Lysicrates at Athens. [*The best specimen of the Roman Corinthian order in Philadelphia is the Banking house of the Old United States Bank in third Street, now the Girard Bank; it was designed by M^r. Samuel Blodget, and executed under his direction about the close of the last century. Its proportions are from the "<u>Maison Quarrée</u>" at Nismes, formerly a Roman province in the south of France.*]

The Corinthian Order from the Temple of Jupiter Stator. George Ledwell Taylor and Edward Cresy,
The Architectural Antiquities of Ancient Rome *(London, 1821-22). Courtesy, Anne and Jerome*
Fisher Fine Arts Library, University of Pennsylvania.

We now proceed to the fifth and last order in the Roman system. It is usually denominated the <u>composite</u> order, from the circumstance of its having been composed of portions of the other orders.—(This drawing represents and example of it from the arch of Titus.) The same base which is used in the Doric, the Ionic, and the Corinthian, is employed in this order [25] also;—the shaft of the column is of Corinthian proportions, and the capital is composed of the foliage of the Corinthian, and the volutes of the Ionic.

The ancients seem to have affected to this order no particular form of Entablature:—Sometimes they used the Corinthian with very little alteration, at others the Ionic, and in some instances they have made compositions from both.

The height of the composite column is usually about ten diameters, and the entablature two and a half.—The base is <u>attic</u>, being about half a diameter in height; and the elevation of the capital is generally about one diameter and a third. [*The shaft is enriched with 24 flutes similar to the Ionic and Corinthian.*]

There are many existing remains of this order in Rome, nearly all of which are widely different from each other. The example that bears the highest reputation is the triumphal arch erected by the Roman Senate in honor of Titus, after his conquest of Jerusalem. The walls [26] of this arch contain representations in relief of the splendid pageant of Jerusalem's conqueror, on his entry into Rome, with his apotheosis,—and the spoils he brought from the temple of the holy city, all sculptured in marble by artists who lived when Titus lived, and who were probably engaged in executing the very forms which here exist, to conjure up the distant past; before the ruins of Jerusalem had ceased to smoke, or the victims of that sanguinary war had found a grave:—here we see the vessels of incence, the golden table, the golden candlestick with seven branches, and the trumpets mentioned in the bible, all engraved upon the stone.—Thus have the images—the very reflections of the furniture of GOD's own house on mount Moriah been handed down thro' more than seventeen centuries.

Arched Construction

Having considered the orders, the next subject we shall notice is the mode of building with arches.—This method of construction was extensively practiced by the Romans, and may [27] be considered as peculiar to the architecture of that people;—in some instances they have used it with excellent effect, but more frequently we find it employed without the slightest regard to harmony, proportion, or even utility.—Entablatures

The Composite Order from the Arch of Titus. Antoine Desgodetz, Les edifices antiques de Rome *(London, 1771). The Athenæum of Philadelphia.*

were often entirely omitted, and arches constructed from column to column; — arcades were substituted for Porticoes; — a curvilinear finish was given to the smallest openings; and in many of the most important Roman structures some windows are crowned with Pediments, and others in the same façade finished with arches: — this is obviously at variance with every principle of beauty, and has no apology even in utility.

It cannot be denied that the arch is a convenient, and in some situations, an agreeable form of building, and when properly managed may be made to produce the most pleasing effects; but its abuse has probably led to a greater corruption of style, than would ever have been witnessed had it never existed.

The evident intention of the arch is to [28] span over openings which are too large to admit of being covered with a single stone; it is therefore always misapplied when used over openings which are smaller, or of equal size with other apertures, which are not arched.

[*This defect is nowhere more evident than in many of our ordinary dwelling houses. — We frequently see the windows lintelled with stone, and the front door crowned with an arch; and to heighten the incongruity, neither the springing line, nor the crown of the arch agrees with any horizontal line in the building: — this is even worse than Roman.*

I am happy however to say that the public taste in this particular is improving: — builders seem almost universally to have given up their attachment to circular headed doors, and if they would now pay a little more attention to having the upper horizontal line of the opening of the door to agree with that of the widows, and be more careful to make the windows in the different stories over [29] *each other, our street architecture would be still further improved.*]

Notwithstanding the importance of the arch in building, when judiciously applied, and the great changes its introduction has produced in architecture, the era of its invention is completely involved in obscurity; — some have endeavoured to trace its origin to the shores of the Nile; others suppose the builders of Babylon to have been familiar with its properties, and refer in support of the conjecture to the bridge over the Euphrates, the hanging gardens, and the subterranean passage made by Queen Semiramis under the bed of the river; — Herodotus however describes the bridge alluded to, as having been composed of stone piers supporting squarred beams, and the recent investigations of Rennel and others prove beyond a doubt that the Babylonians knew nothing at all of the principles of arching.

It is necessary however in considering this question to keep in mind the difference between an arch constructed of wedge-formed [30] stones, whose joints if prolonged would meet in a center, and one produce merely by the gradual projection of horizontal courses of stones until they meet.

Examples of arches of this last description may be found in all ages, they cannot however be considered as any thing more than a species of horizontal masonry.

No specimen of the arch scientifically constructed seems to have been found of higher antiquity than the age of Alexander, either in existing remains, or described in the works of writers who florished previous to that period.

Arches it is true are found in Egypt, Æthiopia, and other ancient countries, [31] but they were, no doubt erected at much later date than some modern writers are willing to admit: Mʳ. Hoskins, in the account of his travels in the higher parts of Ethiopia¹ in 1833 describes an arch he found at Gibel el Birkel, one at the Capital of Ethiopia, and two at Thebes, which, he remarks "will satisfy the most skeptical that the Romans were not the first who were acquainted with the power and principles of the arch."* — The arguments of this learned traveller are not however sufficiently strong to justify his conclusion; — the architectural remains of Ethiopia in which arches are found, were no doubt the work of the Romans: — both Strabo and Pliny tell us of an expedition under Petronius some 20 years before Christ, to the very region in which Mʳ. Hoskins discovered the arches alluded to, and we are told that a garrison of 400 Romans was left there for the space of two years; it is therefore a matter of surprise that these famous arch-builders have left so few evidences of their visit to Ethiopia.

Again, if the Egyptians, Ethiopians or even the Greeks had understood the principles of the arch, they would undoubtedly have applied them, more or less, in most of their best edifices.² The existence therefore of the arch in these countries only shows the extent to which the Romans carried their arts, as well as their arms.

Aqueducts and Bridges

The principles of the arch were applied with greater effect and usefulness in the construction of aqueducts and Bridges than in any other department of Roman architecture. — Numerous fragments of Aqueducts are still to be seen both within, and without the walls of the city; — and many of them bespeak the solid and massy architecture of the best ages of Rome.

Appius Claudius the censor is said to have been the first to employ arches in the construction of Aqueducts: — about the year of Rome 441, he

---

* 334 [Of the several temples at Gebel Barkal in Nubia, Hoskins shows a small temple constructed about 650 BC as having arched construction. Ed.]

¹ Appearing in the original manuscript, the term "Æthiopia" was later updated to "Ethiopia."
² A large section of text was added on the facing page, starting in the preceding paragraph from "Mr. Hoskins" to the end of this paragraph, reflecting continued research.

Aqueduct of Tarragona. Comte de Alexandre Laborde, Voyage de l'Espagne *(Paris, 1806-1820). Courtesy, Annenberg Rare Book and Manuscript Library, University of Pennsylvania.*

brought a stream of water into the city from a distance of about seven [32] miles; previous to which Rome had no other supply of water than that which was derived from the Tiber.

I made a careful examination of this aqueduct. Many of its arches are still perfect, and the whole line may be traced, winding through the country from its starting point to its termination. Some of its arches were 109 feet above the valley, and its cost, according to Palladio, was 1.395.000 gold Crowns. This was the greatest of all the hydraulic works of the Romans.[1]

Another work of the same description was constructed near the Porta San Lorenzo;—this aqueduct had three water courses, one above another, and is said to have conveyed the waters of the three rivers Martia, Tepula, and Julia to Rome. [*The greatest however of all the hydraulic works of the Romans was the Claudian aqueduct, which was begun by Caligula, and finished by Claudius;—its arches were 109 feet in height, and its cost according to Palladio, one million, three hundred and ninety five thousand gold crowns. A great portion of this stupendous work still remains.*]

The number of Aqueducts in the time of Procopius (who wrote in the sixth century of Rome) is stated by him to have been fourteen; the ruins of most of which are still to be seen.

The same causes, and the same ambitious spirit which led the Romans to construct [33] their Metropolitan aqueducts incited them to the formation of similar structures in many of the countries which fell

[1] This paragraph appears on the page facing [32].

under their dominion; hence we find Roman aqueducts at Catanea, Salona, Smyrna, Ephesus, Alexandria Troas, Evora, Athens, Segovia, Mentz and Nismes. — This last work is now known by the name of the Pont du gard, and is supposed to have been erected by Agrippa; it is one hundred and sixty feet in height and presents a very superior specimen of masonry.

The Aqueducts built by the Romans have, it is true, been surpassed in our own country and in our own times, but it must be borne in mind that the Roman works were constructed 17 centuries ago — The Croton Aqueduct in New York carries more water than all the aqueducts of Rome put together, and is longer than any except the Julian aqueduct, which exceeded it only by 2 miles in length.[1] [34] The piers were generally made equal to about one third of the openings, and never less than one fifth; and their largest spans seldom exceeded seventy feet.

The first bridge of which we have any account was composed of wood, whence it was called sublicus; it was built by Ancus Martius at the foot of the Aventine hill, and is the same bridge which was defended with so much courage by Horatius Coles, against the army of Porsena: — Emilius Lepidus rebuilt it of stone from whom it took the name of Pons Emilianus: — after having been repaired by Tiberius it went to decay, and was subsequently rebuilt of marble by Antoninus Pius, whence it received the name of Pons marmoratus. — In the year 780 it was carried away by a flood, and has never since been replaced.

Another of the celebrated bridges of ancient Rome is called Pons Triumphalis, it extended from the Campus Martius to the Vatican, and is said to have been the longest bridge ever built in Rome; — it was destroyed in the fourth century, and all that can now [35] be seen of it, is the agitation of the water produced by passing over its ruins.

The ponte Rotto, or as it is called by some antiquaries, the pons Senatorius, was the first stone bridge every built in Rome; — it was commenced 179 years before our era, and 37 years were occupied in building it; — five arches of this bridge are yet remaining.

Besides these, there were many other similar works of considerable importance in Rome and its vicinity; one of later date built over the Danube by Trajan is particularly worthy of remark: — this bridge, according to Dio Cassius consisted of twenty piers of one hundred and sixty feet in height, by sixty feet in width, united by arches of one hundred and seventy feet span: — this noble structure was wantonly demolished by Hadrian shortly after its completion, and its Architect, the great Apollodorus was as wantonly destroyed by the same Emperor [for his frankness in criticizing a design for a temple made by Hadrian himself: — thus was an eminent professor cut

---

[1] To this point, this paragraph is an addition; with it Walter brings contemporary American engineering achievements into the discussion. By the time of Walter's rewriting in Washington the Croton Aqueduct (1842) had well proved its potential.

off, because he presumed [36] *to have more knowledge of his art than was possessed by one of its most superficial amateurs*].

We have, in these structures, the developement of the principles of building with arches; we will now refer briefly to other remarkable edifices of Roman origin, which seem to claim a passing notice.

Significant Roman Buildings

The temple of Jupiter Capitolinus was probably the most magnificent structure in Rome; it was begun by Tarquinius Priscus, and finished by Tarquinius Superbus; — Dionysius describes it as standing upon lofty foundations surrounded with pillars, having three rows on the fronts and two on the sides; it contained three chapels, one dedicated to Jupiter, one to Juno, and the other to Minerva. — Livy tells us that the original doorways of the building were of brass; the roof was made of wood, and Pliny says, that after the destruction of Carthage the timbers of the interior were gilt, and the pavement laid in mosaic.

This splendid edifice was burnt, in [37] the wars of Marius and Sylla, and restored by the latter upon the same foundation. — It was again burnt in the time of Vitellius in the 69th year of the Christian era, and rebuilt by Vespasian. — It suffered by fire a third time under Titus, and was restored by Domitian, who gilded the outside of the roof [*and Plutarch tells us that these last repairs cost upwards of 12,000 talents*].

Another wonderful production of Roman power is the Flavian Amphitheatre, now known by the name of the Colosseum. [This gigantic ruin still stands amid surrounding desolation.] — The massy walls of this gigantic ruin have served for ages as a quarry from which the builders of Modern Rome have been supplied with materials for other works, and yet enough remains to enable the imagination to fill up with accuracy its huge proportions.

This enormous edifice was commenced [38] by Vespasian and finished by his son Titus about the 79th year of the Christian era; — its form is eliptical, measuring 620 feet on the conjugate diameter, and 513 on the transverse; — the whole height of the building is 157 feet, which is divided into four stories, each of which is decorated with a separate order of Architecture; — the first, or lower story is Doric, the second Ionic, the third Corinthian, and the fourth Composite. — The three lower stories consist of columns, and the upper one of pilasters, all of which are attached to the wall and support their respective entablatures; every intercolumniation around the whole building is pierced with an arch, and the entire mass consists of a succession of arches beginning on the ground before the arena and ascending—and receeding until they reach the height of 157 feet.

> "Arches on Arches! as it were that Rome
> Collecting the chief trophies of her line
> Would build up all her triumphs in one dome."[*]

[39] This building is chiefly composed of Travertine, and has never been considered a very superior specimen of workmanship;—it is said to have been sufficiently large to contain <u>one hundred and seven thousand persons</u>; and according to Victor eighty seven thousand could be accommodated in the seats.

The space in the middle where the shows were exhibited was called <u>arena</u>, from the sand that was strewed over it, to absorb the blood of the beasts that were slain there;—the greater part of the wall which was built around this space to keep the wild beats from the audience still remains.

The emotions awakened in my own mind on looking around from the arena of this immense pile seemed however to derive their power chiefly from association;—as the scene itself presented nothing [*intrinsically interesting*] to excite admiration except its magnitude.

> —"here the buzz of eager nations ran,
> In murmur'd pity, or loud-roar'd applause,
> As man was slaughter'd by his fellow man."[†]

On this spot barbarian gladiators met in fearful combat, and died to amuse the savage multitude;—these seats have contained at a single fête, an hundred thousand Romans; looking with eager and delighted eyes on scenes of blood and death. [40] The subterranean passage through which the victims were introduced, still shows its gloomy entrance;—through that dark avenue 5000 wild beasts were brought from the Lybian deserts, and the forests of Anatolia, and suddenly let loose, to exhibit to the Roman people a spectacle of blood more gorgeous than had ever been known before;—thus were consecrated the hundred holidays that marked the dedication of this pondrous structure.

The regal arch where once the Roman Emperors appeared in state to see these sands made sick with gore—the spot that Titus the despoiler of Jerusalem occupied during the murdrous dedication of this "imperial slaughter house" still stands entire.

No wonder that "the pomp of Rome is [41] fled!"—no wonder that the glories of the "eternal city" are only to be found amongst the things that were!

The next building which claims our attention is the Pantheon of Agrippa.—This is the most perfect edifice remaining of the better days of Roman Architecture;—it stands in the Campus Martius, and is supposed to have been built by Agrippa about 26 years before the Christian era, in

---

[*] Childe Har. Canto 4. v 128
[†] Childe Har can. 4. 139

memory of the victory of Augustus over Anthony;—it was dedicated to Jupiter Ultor, and all the gods.—In the time of Titus it suffered by fire, and was afterwards repaired by Domitian; and in the 12th year of Trajan it was injured by lightning and subsequently repaired by Hadrian.

The form of the building is circular being 144 feet in diameter in the clear, and 144 feet in height;—the front is ornamented with a portico in the Corinthian order 110 feet in width by 44 feet in depth supporting an entablature and Pediment. The shaft of each of the columns consists of a single [42] piece of oriental granite of 5 feet in diameter and 39 feet in height, and the capitals and bases are composed of white Pentelic marble.—The whole cell of the building is said to have been originally <u>faced</u> with marble, all of which has been carried away, leaving nothing exposed to view but the rough bricks:—it is however somewhat doubtful that the Pantheon ever had any other facing than brickwork or roughcasting.

The portico of this edifice, grand as it is, has no agreement with the circular building to which it is attached, and the wall and Pediment which rises above it, present an example of great deformity.

The ceiling of the portico was of gilt bronze, which was taken away, after it had become dilapidated, by Urban VIII from which he formed the four twisted columns which support the canopy over the high alter of S[t]. Peters.—The metal in this ceiling weighed upwards of 450.000 pounds.

After the transfer of the seat of [43] empire to Constantinople, the Pantheon became an object of plunder; numerous depredations were made upon it, until about the year 608 when Pope Boniface the 4th consecrated it as a Church; and it still stands, a mutilated monument of other times [—*a link to connect the distant past with future ages – once the Pantheon, or fane of all the heathen gods – now a temple consecrated to the Christian's GOD.*

"Spared and blest by time
Looking tranquility, while falls, or nods
Arch, empire, each thing round thee, and man plods
His way, through thorns to ashes – glorious dome!
Shalt thou not last? Time's scythe, and tyrant's rods
Shiver upon thee – Sanctuary and home
Of art and piety – Pantheon! – Pride of Rome."]

The Theatres of Rome seem also to claim a passing remark;—of these there were three; the oldest was the Theatre of Pompey which was built about 55 years before the Christian era, and was large enough to [44] contain 40.000 persons:—of this building there are now no remains.

The next in point of age is the Theatre of Balbus, which was built about 12 years before Christ, and was capable of containing 30,000 people:—this Theatre was dedicated by Claudius, and, according to Pliny it contained four very remarkable columns of onix;—no remains of this building

* Childe Har can 4 v 146

The Pantheon. George Ledwell Taylor and Edward Cresy, The Architectural Antiquities of Ancient Rome *(London, 1821-22). Courtesy, Anne and Jerome Fisher Fine Arts Library, University of Pennsylvania.*

are however to be found, nor is their any certainty even as to its former location.

The third Theatre of Rome is that of Marcellus, of which it has been supposed that Vitruvius was the Architect: — this building was erected about 10 years before our era, and was designed to accommodate 30,000 persons. — The remains of this structure are still to be seen in the Piazza Montanard; its ruins have formed a hill upon which the Savellia pallace now stands.

An evidence of the wealth and luxury of the Romans is found in the extent and grandeur of their establishments for bathing; — Sextus Rufus estimates the whole [45] number of bath houses in Rome at eight hundred.

Of the Baths of Titus, called by Pliny the <u>palace</u> of Titus, considerable remains are still to be seen: — on the walls of these ruins many paintings have been found almost in a perfect state.

The Baths of Caracalla which form the principal ruin on mount Aventine were even larger than those of Titus: — this establishment measured 1840 feet in length and 1476 in width covering about 70 acres — Olympidorus tells us that 1600 seats were made of polished marble for the use of persons bathing. The lower story which contains the baths is now entirely buried under the mass of ruin, which in point of magnitude is very little inferior to the Colosseum.

But the largest bathing establishment in Rome was that of Diocletian. These baths were commenced in the 298th year of our era, and finished in 305: — 40,000 Christians are said to have been employed on this enormous work as a species of persecution.

The Triumphal arches of Rome [46] form another grade of architecture; these works were however of but little importance and are generally in very bad taste: — they were raised to perpetuate the fame of Roman conquerors, and serve only to bring up through the lapse of ages the names and deeds of whose to whom they were erected.

The Arch of Titus which stands at the foot of the Palatine hill is of better architecture than either of the others; and as already remarked, is generally considered as the best specimen of the composite order in Rome.

The Arch of Septimius Severus, the ruins of which stand at the foot of the Capitoline hill, and the arch of Constantine at the foot of the Palatine hill were both of inferior design, and workmanship. — The ornamental parts of the latter structure were barbarously stripped from the arch of Trajan, and absurdly applied by the despoilers in the decoration of this edifice.

The Arch of the Goldsmiths, which was erected by the merchants and goldsmiths [47] of Rome in honor of the victories of Septemius Severus in the east, differs from all others in being no arch at all; — it consists simply of two piers supporting an horizontal entablature, the whole of which is charged with a profusion of sculpture miserably designed and badly executed.

Triumphal columns were also erected by the Romans. They were chiefly designed to honor those who won laurels for the state, or power for themselves.

The Column of Phocas near the Temple of Concord is supposed to be the oldest in Rome; — it is composed of Greek marble and measures four feet in diameter at the base, and 54 feet in height including its pedestal.

Another column worthy of notice is that which was erected by the Roman senate in honor of Marcus Aurelius, and which has since been called the column of Antoninus: — its order is Doric, and its dimentions eleven feet six inches in diameter and one hundred and forty eight feet in height.

The most celebrated column in Rome is that of Trajan. It is about 12 feet in diameter and stands on a pedestal in the midst of the forum of Trajan, rising majestically above the ruins that surround it; having braved the storms and wars of 17 centuries, almost uninjured. Its whole height, including the pedestal on which it stands and the statue that surmounts it is 150 feet. The whole work is composed of white statuary marble. The shaft consists of 34 frusta, secured in the building by bronze cramps. A stairway runs up through the middle, cut out of the solid marble.

The outside is embellished with a series of sculptures extending around it in a spiral form from bottom to top; — of these, Dyer beautifully observes,

> "From whose low base the sculptures wind aloft,
> And lead through various toils, up the rough steep,
> Its hero to the skies."[1]

This is undoubtedly the finest triumphal column in the world.

[48] One of the most attractive objects now standing in Rome is the celebrated church of S^t. Peter [*This edifice, it is true, belongs more properly to modern, than to Ancient Architecture; to mention it here may therefore seem to be a digression from our subject, but to go to Rome without going to S^t. Peter's would be, not to go to Rome at all. I shall therefore venture to detain you with a general, but brief description of it*].

This immense structure is considered by some as the very beau-ideal of beauty, and grandeur in Architecture, while others look upon it as the most unsightly mass ever put together by the hand of man. I am not however prepared to subscribe to either of these opinions; — there are many things in S^t. Peter's to admire [49] — much to excite wonder and astonishment, — and not a little to condemn. — As a mass its magnitude excites strong emotions

---
[1] John Dyer, "The Ruins of Rome" (1740)

The Basilica of St. Peter (San Pietro in Vaticano). Ridolfino Venuti, Accurata, e succinta descrizione topografica e istorica di Roma moderna *(Rome, 1766). Courtesy, the Winterthur Library: Printed Book and Periodical Collection.*

of sublimity, which proceed from ideas of power, awakened by its vastness and gigantic proportions;—and these effects are greatly enhanced by the richness and splendor of its decorations:—but when we take
"To separate contemplation the great whole"*
we find a discordance in the various parts—a want of unity of design which oppresses the mind with a feeling of regret that so stupendous a pile should not have been more beautiful.

The impressions produced on my own mind by the magnitude of this enormous structure were stronger on viewing it from the <u>roof</u> than from any other position;—it appears more like a town crowning the summit of a mountain, than like the roof of a building;—its two small cupolas rise like two great churches, and the immense dome, the outside diameter of [50] which is 160 feet, rises into the clouds with a majesty and grandeur which attones for many a fault in the details of its deign.

On entering S^t. Peter's one is awed with the magnitude of space enclosed by the immense walls and Dome, as well as by the colossal proportions of all surrounding objects;—the eye stretches from the entrance, through the nave, and in the distance rests upon the high altar, the canopy of which rises to the height of <u>ninety</u> feet:—before this shrine is the <u>sacra conféssioné</u> embellished with the richest marbles, and surrounded with a hundred lamps constantly burning.

The walls are inlaid with costly marbles,—the ceiling is gilt,—and the aisles are adorned with rich mosaics and colossal sculptures. The softened emotions of a refined and delicate taste are rather suppressed than heightened.

In this vast pile, <u>genius</u> has been united with <u>riches,</u> and <u>power,</u> to produce [51] sublimity; and <u>science</u> has contributed all <u>her</u> stores to consummate the work:—nothing has therefore been wanted in the design of S^t. Peter's, but taste—a refined, a cultivated taste; the absence of which is evident in every part of the composition.

The length of the building is 654 feet and its breadth 220.—The inside diameter of the dome is 148 feet, and the whole exterior height 477.—The columns of the main edifice are 9 feet in diameter and 93 feet high.

The original design was by Bramante, and its successive Architects were Sangallo, Raphael, Peruzzi, Michael Angelo, Ligorio, Vignola, Fontana, Carlo Maderno, and Bernini.—It was commenced in 1506 and finished in 1592 being the work of nearly a whole century the cost of its construction was equal to $47,000,000.

---

* Childe Har. Can 4 v. 157

Architecture in the Roman Colonies

Roman Architecture was by no means confined to the imperial city, but was introduced into every province under the dominion of this once powerful nation: — we shall not however have time to do more than allude [52] very briefly to a few of their most extraordinary efforts, beyond the borders of Rome.

The remains at Palmyra and Balbec are more wonderful in some particulars than those of Rome itself. Palmyra was originally founded by Solomon, and is called in the Scriptures Tedmor in the wilderness; — but existing monuments show that a taste for the fine arts was not introduced in that country until after it was conquered by Pompey: — Stephanus mentions it as having been repaired by Adrian, and hence called Adrianople; and on the coins of Caracalla it is called a Roman colony: — we find also that the inhabitants joined Alexander Severus in his expedition against the Persians under Artaxerxes in the 227th year of the Christian era.

Palmyra is surrounded on all sides by a vast sandy desert, which totally separates it from the rest of the world; it lies about 60 miles from the Euphrates, and 180 from the Mediteranean Sea. — Its architecture is nearly all of the Corinthian order, there being but a single exception; — the ruins are in [53] a much more perfect state than those of Rome, which is no doubt owing to their being but few inhabitants to deface them, — to a dry climate, and to their distance from any other city.

M[r]. Robert Wood, who visited these ruins in 1751 describes their appearance in the following language: — "the hills opening discovered to us all at once the greatest quantity of ruins we had ever seen, all of white marble, and beyond them, towards the Euphrates, a flat waste as far as the eye could reach without any object which showed either life or motion. It is scarcely possible to imagine anything more striking than this view; — so great a number of Corinthian pillars mixed with so little wall or solid building, afforded a most romantic variety of prospect."[*]

The ruins of Palmyra present the remains of a stupendous portico of about 4000 feet in length composed of hundreds of columns, the most of which still bear up their elaborate entablatures. — Along the line of this great Portico are the remains of numerous temples of every description, all [54] in the Corinthian order, and M[r]. Wood thinks he could trace amongst them the ruins of a Roman circus.

The temple of the Sun is the most magnificent of all the remnants of this once beautiful city; — its columns are four-and-a-half feet in diameter, by about 45 feet in height, and their number was originally 424.

[*] Woods Palmyra p 35

The Great Arch (seen from the west), Palmyra. Robert Wood, The Ruins Of Palmyra, Otherwise Tedmor, In The Desart *(London: 1753). Courtesy, Winterthur Library: Printed Book and Periodical Collection.*

The Palmyrenes must have been a powerful, and a wealthy people; and it is to be regretted that their country, so rich in monuments of ancient splendor — the seat of Zenobias power, should be so little known.

Balbec, the city alluded to in connection with Palmyra, is situated at the foot of Mount Libanus in Syria, and until the year 1759, when it was severely visited by an earthquake, it rivaled Palmyra. The gigantic proportions and splendor of its Architecture are even now, ruined and dismantled as it is, a subject of the highest wonder and admiration. This city is sometimes called Heliopolis, a term which has the same signification (though in another language) with Balbec; both referring to the favorite idolatry of the place; the worship of the sun.

[55] Balbec contains the ruins of several ages remote from each other, and these wonders are frequently supposed to be altogether the woks of a people who lived long before the Romans; but such is not the fact; — the several ages are distinctly marked in the character of the ruins, and intelligent travelers have no difficulty in assigning to each its proper place.

The eloquent Lamartine in describing the immense walls which once served as the defence of the city, says, "These wonders are evidently not of the date of the temples, — they were mysteries to the ancients, as they are to us. They belong to an unknown age, and are perhaps ante-diluvian."* Some of these stones "are sixty two feet long, twenty feet broad and fifteen feet thick, weighing each about 1800 tons are the most prodigious masses which have ever been moved by human power." — In speaking of the beauty of the congregated ruins this elegant writer continues — "The grave and somber color of the stones of the base, contrasts with the golden hues of [56] walls and the avenues of columns, and just before the setting of the sun, when its rays fall aslant among the pillars and ripple in firey beams amongst the volutes and acanthus of the capitals, the temples glitter as if they were sculptured out of pure gold, and were standing on Pedestals of bronze."

Balbec is said to be indebted chiefly to Antoninus Pius for the magnificence of its buildings; its grandest structure is the temple of the sun, which is no doubt the best effort in Architecture of that period: — a representation of it is found on the reverse of a medal of Septemius Severus, which proves that in the time of that Emperor it was either finished or in progress.

This temple consists of a cell surrounded by 50 columns measuring 7 feet in diameter and 62 feet in height; the architecture is Corinthian, of the best Roman age, but the columns are not fluted.

The worship of the sun constituted all the religious devotions both of Balbec and Palmyra; [57] the violence of the heat, and its destructive

* Lamartine, Voyages en orient tom. 3 p. 323

power on vegetation, rendered that luminary an object of peculiar awe to the inhabitants, and all their religious efforts seem to have been bestowed to appease their angry deity.

In more northern countries, where hills, vallies, groves, and water, blend in picturesque combinations, we find the oreades, or nymphs of the mountains,—the Dryades, or nymphs of the groves,—the Naiades, or nymphs of the waters, and a boundless variety of fanciful mythology, grouped and connected by the fertile imagination of Grecian poets; but in the parched regions of Balbec and Palmyra no supernatural power was acknowledged but that of the sun.

Pompeii and Herculaneum

Another, and a most interesting development of Roman architecture is found in the disinterred cities of Pompeii and Herculaneum in the Campania near Naples.

These cities were overwhelmed in the full tide of their prosperity by an eruption of Vesuvius in the 79th year of the Christian era,—and so effectually were they buried that all [58] traces of them were lost, and their history was considered for many generations as nothing more than a legendary tale.—Herculaneum was discovered in 1713 by some laborers digging a well, and Pompeii was found about 40 years afterwards.—Thus have two Roman cities been sealed up and forgotten for 1700 years, and then laid open with all the freshness of their original character.—No sacrilegious alterations and pillagings have been perpetrated by intervening ages, no changes to suit newer fashions, nor patchwork to meet the exigencies of other times; but every thing is exactly as it was in the days of Roman pride and power;—paintings undimmed by time; household furniture left in the confusion of use; and articles even of intrinsic value abandoned in the hurry of escape, or scattered as they fell from the hands of affrighted owners.

In the year 1826 as many as 400 skeletons of the inhabitants had already been found in the streets and houses of Pompeii, and every week makes new and interesting developments.[*]

[59] A recent traveller, (Mr. Simond) says that he observed "opposite to the temple of Jupiter in the Forum a new alter of white marble exquisitely beautiful, and apparently just out of the hands of the sculptor; and around it an enclosure partly finished, on the walls of which the morter had just been dashed, and but half spread out, exhibiting the long sliding stroke of the trowel, about to return and obliterate its own track;—but it never did return: the hand of the workman was suddenly arrested, and, after the lapse of almost 1800 years, the whole looks so fresh and new, that you can

[*] notes on Bulever's Pompeii

scarcely resist the idea that the mason has only gone to his dinner, and is about to come back to finish his work."

The following quotation from one of the reports of the overseers of the excavations to the Court of Naples, will give you some idea of the incalculable riches of Pompeii, and the rapidity with which they are brought to light.

"November 10ᵗʰ 1823. In the third and fourth [60] houses on the right of the street running from the temple of Fortune, were found several articles in the presence of the English Minister. These were: a vase with a handle; an oil vessel with a handle and cover; six coins of middle size, and some ornaments of a door, all of bronze; ten lamps of terra cotta, one of a circular form, with an eagle in relief; five cups, two earthen pots, into which money was slipped through a hole; and a number of bronze sockets on which doors had turned." — This, it will be recollected was but a single days work, and the account includes nothing but such moveable articles as admitted of being transferred to the Museum.

Conclusion

The influence exerted by Rome over her conquered provinces is as astonishing in architecture as it is in arms; — no place was too remote from [the] Tiber to receive the impress of the "seven hill'd city;" — in every [61] part of Greece, — in Egypt, — in Ethiopia, as far from the Delta, as the sixth cataract of the Nile, — in the sandy deserts of Arabia, — in the rocky bounds of Petra, the desolate capital of Edom, — and even in Britain are to be found the works of this mighty people, pointing to Rome, as to a polar star. — Wherever Roman arms penetrated, we find Roman monuments to mark the way.

But, (in the words of the Poet Wordsworth)
"Where now the haughty empire that was spread
With such fond hope? — her very speech is dead."
"She who veiled
Earth with her haughty shadow, and display'd,
Until the o'er-canopied horizon fail'd
Her rushing wings,"*
Was doomed to the saddest reverses; — torn by internal factions, and enervated by her very triumphs, she gradually yeilded to the barbarians of the north, and became at last a shattered wreck of gaudy splendor leaving desolation and ruin triumphant
"Where lords of nations knelt in ages flown."

---

* Childe Har. P 163 [These lines are the first two from the last stanza of Wordsworth's "The Pillar of Trajan." The following four are from Byron's "Childe Harold," Canto Four. Both poems date to 1826. *Ed.*]

Lecture 4th

On the Architecture of the Middle ages

Thos. U. Walter

Philad.ª Nov. 4. 1841

Delivered Dec. 2. 1841

Salisbury Cathedral. *John Britton,* The History and Antiquities of the Cathedral Church of Salisbury *(London: 1814). Courtesy, The Winterthur Library Printed Book and Periodical Collection.*

LECTURE IV
ON THE ARCHITECTURE OF THE MIDDLE AGES

Introduction

[1] The mind is so constituted that its energies can never remain stationary. — Nations, as well as individuals, are either found advancing in knowledge and skill, or receding from the lights of science and literature, into the shades of ignorance and superstition.

Thus, when learning and the arts began to lose their influence over the classic inhabitants of Rome, a gradual decline in liberal studies became apparent, Philosophy grew dim, and glimmered with a flickering light, taste sunk in the general wreck of intellect, and the commencement of the fourth century found the Roman nation [2] enveloped in ignorance, and tending rapidly, by its own intrinsic weakness, to irretrievable ruin.

Europe and Arabia in the Middle Ages

The early part of this gloomy century was characterized by a sickly tranquility, and its close by storms. — A people of Germany called Goths, Vandals, and Burgundians invaded the country, and consummated the degradation of Rome by the complete overthrow of the whole western empire.

The invaders, according to Pliny and Procopius, were of one nation, agreeing in manners, and speaking the same language: they were all called Goths — they inhabited the banks of the Vistula, and their settlements reached to the Baltic: — those who came from the east of Scandinavia were called Ostrogoths, and those from the west, Westrogoths, or Visigoths, in allusion to their localities.

They began to be troublesome to the Romans as early as the second century, but at that time they were too wild and undisciplined to cause much apprehension; [3] their martial prowess and skill, however, increased with each succeeding combat, and their numerical force was gradually augmented by other hordes of Scandinavians, until their power became irrestistible; and in the year 409, under the notorious Alaric, they entered Rome without even the ceremony of a battle;

"That Rome which witnessed, in her sceptred days,
So much of noble death; — when shrine and dome,
'Midst clouds of incense, rung with choral lays,
As the long triumph passed with all its blaze
Of regal spoil"*

The invaders subsequently took possession of all the fairest provinces in the west of Europe, reducing the inhabitants to degrading servitude.

With this barbarian conquest begins the period denominated the Middle ages, and the length of time it is usually estimated to comprise, is about one thousand years; or from the beginning of the fifth, to [4] the close of the fourteenth century.

Some have denominated this portion of history "the dark ages," from the ignorance and superstition in which all ranks of society seem to have been enveloped; and others, "the barbarous ages" in allusion to the want of refinement which is said to have characterized all Europe during the period in question.

The Goths, with whose triumph the Middle ages commenced, were, according to some historians, a rude, warlike, and barbarous race, delighting in the work of destruction, and regarding literature, and the arts with unmingled contempt. — Others contend that they were a very clever people, excelling, in many respects, the Romans themselves; some of their Kings are said to have been exceedingly humane and civil, while their subjects aspired at a character of refinement, moderation, and humanity, which would have done honor to the fallen state. — It is not, however, [5] reasonable to suppose that civilization and refinement, were in any degree promoted by the invaders: — they came from inclement and uncultivated regions, and were unquestionably a wild and ferocious people; — a people whose religion taught them to court death, and to hold danger, and bodily pain in contempt, and whose sole delight was in war, and in the slaughter of their enemies. — They subsequently, it is true, became softened in their manners, under the influence of a milder climate, and in the atmosphere of literature and the arts; but at the time of their conquest they were characterized, as a nation, by ignorance and barbarity. — Theodoric, the most famous of their Kings could not even write his name; — his prime minister, Cassiodorus, was, however, an educated Greek, and, true to the

* Hemans / 187 p.

The Alhambra: Court of the Lions, Grenada. Henry Swinburne, Travels through Spain, in the Years 1775 and 1776 *(London, 1787). The Athenæum of Philadelphia.*

taste of his native country, he attempted the revival of literature; but we are told by historians that the uneducated sovreign treated his efforts with ridicule.[1]

But while the Goths were consummating the ruin of letters and the arts in Europe, the torch of literature was kept alive in Arabia. — In the gloomy period which occurred between the <u>sixth</u> and the <u>twelfth</u> centuries, when ignorance had thrown its mantle over the whole of Europe, and superstition had imposed its fetters on the fairest portions of the Globe, learning was shedding its radiant beams from the Saracen halls of Bagdad, Damascus, and Medina — from Cordova and from Cairo. — Here, among the followers of Mahomet — that impious but successful imposter, it found a safe asylum; and when the last rays of Greek and Roman literature were almost [6] quenched by the barbarian possessors of Italy, and scarcely an unmutilated monument of art or genius was left in Europe, the Saracens were cultivating every department of knowledge. — They had, it is true, been plunged for centuries in the grossest ignorance, but they emerged with a lustre not more remarkable for its brilliancy than its strength: — this sudden blaze of genius illuminated every corner of the Moslem domains, and its influence as coextensive with Moslem arms. — Many of the califs surrounded themselves with poets and orators; their palaces became halls

---

[1] The following paragraph, to the end of manuscript page [5], was added to the original manuscript.

of learning and refinement; and the beautiful—the enchanting fictions which made their country a "fairy land, will continue to difuse a charm until taste and imagination shall become extinct."*

Cairo, Fez, and Morroco were famous for the magnificence of their establishments for learning, and extensive colleges were instituted throughout the whole Empire; [7] many invaluable literary treasures of antiquity were preserved, and every department of science and letters received valuable accessions from Arab enterprise and enthusiasm; while some of the most useful and important inventions which minister to the comfort and happiness of mankind have been handed down through this extraordinary people.

Thus we find that during the gloomiest period of European night, the reigning influence of literature and the arts was enjoyed by the Saracens to its fullest extent. The ages therefore which were dark in Europe, were bright in Arabia; and while the Goths were prostrating the last hope of science with the falling fanes of classic ages, the Arabians were assiduously engaged in cultivating letters and the arts, until the sun of science and philosophy shone in full splendor; and, outstripping the bounds of "Araby the blest" shed a humanizing and exalting influence to the [8] farthest limits of their vast domains;—and although the monuments they have left are not to be compared with the stupendous and imperishable relics of classic Greece and Rome, or the more ancient cities of the Nile, yet they possess an interest—a peculiar charm, which never fails to awaken the most agreeable emotions of taste.

Many of the melancholy ruins of this elegant and graceful people, delicate and fairy like as they are, after having contended against the wasting powers of time for a thousand years, are still to be seen crowning the verdant hills, or embosomed amid the spicy plains of Araby,

"Where the young leaves by vernal winds are swayed,
And the reeds whisper with a dreamy tone
Of Melody, that seems to breathe from worlds unknown"†

Gothic Architecture

[9] The Architecture of these mysterious ages especially that of northern Europe, is usually denominated Gothic; a term strongly objected to by many authors, but nevertheless an appropriate one.

It is certain however that the Goths had no part either in inventing or perfecting any of the ramifications of the Architecture of the period in question; they were entirely swept off from the civilized world, before any

---

* Arabia / v.1 p. 24
† Mrs. Hemans / v 3. p 191

progress whatever was made in the arts, after their conquest of Italy: — the beginning of the sixth century found their power extinguished in France by Clovis, the King of the Franks; — in the year 534 the Emperor Justinian exterminated them from Africa, and in 583 from Italy; while in Spain they remained until the year 713, when they were conquered by the Moors. — Thus we find Gothic power extinct in the beginning of the <u>eighth</u> century, while the style of building which bears the name of Gothic, can scarcely be said to have had an existence before the [10] days of William the Conqueror in the <u>eleventh</u> century. — But the havock these barbarian invaders made in Italy, produced, indirectly, a new epoch in Architecture; — although they did little else than pull down what other people had built up, the devastation and ruin they consummated led eventually to that wide departure from classic taste which characterized the Middle ages. — There is therefore some propriety in the application of the term Gothic to the Architecture of the period in question, and as its meaning is generally understood there can be no objection to its use.

England

The first description of Gothic Architecture to which your attention is invited is that of England; the country in which it reached perfection, and which justly claims as her own, some of its most beautiful developements.

The Architecture of England naturally divides itself into <u>five</u> distinct periods, or styles, which are usually denominated the Saxon, the Anglo-Norman, the early pointed, [11] the decorated, and the Florid pointed, — an example of each of these styles is here exhibited.

(See illustrations representing)

($1^{st.}$ Period — $2^{nd.}$ Period — $3^{rd.}$ Period — $4^{th.}$ Period — $5^{th.}$ Period)

The Saxon Style, which is the first to be considered, was practised under the Saxon Kings from the time of their conquest of England in the fifth century, to the triumph of the Normans in the year 1066, embracing a period of about five centuries.

The Architecture of this people exhibits strong evidences of a rude and degenerate age [— *as a nation they possessed, in their original forests as much roughness as the Goths themselves, and their long struggle with the Britons tended rather to brutalize than improve their manners*].

Its principal characteristics are thick walls built of small rough [12] stones, without Buttresses; semicircular arches springing from short and massy columns somewhat in the form of Roman balusters; rudely sculptured figures; zig-zag mouldings; and other coarse adaptations of classic forms.

Peterborough Cathedral. Rev. T. Warton, Rev. J. Bentham, Captain Grose, and Rev. J. Milner, Essays on Gothic Architecture *(London, 1802). The Athenæum of Philadelphia.*

This sketch (see drawing) furnishes a general idea of the style; and when we consider it as the starting point of the architecture of our anglo-Saxon ancestors it is certainly not without interest. — The lower arch is from S^t. Albans Church and the upper one from S^t. Benet's Cambridge.

Writers generally agree that the first ideas the Saxons ever had of Architecture were derived from the Romans: — in the language of M^r. Robert Stuart "the Saxon style was doubtless but a barbarous imitation of the architecture of Rome"[*] and Bede, who wrote in the early part of the eighth century says, that in the year 675 the famous Abbot Benedict Biscopius went over to France to engage workmen to build his church after the <u>Roman manner</u>; and when the building was nearly [13] finished he procured artificers from the same country skilled in the mystery of making glass to glaze the windows.[†] — D^r. Milner observes that "the well known Saxon mouldings, the chevron or zig-zag, the billet, the cable, the embattled fret, the lozenge, the corbel-table, and a variety of such other ornaments as are supposed to be peculiar to Saxon architecture will be found to have their archetypes in Italy."

Anglo-Saxon structures are supposed to have been chiefly built of wood, and indeed the Saxon verb <u>getymbrian,</u> to build, indicates that timber, (from which the word is obviously formed,) was once the common material for building.

[*] Stuarts dic. / Saxon arch^t.
[†] Nights' Normandy / p. 219.

It is, however, certain that as early as the middle of the 7th century wood was superceeded in many instances by stone;—and D[r]. Sayers remarks, that under the influence of Wilfred and Biscopius the practise of building with stone became general.[*]

Bentham says, that we have sufficient testimony from authentic history to show that the Saxons not only built their walls of stone, [*from the fact that Edwin, King of Northumberland, ordered a wooden chapel to be taken down, and a larger and nobler church of stone erected in its stead, in commemoration of his baptism; this was however but an exception to a general practise;*] but that they constructed pillars, arches, and vaultings of the same material of which there are still undoubted remains.

[14] We learn from the early chronicles that in the latter part of the seventh century Wilfred built the conventual church of Ripon, and the Cathedral Church of Hexham, and that both were constructed of stone with columns and arches by workmen from Rome Italy and France.—We also read that in the eighth century Ethelbald built the monastery of Croyland, and archbishop Albert rebuilt the church of S[t]. Peter at York, both of which were constructed of stone.

In the ninth century a stop was put to the progress of art by the incursions of the Danes, and every Saxon building was either wholly or partially destroyed, these [15] formidable invaders having infested nearly every part of the Island.—They were at length subjugated by Alfred whose signal triumph diffused a confidence throughout the land, which gave a new impetus to art, and placed it on a surer basis;—the ruined monasteries were rebuilt,—new churches were erected of stone, and military edifices were everywhere constructed for the defense of the Island.

There are however but few remains of buildings erected by the Saxons now to be found in England, and these consist chiefly of doorways or other ornamental features which have been incorporated into the structures of the succeeding style; thus rendering it difficult to determine to which age some of the most interesting examples of English architecture really belong.

The next period is the Anglo-Norman style, so called from its having been introduced into England by the Normans, after their [16] conquest, under William, duke of Normandy in the year 1066.

When we consider the great change produced by the Norman invasion in the political affairs of England, we can readily account for the total abandonment of one style of architecture, and the sudden and unceremonious introduction of another.

With the battle of Hastings the power of the Saxon heptarchy received a complete overthrow, and the Norman conqueror took full possession of the government;—the property of the inhabitants was either tyrannically

[*] Arch. Antiq. / v. 5 p. 102

confiscated, or indiscriminately sacrificed [*– while the native lords of the soil frequently perished in the wreck of their own fortunes;*] – the very name of Englishmen became a reproach; – their language, and the character in which it was written were rejected as barbarous; and in order to extinguish if possible the last glimmer of English character, the children in every school in the land were taught French, and the laws were administered [17] in the same tongue.*

The style of architecture introduced by the invaders soon became general, and we are told by William of Malmsbury that magnificent churches and monastries were everywhere seen rising up with a splendor which had never before been witnessed in England.

Thus began the Norman dynasty, and from this epoch in history the Anglo-Norman style of architecture takes its date.

Previous to the conquest, the Normans were a far more civilized race than the Saxons, but the architecture of both nations having had a Roman origin exhibited the same general character; the Norman style is therefore but little more than a refinement of the Saxon, executed on a grander scale and in a more scientific manner. Norman structures were loftier than those of the Saxons, and the ornaments more elaborately finished; – towers embellished with tiers of interlaced arches were often built in connection with their cathedral and conventual [18] churches; and some of their best examples were enriched with sculptured capitals, animals, leaves and flowers.

This sketch exhibits some of the principal features of the style, and when compared with its predecessor the Saxon the superiority of the Normans in taste and skill will be obvious. – The lower window on the drawing is from Chichester cathedral and the upper one, with the Buttresses and Battlements from S^t. Albans.

Norman arches were always semi-circular, and in this style as well as in the Saxon, there is a total absence of Pediments and pinnacles, these features belonging exclusively to the works of subsequent ages.

In consequence of the immense thickness of the walls in structures of this period, the doors were deeply recessed, and the jambs ornamented with receding rows of columns and arches; – the interior walls of many of the churches were ornamented with [19] mural arcades of intersecting arches springing from attached columns, thus, (see drawing). Some contend that the point thus produced by the intersection of the circles first suggested the idea of the pointed arch.

When the ceilings of Norman structures were not vaulted, the timbers which composed them were always exposed to view, and the carpentry in

---

*Hallam on / the Middle Ages / p. 334

many instances exhibits considerable taste and skill — the "white tower" in London affords a Norman example, and I believe, a solitary one, of a ceiling covered with an original vaulting of stone.

The administration of affairs under the Norman dynasty seems to have been peculiarly favorable to the advancement of architectural science: — the conqueror and his successors took care to bestow all the best ecclesiastical preferments on talented and tasteful Normans, thus placing the means of diffusing Norman [20] Architecture in the hands of those who were the most interested in its promotion. — This policy resulted in the improvement, or entire rebuilding of all the cathedrals, and abby churches in England, besides the construction of innumerable Parish churches in every part of the Kingdom; — and it is a fact worthy of remark that fifteen of the twenty two cathedrals of England, still retain parts which are undoubtedly of Norman origin.

The period usually assigned to the Anglo Norman style terminated on the first transition from the semicircular arch to the one slightly pointed, which is said to have taken place in the latter part of the reign of Stephen, the last of the Kings of the Norman line, about the middle of the twelfth century.

Thus we find that Norman architecture had only prevailed in England about [21] 80 years when the introduction of the pointed arch, and other improvements changed its entire character, and produced what is now called the "early pointed" or the "Early English" and by some, the "lancet" style.

In this age of gothic architecture, circular and pointed arches were used in the same structure; the heavy Norman pillar was cut into a cluster of small columns with bell-shaped capitals ornamented with bold but plain mouldings; windows were made long, narrow, and lancet headed; Buttresses were used more frequently, and their proportions greatly improved; battlements were ornamented with sunken panels and tracery; and towards the end of the style finials and crockets were frequently introduced, and vaulted ceilings became general.

Shortly after the confirmation of this style, the practise was introduced of foiling arches, or uniting a series of three or more small arches at their bases so as to form one thus (see diagram). Arches [22] thus foliated are denominated trefoil, quatrefoil, cinquefoil and so on according to the number of circles or foils of which they are composed.

The spaces between the foiling and the outside line of the arch is generally ornamented with panels formed by concentric circles producing a feature called tracery, thus,

foliation,

tracery.

Where there are no concentric circles the arch is simply said to be foliated.

The general character of the Early pointed style is represented by this sketch

(see drawing).

Portions of several of the best examples of this period are here brought together for the purpose of presenting on a single drawing as many features of the style as possible; the window is from east Dereham Church Norfolk, the buttresses [23] from Beverly Minster, and the parapet from Salisbury Cathedral.

By comparing this style with the preceding one it is evident that the transition was too great, and too sudden to have been produced by gradual improvement; it is therefore probable that the first ideas the English ever entertained of Pointed architecture were derived from France and Germany; as the pointed arch, foliation and tracery were in use in those countries more than a century before they were known in England,* and there is little doubt that the Germans were the first to connect and resolve these features into a distinct style, although their <u>first</u> notions of them were probably derived from other sources.[1]

One of the most important characteristics of the architecture of this period being the pointed arch, it will be proper to advert to some of the various notions which have been advanced respecting its supposed origin. — Many [24] have endeavoured to trace its invention to the Moslems, and imagine it to have been copied by European crusaders from Moorish buildings in Palestine; — others contend that it resulted from the intersection of semicircular arches; and the Romans, the Germans, the French, and the English have each in turn been reputed as its originators; — some indeed would have us to believe the pointed arch to have come down from the remotest antiquity; — D[r]. Clark thinks he can trace it almost to the

---

* Hope's archt. / v. 1. p 394

[1] Identifying the origin of the pointed arch was a main focus of writers on the middle ages. Walter agrees with Thomas Hope, who favors the Germans. Thomas Hope, *Historical Essay on Architecture* (1835), 374.

time of Abraham*, and gravely says that examples of it may be referred to in buildings which were erected before the Trojan war; — the Rev Mr. Gunn in his "inquiry into the influence and origin of Gothic architecture"† talks about a pointed arch at Memphis; Mr. Hoskins finds one in the Pyramids of Meroe, which he thinks is 3300 years old and Hamilton in his "remarks on the fortresses of ancient Greece,"‡ alludes to a Gothic arch over the doorway of a small fort on a rock above Ephesus; — "But," in the language of Mr. Britton, "on these examples [25] no reliance can be placed," they have no doubt, "arisen from alterations in comparatively modern times."§

The learned Bishop Warburton has imagined not only the pointed arch, but the whole system of Gothic vaulting to have been derived from the natural arbour formed by trees in a forest.** — This hypothesis is certainly an ingenious one; and it cannot be denied that something of the effect of the interior of a Gothic Cathedral is produced by the natural interlacing of trees in an avenue; — but we cannot for a moment suppose the origin of Gothic architecture to have been quite so romantic while countless monuments still exist, through which we trace with certainty its slow but constant progress from Saxon coarseness to Tudor luxuriance: — we are moreover told that Warburton himself afterwards discarded the idea as utterly absurd and fanciful. — Lord Orford says in his "Walpoleana" that "Warburtons groves are nonsense, it was not [26] a passage from barbarism to art, but from one species of art to another."

The analogy which exists between Gothic vaulting and a natural arbor — between the divaricating branches of trees, and the ribs which spring out of Gothic columns affords however a beautiful coincidence in the works of nature and art, but the idea of the woods being the prototype of the vaults is wholly imaginary.

Many other chimerical notions as to the origin of Gothic vaulting have been propagated, and in several instances the subject has been treated by confessedly able writers, but no satisfactory conclusion has ever yet been arrived at, and the question continues to be involved in obscurity. — We have however the satisfaction to know that its solution is as unimportant as it is difficult.

The early pointed style attained its most perfect state in the thirteenth century, and some of its best examples are the chapter house, transepts and part of the choir [27] of Westminster Abbey; the choir of St. Albans; the nave of Lincoln; the nave and spire of Lichfield; the south transept of York; and the Cathedrals of Salisbury and Durham; — but of all the specimens of this period now existing in England, Salisbury is unquestionably the

---

* Clark's travels / v. 3 p. 654
† p. 98
‡ 323
§ Archl. Antiq. / v. 5. p 37
** Hope's archt. / v. 1 p 370

most beautiful;—its architecture is almost wholly of one species, and one era of construction;—it presents one uniform whole,—grand without coarsness,—rich without exuberance.—It was begun in the year 1220, and nothing having interposed to arrest its progress during the whole time of its execution; it presents more oneness of expression in design—a chaster and more harmonious combination of forms than we find in any other building of a corresponding age;—its

> "shapes minute
> At once distinct and blended, boldly form
> One vast majestic whole."*

It embraces in an eminent degree an association of the beautiful,—and the [28] sublime;—its boldness, and strength impress the mind with ideas of grandeur and magnificence, while its loftiness, and lightness, awaken the most delicate emotions of taste.—Its slender, but stately spire, all built of stone, rises gracefully to the height of 404 feet [*or more than twice the height of Christ Church Steeple*], thus terminating the Pyramidal arrangement of the group in a misty altitude amongst the clouds.

The interior is no less imposing than the exterior;—an atmosphere of sacredness seems to pervade the whole space;—the windows of richly stained glass admit a softened radiance which gleams in a countless variety of tints, on walls and arches and vaulted roof producing a subdued and harmonious effect:

> "the very light
> Streams with a colouring of heroic days
> In every ray, which leads through arch and aisle
> A path of dreamy lustre wandering back
> To other years."†

[29] When seen by the pale and silvery light of the moon, amid the solemn azure and fleecy vapours of an English summers evening, the effect of this beautiful structure is particularly impressive and enchanting [;—*the mind swells before it with lofty and harmonious emotions, and the imagination "darts from heaven to earth, from earth to heaven in rapid and daring flights."*]

> "They dreamt not of a perishable home
> Who thus could build."‡

We now proceed to the fourth period of English gothic, which is frequently designated by the simple term "the pointed style," in contradistinction to the early pointed with preceeded it, and the florid pointed which followed;—some call it the decorated style; others the decorated English; and it is not unfrequently denominated the Pure Gothic par excellence.

---

* Mason's Garden [Lines drawn from Book 4, lines 65-74. See App. A *Ed.*]
† Mrs. Hemans / p 354
‡ Wordsworth / p. 186 ["Ecclesiastical Sonnets" (1821-22), Part III: XLV. *Ed.*]

This drawing (see sketch) exhibits a composition from three [30] of its best examples; — the window is from Worstead church Norfolk, the buttresses are from Beverly Minster and the battlement is from the West front of the Cathedral at York.

The commencement of this period is generally dated in the reign of the first Edward about the close of the thirteenth century; and the length of time it flourished as a distinct style is usually estimated at 110 years.

This age of pointed architecture is characterized by lightness, gracefulness and harmony combined with an astonishing degree of strength; — many of its structures most remarkable for lightness and delicacy, have withstood the ravages of time for more than five centuries; and the violence of enfuriated revolutionists seem to have fallen powerless upon its slender but firm supports and well poised arches.

In this style the windows are made [31] larger and divided by mullions into several compartments, which are always ornamented with foliation and tracery; — corbels and canopies are freely introduced; — arches are formed with increased gracefulness and elegance; — the use of crockets, pinnacles, spires and finials is fully confirmed; — the ribs of groin vaulting are made lighter and more elaborate; — and in short the whole style is one great movement onward in richness and splendor, — a movement which raised Gothic architecture to its greatest perfection.

The Capitals of columns to doorways in this style differ from those of the preceding one in being composed of woven foliage instead of upright leaves; and in may instances they present the appearance of a round ball of open work.

The arch peculiar to this period is equilateral, though in some instances other forms are used; — architrave mouldings are bolder and larger than in the last style, [32] and in some examples we find ogee arches ornamented with foliated heads and canopies.

As rapid an advance in taste is exhibited in the Buttresses of this age as in any other of its features; the corner ones are often placed diagonally, and there are some buildings in which small turrets are used instead of buttresses.

There is no one entire structure to be found in England in which the pointed or decorated style prevails throughout as the early pointed does in the cathedral of Salisbury: — there are however several in which the most important portions of the buildings are in this style, and which afford models of superior taste and elegance: — amongst these are York, Ely, Exeter, and Lincoln cathedrals and Melrose Abby. — York is however the finest and presents one of the most interesting studies of this style in the

Salisbury Cathedral. John Britton, The History and Antiquities of the Cathedral Church of Salisbury *(London: 1814). Winterthur Museum and Library.*

Kingdom: M^r. Elmes calls it "the Parthenon of Gothic [33] architecture," and the author of Ivanhoe denominates it "the most august of Temples."

The Choir of this venerable structure was destroyed by fire in 1829, and subsequently restored with great faithfulness and beauty, by M^r. Smirk at a cost of above $250,000. [*In 1839 this matchless fabric again became a prey to the devouring element, and the roof of the nave, with the south-western tower were reduced to ruins. It will no doubt be again restored, but we shall still have to lament a broken link in its associations with departed ages, — associations which "time alone can give."*]

The interior of the building measures 524 feet in length 222 feet in width through the trancepts or cross aisles, and 100 feet in height from the floor to the ceiling.

The view of this magnificent chamber from the western door is probably without a parallel in Architecture. The numerous clusters of delicate and graceful columns, [34] arranged on either side, bearing a ceiling of the most beautiful proportions, present a vista of overpowering grandeur. — The whole atmosphere, mellowed by the richly coloured windows, impart to the long perspective of its majestic aisles a mysterious and glowing splendor.

The celebrated window which terminates the view on the eastern end is 75 feet high and 32 feet wide, the whole of which is ornamented with representations of Scripture history.

Every window in the church was once entirely glazed with richly coloured glass, and all but two or three of them seem to have escaped the reckless spoliation which characterized the civil wars, and which left almost every other monument of ancient English architecture in a much more mutilated condition.

This edifice was commenced in 1227, and one hundred and forty three years were occupied in building it. — Nearly five [35] centuries have therefore elapsed since its final completion.

We have now come to the fifth, and last period of English Gothic usually called the florid pointed style, its decorations being richer than those of any preceding age. — The architecture of this period is also called the perpendicular style, from the perpendicular mullions which run through the tracery of the windows: — and some denominate it the Tudor style in allusion to the Tudor family under whose dynasty it flourished most.

This period is generally dated from the commencement of the reign of Richard the second, in the year 1377, to the time of the Eighth Henry in the early part of the sixteenth century.

Some of the principal features of the style are exhibited in the drawing before you, which represents the front of Bishop Longlands chapel, Lincoln Minster.

York Minster. Rev. John Milner, A Treatise on the Ecclesiastical Architecture of England during the Middle Ages *(London, 1835). The Athenæum of Philadelphia.*

This style succeeded the Decorated, [36] and is distinguished from it by the introduction of obtucely pointed arches formed from four centres; embattled transoms to the windows; Heraldic ornaments; fanlike tracery in the vaultings of the ceilings; and perpendicular mullions running through the tracery of the window heads, no vertical lines having ever been made above the spring of the arches of windows previous to the changes which were wrought on the architecture of England on the accession of Richard the Second; — hence this feature alone has given to the style the name of perpendicular.

Another prominent distinction between this period and the preceeding one is the use of horizontal architraves over arched windows and doors with the spandrils ornamented with tracery.

Every conceivable variety of buttresses, battlements and pinnacles are used in this style, while there are some examples without any buttresses at all, and some even without [38] pinnacles.

Grotesque figures are frequently introduced, and in some instances we find ludicrous representations of Chases composed of cats, rats, mice, dogs, monkeys and a variety of curious imaginary forms which do but little credit to the genius of the inventors.

The whole exterior of the best examples of this style is covered with a series of rich panels by which all repose for the eye is destroyed, and as the natural consequence the power of producing agreeable emotions of taste is lost. Figures of Angels carved in stone [*or in other words petrified spirits*], are frequently introduced to support shields &c, and sometimes they are even used as corbels to support roof beams.

The spires of this period differ but little from those of the last; — their age is however evident from the details of their ornaments, such as arches formed from four centers; perpendicular lines running through [39] the tracery of the window heads &c.

The finest examples of the Florid pointed style are the chapel of Henry the Seventh, Westminster; the Kings College Cambridge, and S^t. Georges, Windsor.

The Chapel of Henry the Seventh is probably the richest and most highly wrought specimen of architecture ever executed; — it stands in connection with Westminster Abbey, and measures 77 feet wide 113 feet long, and 77 feet high; the cost of building it was equal to one million of dollars; and some recent repairs effected under the late James Wyatt cost of $210,000.

The most highly embellished portion of this edifice is the ceiling, the strength, richness and airy lightness of which characterizes it as a prodigy of art [*and exhibit the profoundest knowledge of geometry combined with the utmost degree of practical skill and science in mechanics:* —] it is altogether

[40] composed of stone, and appears to hang in air like elegantly wrought net work; — the architecture of this edifice is however too elaborate and too complex to admit of being intelligibly described without extensive illustrations.

In every example of the Florid pointed style the details are overwrought, and although there are numerous specimens in this age of Gothic architecture which exhibit astonishing skill in execution, there is never the less an obvious decline in taste: — a love of gaudy show seems to have predominated in the public mind, and the close of this style, which terminated the period usually assigned to the middle ages left England rapidly retrograding in art.

> ["Hence doom'd to hide her banish'd head
> Forever, Gothic architecture fled;
> Forewarn'd she left in one most beautious place
> That much might of her ancient fame be said
> Her pendant roof, her windows' branching grace,
> Pillar of cluster'd reed and tracery of lace."]

Glass[1]

[1+][2] The beautiful effects produced in the interiors of midæval structures by the introduction of stained glass, having been alluded to, it will be proper to speak more particularly to this species of ornamentation; and, in this connection, it may not be out of place to refer to glass in general.

The first ancient writer by whom any mention is made of glass, as an artificial substance, is Theophrastus, who wrote about 300 years before Christ; he describes it as having been made of the sands of the River Belus, and seems to have had considerable knowledge of its nature. About a century later, we have a description of the celebrated sphere of Archimedes, which, if the account of it be true, goes to show that the art had then attained a good degree of perfection.

Lucian speaks of "drinking glasses," and Plutarch, Lucretius, Virgil, Horace, Strabo, Senaca, and Pliny, all mention glass; indeed Pliny, who wrote in the 77th year of Christ, gives a full description of the way in which it was then manufactured. He says that some forms were brought into the

---

[1] Part of this section parallels Walter's article "On Glass as Applied to Architecture" *JFI* 1, no. 4 (May 1841), 266-67.
[2] The five following pages are rewritten additions which replace four original pages that Walter cut out of the original manuscript. The only writing that remains from the original draft (and which Walter deleted) notes that one Robert A. Caldeleigh Esquire obtained the windows for St. John's Catholic church in 1818 during a European tour (see manuscript page [5+]). In 1832 *Poulson's American Daily Advertizer* described them as Biblical scenes of "Ancient Stained Glass" removed from a "dilapidated" church in Rouen.

Chapel of Henry VII. Rev. John Milner, A Treatise on the Ecclesiastical Architecture of England during the Middle Ages *(London, 1835). The Athenæum of Philadelphia.*

required shape by [2+] blowing with the breath, some were ground on a lathe, and others were embossed; Sidon, he tells us, was formerly famous for these manufactures, and specula, or looking glasses, were first invented there. He further remarks, that no substance was more manageable in receiving colors, than glass, and that it might be cut, or engraved upon by diamonds.

The ancients did not, however, make use of glass for widows. That application of it is comparatively modern, while its use in the manufacturing of vessels and ornaments, dates back some 3500 years. The process of blowing glass is plainly shown by the sculptures on the Egyptian Temples. Wilkinson has given us the fullest evidence that the Egyptians were expert glass-blowers.

A glass lens has been found at Pompeii, which explains the mystery of the fine engraving on ancient gems, which cannot even be seen by the naked eye, much less executed.[1]

[3+] Notwithstanding these facts, as to the antiquity of glass, we have no positive authority relating to its use for windows earlier than the close of the third century. S[t]. Jerome, who wrote in 422, speaks of windows formed of glass, melted and cast into thin plates; and in the year 571 Gregory of Tours alludes to the devastations committed on the windows of Churches, by the ravages of war. Johannes Philoponus, who wrote about the same, speaks of the panes of glass being fastened in the windows with plaster.

Felibien, in his principes de l'architeture, says that the first attempts at ornamenting windows with figures, were made by arranging glass of different colors, like mosaic, and that the beautiful effects thus obtained, led gradually to the art of infusing various tints into each pane, so as to produce compositions of any required design.

Fortunatus, who lived towards the end of the sixth century, alludes in glowing terms to the painted glass in the windows of the Church of Notre Dame, in Paris; and Benedict Biscopius is said to have imported the art into Britain in the year 675.

[4+] Stained glass was not, however, connected with architecture, to any great extent, until the 13th century; and it reached its zenith under the kings of the house of York, in the 15th century.

A popular idea prevails that the art of staining glass is lost. Such is not the fact. When architecture began to decline under the Tudor family, all the arts connected with it declined also, as a natural result. — Felibien,[*] who wrote in the year 1699, says that in ancient stained glass, some very beautiful, and very lively colors are seen, which are not now to be found;

---

[*] p. 182

[1] A note here reads "Refer to ruins in Northumberland—."

it is not, however, that the invention is lost, but because persons will not incur so great an expense or take the same pains to make them, that they formerly did.

Dallaway,* in his "Discourses upon Architecture in England" says: —"the history of stained glass in England, would require a distinct work to offer all the information concerning it, which has been collected by myself and others. It may be merely necessary to observe, that it was first connected with architecture in the reign [5+] of Henry the third, and reached its zenith in the 15th century; and that we had eminent professors in the reign of Charles the First. That the art was ever lost is a vulgar error."

So far from the art of staining glass having been lost, it is practised at the present day in far greater perfection than in any preceding age; the designs are more beautiful, and artistic, and the colors more brilliant and harmonious than any ever executed by the ancients. The compositions in stained glass of the times in which we live, embrace all the brilliancy and variety of color, and all the perfection of manipulation ever attained in the Middle ages, combined with a style of pictorial illustration equal in drawing to the best representations on canvas, and far more brilliant in color. The art of stained glass, as practiced by the ancients, is not lost. All that was ever known about it in midæval times is known about it now, and infinitely more.

Two specimens of ancient stained glass may be seen in S[t]. John's Church, in 13th near Chestnut S[t]., Phil[a]. in the windows on each side of the altar; they were [45] obtained in 1818, from an Old Church now occupied as a stable at Rouen in Normandy.

From this cursory glance at the introduction of glass in building we find that architecture went through all its earliest stages in the east, attained the zenith of its glory in Attica, and sunk in ruin with the city of the Cæsars, before glass was used at all, as a material for keeping out the weather, and transmitting light:—hence classic architecture ran its whole course without any influence whatever from this invention; while on the other hand Gothic architecture depends for its character almost exclusively upon it.—To the introduction of glass in building may therefore be attributed much of the wide difference which exists between classic and Gothic architecture.

France

Having considered the five periods or styles practised in England during the [46] middle ages, I shall proceed to notice briefly the progress of the building art in France through the same period.

---

* p. 63

About the close of the ninth century the northern part of France was overrun by a tribe of Scandinavians under Rolla, afterwards called Robert; who compelled the French king, Charles the Simple to cede this portion of his territory to them about the year 912.

The new settlers were called north men, or Normen, and the portion of France they inhabited was called Normandy.

After the cessation of hostilities between the French and their new neighbours, the Princes, Nobles, and Bishops of France set about architecture in good earnest; and we are told that Robert the Pious during his reign in the beginning of the eleventh century built no less than fourteen monastries and seven other churches.* — At the same time a corresponding spirit was displayed in Normandy, and William the first, before [47] his invasion of England constructed two Abbeys himself at Caen, and his nobles built thirty eight others in the same province, many of which were of great magnificence; — thus we find architecture extensively cultivated in France and Normandy even before the Norman conquest.

Among other reasons for the very extraordinary developments in building which signalised this period is the fact that before the close of the tenth century an idea began to prevail that our Saviour would reappear in the year 1000, and that the world would certainly be destroyed. — This impression rapidly gained ground, and eventually produced a total suspension of all kinds of building; the coffers of the church were filled to overflowing with the donations of those who had sought in this way to calm the turbulence of their conciences; and the first dawnings of the eleventh century were watched with a breathless suspense. — It is scarcely necessary however to attempt on the present occasion to prove that the world did not come [48] to an end, as that is a point which the most industrious unsettlers of history have not yet assailed.[1] — When the period of the millenium had passed away, and the people recovered from their fright, they began every where to construct new churches and monastries and to rebuild old ones, so that in every country we find more fine ecclesiastical edifices founded in the first century of the second millenium, than in any other period of the middle ages. — We learn from Spelman's Glossary that the frequent and extravagant grants of land bestowed on Cathedrals, monastries, and other churches from the beginning of the tenth to the middle of the eleventh centuries, placed more than one third of all the lands of England in possession of the clergy, exempt from all taxes.†

---

* Milner / p. 39
† p. 396

[1] It is likely that these "industrious unsettlers of history" were historians, geologists, archaeologists, and others whose findings were contrary to biblical record. Walter underscored the work of those scientists and scholars who supported the Bible.

The style of building in France and Normandy continued to be similar in its general features, to that of the Norman period in England until the beginning of the twelfth century, when it underwent a total change by the introduction of the Lombard style from [49] Italy.

About half a century later another change was produced by the appearance of the pointed arch from Germany; — and as early as the commencement of the thirteenth century, pointed architecture triumphed over all Italian admixtures, and generally prevailed.

After this period the Architecture of France varied but little in any of its ramifications from that of England, the chief differences between the two styles consisting in the French buildings being higher in proportion to their horizontal dimensions than English ones, and in the existence of some peculiarities in their details.

Germany

Another interesting portion of the architecture of the middle ages is found in Germany; the industrious and opulent inhabitants of that country were evidently in advance of their neighbours in bringing to perfection the rich pointed styles which embellish Northern Europe.

[50] Pointed architecture was not only promoted in Germany, but, there, unquestionably, was its native soil, and there it existed more than a century before its introduction into England, and half that period before it reached France; — the best German examples are more grand, perfect, and varied than those of other countries, and in some of them, from their very foundations to the summit of their towering spires, a degree of compactness, consistency and harmony is exhibited, which is equaled in no other country; — it should however be remarked that their whole appearance is coarser and their details more clumsy than corresponding works in England; as far as it regards chasteness, elegance, and brilliancy of effect, the English have the undoubted preeminence; while in point of magnitude and unity of design the Germans excel. — Their architects were everywhere in demand, and nearly all the best edifices of Italy were executed from their designs. — Vasari, who wrote in the 16th century [51] speaks of Gothic architecture as a curse brought from Germany which eventually overrun Italy; thus giving to the Germans the credit, or as he thought the reproach of its invention.

The Cathedrals of Strasburg, Friburg, Oppenheim, Oberwesel, and many other German cities present magnificent examples of the Gothic of that country, but we should not have time on the present occasion to examine them without running far beyond our limits; we therefore take leave of the Germans and proceed to notice briefly the architecture of Lombardy.

Lombardy

The Lombards were the first people after the downfal of the Roman empire to awaken to trade and industry; their commerce soon expanded into importance both on the Adriatic and the Mediteranean Seas, and their influence extended to the shores of the Baltic: — they systematized their architecture upon principles drawn from Roman and Byzantine structures, and the style thus compiled soon found its way into every part of Europe.

[52] This description of Building is usually called the Lombard style; and its general character as well as details differ very materially from any thing we have yet considered.

In order to convey by means of a single sketch as many of the characteristic features of the style as possible, I have composed the drawing before you (see sketch) of several of the best Lombard examples; the contour and general proportions of the building, with the centre door and the window over it are from San Zeno at Verona; the side doors are from the Duomo of Piacenza, and the galleries under the cornice from San Michele at Pavia.

Columns in the Lombard style have no fixed proportions; they are generally made without taper, and are frequently started from brackets, having no other foundation; sometimes they rest on the backs of animals, as in the churches of Mantua, Modena, and Verona, as here represented; and [53] in some instances small columns are twisted together spirally, in others they are formed with a kink in them so as to appear as if they were broken and about to fall; — this absurd idea is found in the Cathedral at Vienne in Dauphiné, and in the south porch of the Cathedral of Worms.

A continuous entablature is sometimes used, but more frequently the columns are surmounted simply by arches as in the pointed styles, and in some of the lastest works of Rome.

The Capitals of columns in the earliest Lombard buildings are rude imitations of the Roman orders, but in later works we find representations of all kinds of animated beings, real and monstrous, many specimens of which exist at Bologna, Modena, Parma, at Paris in the church of S^t. Germain-des-Pres; and at Canterbury in the Cathedral.

One of the most remarkable features of the style is the arched galleries or arcades [54] under the raking cornice thus. These galleries are certain characteristics of Lombard architecture, never having been used in any other description of building. — They are generally formed within the thickness

San Zeno, Verona. Thomas Hope, An Historical Essay on Architecture *(London, 1835),*
The Athenæum of Philadelphia.

of the walls, and are approached by means of inside stairways: — in some examples the base of the arcade is made horizontal, and the arches rise in height so as to follow the slope of the roof, as in the cathedral of Modena, and the church of Santa Maria at Murano; — but in other specimens we find the whole arcade inclined so as to coincide with the inclination of the pediment as here exhibited. (see drawing) These archways gave rise to the scolloped curtain so often used under cornices in the rural architecture of the present day.

Lombard arches are generally semicircular; — sometimes however the horse-shoe form is used, and in a few instances the pointed arch.

The windows of this style are very narrow in proportion to their height, and often [55] present the appearance of mere loop-holes.

In most Lombard buildings the front walls are ornamented with horizontal bands, but in no instance that I now recollect are these bands suffered to intercept the vertical lines. — Each extremity of the front is usually bounded by a sort of pilaster buttress, and in all the best examples two intermediate buttresses are placed so as to divide the façade into compartments corresponding with the interior aisles, thus. — The later Lombard churches are each ornamented with an immense circular windows composed of spokes radiating from a centre, and connected at the periphery with arches as in the design before you: — this windows is commonly called S^t. Catherine's wheel.

The Campaniles, or towers, of the middle ages so frequently noticed by travellers are nearly all in the Lombard style, some of them are very lofty, and they generally continue their thickness throughout. Several of [56] these structures have been built on bad foundations, which has caused them to decline from the perpendicular: — many suppose them to have been built so intentionally for the purpose of exhibiting the skill of their builders; but the towers themselves exhibit proof to the contrary: Mess^r. Cressy and Taylor remarked that in the leaning tower at Pisa (a curious and intricate piece of workmanship) the settlement began before the structure was completed, and that attempts were made to rectify it by increasing the height of the columns and cornices on the lowest side; — they also observed that the scaffold holes incline just as the tower does; — similar peculiarities were noticed by myself in the leaning tower at Bologna.

Lombard towers were often crowned with octagonal spires, thus producing in the change from a square to an octagon, and from a vertical wall to an inclined one, an abruptness which the architects of the Italian states never attempted to overcome: — but in more northern countries where Gothic architecture [57] reached a greater degree of excellence the most beautiful artifices were used to avoid the abruptness of such a combination; and in some examples, especially at Frankfort on the Main, the transition is so gradual as to render it difficult to say where the base terminates and the spire begins.

As Lombard architecture approached the north, it became rude and clumsy; in Normandy and England its developments were extremely coarse and vulgar; and indeed we find but few good specimens of it north of the Alps.

The introduction of pointed architecture into Lombardy wrought a great change on the Lombard style, and produced an incongruous composition of which the Cathedral or Duomo at Milan is the most famous specimen. This celebrated structure was founded in 1385 by a German architect; a portion of the building was erected by Brunnelleschi; and the present front by a modern architect of the name of Amati. — Its general character is that of [58] the Pointed architecture of Northern Europe, and all its details are either Lombard or Roman. The composition is one of utter discordance, but the richness and magnitude of the building command admiration. —

The whole mass is composed of white marble [− *it covers a space equal to one half of Washington Square*]. − The architecture is embellished with four thousand four hundred statues; − the exterior is finished with ninety eight pinnacles each of which is crowned with a statue larger than life.

This building has the reputation of being in the pointed style of Gothic architecture; this is however a great mistake; no genuine example of pointed architecture ever existed in Italy: − the pointed styles flourished with some unimportant local peculiarities in Britain, France, Normandy, Germany, and the Netherlands, but beyond these countries it became mixed with classic forms, and I am not aware of a single example in Italy of the architecture of the [59] middle ages in which that of Rome may not be found to exist in a greater or less degree.

Arab Architecture

Having glanced at the several styles of Architecture practicsed in Europe during the Middle ages, it remains for us to consider that of the Moslems, or followers of Mahomet. − These blinded disciples of that notorious imposter, stimulated by his doctrines, started from Arabia, the birthplace of their leader, and extended their conquest from the frontiers of India to the shores of the Atlantic. − When they had reached their ocean limits on the West, Spain presented to them an easy and inviting prey, − a single battle decided the fate of that romantic country [− *"That sunny land of citron groves and orange bowers"*] − and Islamism, was as firmly planted there as in Arabia.

While the dominion of the Arabs was confined to their native soil, they appear to have made [60] but little progress in the arts, and, indeed in the earliest stages of Islamism they seem to have been decidedly adverse to every species of intellectual cultivation; − but, with the extension of their empire and religion they acquired a relish for mental enjoyment; and at the commencement of the ommiad dynasty in the year 623 the ancient frugality of the nation was thrown off; and a taste for the beautiful in every department of art appears to have been successfully cultivated.[1]

The first Omar removed the seat of empire from Medina to Damascus, and, laying aside the simplicity of former princes he assumed the magnificence of an Asiatic monarch. During his reign, and that of his immediate successors, Damascus was adorned with buildings of great splendor: − the celebrated mosque built by Alwalid the first is among the best works of that period; − a lofty minaret which was erected in connection with it, is said to have been the first example of such an appendage ever constructed.

---

[1] Beneath this paragraph Walter drew a line across the page and noted "omit to page 72 if late," which would remove the greater part of his discussion of Islamic architecture.

[61] The seat of empire was again removed and located on the western frontiers of Persia where in the year 762 the famous city of Bagdad was founded.

In the tenth century the new city of Cairo was built; and the great mosque which adorned it, is celebrated for its magnitude and splendor, having been embellished with 500 columns.

The Arabs derived their earliest notions of Architecture from various sources; — they were surrounded by the Egyptians, the Syrians, the Chaldeans, and the Persians; and in all probability they received the germs of art from these countries and gradually wrought them out into their own peculiar style. — Their architecture is characterized by an extraordinary degree of lightness and elevation, — by the horse-shoe form of its arches, and by a profuse use of ornament in which the representation of animals was strictly prohibited, no work of art being tolerated by the religion of the country [62] which exhibited the likeness of any thing possessing animal life: — these ornaments are called arabesque, a term seldom applied among us in its true sense.

There are however a few instances as in the Alhambra at Grenada in which the anathema denounced in the Koran against all representations of living creatures seems to have been in some degree disregarded; but the prejudices of the nation were too strong to be overcome by these innovations, hence we find little or no progress made either in sculpture or painting during the middle ages in any country under Mahometan influence.

Moslem architecture is frequently distinguished in the present day by the term Saracenic, an appellation which originally pertained exclusively to the inhabitants of Saracene in Arabia; but this people being more zealous than any of their contemporaries in disseminating the doctrines of Mahomet, every description of Mahometan architecture is now called Saracenic whether it be found in Europe, Asia, or Africa.

[63] Arabian architecture was practised to as great an extent in Spain, notwithstanding its remoteness from Arabia, as in any other portion of the Moslem domains. — The Mahometan conquest of 713 put the Moors in full possession of that beautiful country, and wherever they carried their arms and their religion, they carried their arts with equal zeal; — hence we find the Moorish architecture of Spain as truly Arabian as that of Bagdad.

Laborde in his Travels through Spain divides the Moorish architecture of that country into three distinct periods; — the first includes the two centuries following the introduction of Islamism, the finest specimen of which is the Mosque at Cordova; — the second extends from the ninth to the thirteenth centuries, and has its most perfect developement in the Royal palace of the Alhambra at Grenada; — and the third reaches to the subversion of the Mahometan dominions in Spain, and the best example of

The Great Mosque, Cordoba. Comte de Alexandre Laborde, Voyage pittoresque et historique de l'Espagne *(Paris, 1806-1820). Annenberg Rare Book and Manuscript Library, University of Pennsylvania.*

this period is the palace of a Moorish Arab chieftan at Seville, the former capital [64] of Andalusia.

The first period is exemplified by the celebrated Mosque at Cordova.—This edifice covers a space about equal to one of our squares.—Before the principal door are six columns of fine jasper, and the three sides of the building are ornamented with 72 columns.—A tower rises on one side of 51 feet square embellished with Moorish arches resting on 100 columns of black and red marble:—the interior is divided into aisles by 850 columns which support ceilings composed of fragrant wood richly ornamented;—these ceilings contain several thousand cubic feet of timber and notwithstanding they have existed upwards of ten centuries, they have not yet exhibited the slightest sign of decay.

The whole number of columns with which this edifice is embellished amounts to 1018, many of which are made of jasper and the rest of red, yellow, and white marble.

The small chamber in which the Moors kept "the book of the law" is finished with the [65] greatest delicacy and beauty;—its walls are encrusted with rich marbles, and the whole area is crowned with a dome of exquisite workmanship.—But the most remarkable apartment of this vast pile is a octagonal room of only 13 feet in diameter; the walls of which are encrusted with costly stones and the ceiling, composed of a single piece of pure white marble sculptured out in the form of a dome, having a concavity of nine feet.

The Moors held this Mosque in great veneration, coming even from Africa to visit it long after the Castilians had converted it into a church.

The example referred to for a developement of the second period of Arabian architecture in Spain is the palace of the Moorish Kings at Grenada, called the Alhambra; or the red house;[*] probably from the colour of the materials of which it was originally constructed.[†]

[66] This ancient structure is situated upon the brow of a steep hill between the rivers, and the country which surrounds it presents a noble expanse of fertile fields embellished with groves of citron, myrtle, and orange; and enriched with beautiful Moorish structures, imparting to the picture a fairy like aspect; while odoriferous trees fill the atmosphere with constant fragrance.—The climate of this delightful region is so mild that the mercury never rises above 80 degrees of Fahrenheit in the summer, nor sinks below 50 in the Winter; thus uniting "the flowers of spring with the fruits of Autumn"[‡] and rendering the whole country a magnificent garden.

[*] Swinburne / p 2
[†] Stuart, dic.
[‡] Laborde / v. 1. 139

"Here Moslem luxury," —
"Hath held for ages her voluptuous reign"*
The present appearance of the palace of the Alhambra from the outside is that of an old castle;—it is built of free stone, and [67] surrounded with strong walls flanked with numerous towers and bastions; while the interior, though dismantled, solitary, and neglected, is still in a good state of preservation, every where attesting the wealth, power, and splendor of its ancient and romantic Kings.

The whole area occupied by this vast establishment is about 2300 feet in length and six hundred in width. The principal court is encircled with a beautiful portico supporting Moorish arches; and the walls and vaults are filled with arabesque ornaments.

In the centre stands a reservoir of running water, and the whole court is embellished with orange groves, and walks; and beautified with beds of flowers paved around with marble.

But the most celebrated, and far the most beautiful portion of the Alhambra is the court of the Lions;—this apartment is one hundred feet in length and fifty in width surrounded with a corridor [68] of 128 white marble columns of slender but graceful proportions, from which spring as many arches, of the horse-shoe form, supporting a ceiling of great beauty.—The walls are all charged with arabesque ornaments, and an admirable degree of lightness and delicacy pervades the whole.

The fountain which "flung luxuriant coolness round" this celebrated court, and which has been rendered famous by song and story, consists of a large reservoir in which are twelve ill-shaped lions supporting a beautiful basin;—from the middle of the group rises another basin of smaller dimensions, thus producing a pyramidal composition, from the summit of which the water gushed out in large volumns over the basins successively, and through the Lions mouths into the lower reservoir, which constituted a fountain head for the whole establishment.

Smaller fountains were distributed in every court, and streams meandered in marble channels through every room. Here, [69] under flowery shades of towering cypresses waving in the balmy breeze;—or amid fragrant and beautiful gardens, the Moorish Sovreigns of Grenada lived in luxiurient elegance.—Some of their marble halls and grottoes, watered by perpetual streams, and embellished with arabesques, paintings, and mosaics, still look as fresh as they did in the days of Boabdil:—the most of their architecture is, however,

---

* Mrs. Hemans / 119

"Stamped with the touching traces of decline"[*]
"But answering well each vision that pourtrays
Arabian splendor to the poets gaze:
Wild, wondrous, brilliant all—a mingled glow
Of rainbow tints, above, around, below;
Bright-streaming from the many tincture veins,
Of precious marbles—and the vivid stains
Of rich mosaics o'er the light arcade,
In gay festoons and fairy knots displayed."[†]

In the beautiful words of the author of the "Sketch book," after a glowing description [70] of this triumph of Moslem skill, "such is the Alhambra. A Moslem pile in the midst of a Christian land;" "an elegant memento of a brave, intelligent and graceful people who conquered, ruled, and passed away."[‡]

"The character of the whole," says another writer "is so remote from that of any thing with which we are accustomed, that it produces unmingled sensations of pleasure and delight;"—and "we may judge" observes the historian of the Arabian kingdoms in Spain, "what this palace had been in the zenith of the regal power of its possessors, with the courts and halls, baths and fountains, groves and gardens, in all their perfection."[§]

"No wonder" remarks Swinburne in his Picturesque tour through Spain that "the moors regretted Grenada; no wonder they still offer up prayers to God every Friday for the recovery of this city, which they even now esteem a terrestrial paradise.[**]

The third period of Moslem architecture [71] embraces the decline of the art; which, according to Laborde commenced in the thirteenth century, and extended to the end of Arab influence in Spain.—Towards the close of this period, Arabian architecture began to assimilate itself with the Italian styles, thus producing a most unsightly mixture of inharmonious forms.

The best existing example of this period is the Arabian residence at Seville, before alluded to.—This structure is still in a perfect state of preservation, and the whole of it is better contrived more for convenience than beauty;—one of its apartments is only 30 feet square, and its ceiling is 60 feet in height;[††] the walls are ornamented with a curious kind of stucco net work, and the whole pile is a mixture of Arabian and classic forms by no means beautiful.

Notwithstanding the splendor and refinement with which the Saracens were surrounded during the dark ages of Europe they have left but few

[*] Sketch book / v. 2. p 46.
[†] Mrs. Hemans / p. 118
[‡] Irvin's / Alhambra / 74 [misspelled Irving. *Ed.*]
[§] Stuart dic / Alham
[**] p. 14
[††] Stuart dic.

mementoes of their [72] lofty genius: — the remains of some of their cities have however reached our time, telling of the power and wealth of the vanished beings who once inhabited them; — and we may trace, with some degree of certainty, through time-worn Mosque and Minaret, the tracks of Moorish art.

Conclusion

Your attention has now been directed to most of the Architecture of the Middle ages; but in attempting to confine the subject within the limits of the hour allotted, it is necessarily reduced to little more than a passing glance: — it must however be obvious, even from these hasty remarks, that this period of history affords a most fruitful field for amusing and interesting study; especially to those whose attachment to letters is chastened by a love of the beautiful.

The remnants of these days of chivalry date up the march of intellect through ten romantic centuries with beautiful precision; — and the influence of art [73] on mind is here exhibited through all the grades of civilization.

The science developed in the Architecture of a portion of these mysterious ages is as profound as it is astonishing; — and the grandeur, sublimity, and poetry displayed in many of the specimens which still exist, especially in those of modern Europe, tell of a tasteful and a mighty people:

"A glow of lofty hope and daring thought"
is still reflected from many a rich memorial of their "bright and soaring genius," and all their hills and vallies teem

"With proud remembrances that cannot die."

Lecture 5ᵗʰ

On Modern Architecture

Thos. U. Walter

Philadᵃ: Dec: 9, 1841

Delivered before the Franklin Institute

Dec. 9. 1841

Benjamin Henry Latrobe, Bank of Pennsylvania, Philadelphia (1798-1800). William Birch, The City of Philadelphia . . . as it appeared in the year 1800 *(Philadelphia: 1800).*
The Athenæum of Philadelphia.

LECTURE V
ON MODERN ARCHITECTURE

Introduction

[1] The changes and revolutions to which the principles of taste in Architecture have been subjected, by the ever varying progress of civilization, have multiplied styles and modes of building, almost to infinity.

The restless activity which characterizes the human mind—its natural aspirations after something nobler, and better than what the present scene affords, have tended in every age of the world, to the modification and improvement of Architectural forms and proportions, to the production of new combinations, and to the application of new principles;—while the art itself, from its enduring character, has accumulated [2] and treasured up, the taste—the styles—the intellect of other ages, presenting imperishable evidences of high and mighty genius

"Forever speaking to the heart of man."

Architectural Awareness in the Modern World

The advancement and diffusion of knowledge in modern times present all these noble relics of the distant past before us at one view; thus placing Modern Architecture in circumstances widely different from those which have influenced all preceding periods of the art. Ancient nations knew comparatively but little of each other;—they were generally either shut up within their own precincts, or engaged in war. Their national intercourse was consequently too limited, and their prejudices too strong to admit of one nation [3] profiting to any considerable extent from the taste or skill of another; ancient architecture will therefore be found to consist of but few principles, although in some instances those few were carried out to the utmost degree of perfection: — this fact is strikingly obvious in the remains which have come down to us from Greece; — nothing can be more perfect than the proportions of Grecian Architecture, and nothing more exquisite than its execution, but to see one greek temple is to see a thousand, — the chief marks of distinction in most of them being the sculptured representations with which they are embellished. A corresponding uniformity of taste arising out of a restriction to but few principles, is apparent, in some degree, in the works of every ancient nation, thus accounting for the peculiar character which distinguishes the Architecture of each.

But in modern times the case is widely different; — the important [4] inventions and improvements in art, and the rapid advancement of civilization which have characterized the few last centuries open to the present age vast avenues to knowledge which were wholly unknown to the ancients.

The invention of printing alone has had a greater influence on architecture than all the revolutions of antiquity; — previous to the discovery of this invaluable art, the cost and delay which attended the copying of manuscripts rendered literature a most expensive luxury, thus confining the productions of the learned almost exclusively to the halls of opulence and splendor; but now, the press, that most powerful engine of civilization, pours forth its volumes daily by thousands, unfolding to the poor as well as the rich of every nation in its own peculiar tongue the wisdom, the genius, the science of all.

The Architecture of the present day has also been influenced in no small degree by the art of engraving. — The architect [5] may now have before him the most perfect representations of the buildings of all ages and all countries; and instead of receiving his impressions from a few scattered monuments as did the ancients, he is enabled to study and compare, the works of every nation.

Modern improvements in the application of steam have likewise had an important influence on art;[1] and this mighty agent is no doubt destined to achieve results still more wonderful than any thing which has yet been witnessed; — it accelerates the distribution of knowledge, brings distant countries near each other, and is rapidly producing an intercourse between nations which must eventually resolve mankind into one great family.

---

[1] To this discussion of "modern improvements" Walter added "photography" in pencil at this point in the manuscript, indicating his intent to speak on it extemporaneously. Alternately, perhaps Walter meant to include photography as a subject in a future rewrite of the lectures.

Revival of Taste for Classical Forms

The epoch which seems to constitute the most natural boundary between ancient and modern architecture is the decline of the pointed styles, and the revival of a taste for classic forms which took place about the close of the period usually assigned to the [6] Middle ages; — this era may therefore be considered as the starting point of Modern architecture, from whence I propose to trace down the art of building to the present day.

Italy

The pointed styles never having been practised with any great success in Italy, and the clumsy Lombard compositions which were ever a disgrace to that classic land, having sunk, in the last century of the Middle ages, to the very extreme of coarseness, it is by no means difficult to account for the return of the Italians to the ancient orders of their country, the remains of which were still before them.

The first indications of a revival of classic taste appeared in the early part of the fifteenth century, and the mode of building which eventually grew out of the new application of antique forms and proportions has since been called the <u>cinque-cento</u> style, in allusion to the fact of its being a patchwork of the five orders.

The earliest examples of this style, [7] and indeed many of its later and most celebrated specimens are nothing more than so many pattern cards of the five Roman orders, executed in minute parts, and piled story on story like enormous houses built of little temples. — Its first developments contained some of the grossest faults and inconsistencies of the worst age of Pagan Rome, and even in its greatest state of perfection there is nothing about it either attractive or agreeable; but a want of boldness arising from the diminutive subdivisions into which its elevations are dissected is obvious in every example; — hence the broad lights, the deep shadows, the sparkling effects so essential to the beauty, harmony, and repose of an architectural compositions were never attained, nor even affected in the cinque-cento style; notwithstanding its originators had constantly before them many specimens of the antique in which these qualities shone preeminent.

The transition from the Lombard [8] and German styles to classic forms was by no means sudden and complete; — the extremes between these opposite modes of building were too wide to be passed at a single step; — the change was necessarily gradual, and the first productions in the <u>cinque</u>-cento style, were little more than a union of classic and Gothic features.

Brunelleschi, who flourished in 1420 is said to have been the first to attempt a restoration of the antique with any degree of success; but his works can scarcely be said to be in the style of which we are speaking: — one of his most celebrated buildings is the Pitti palace at Florence.

The most renowned and tasteful architect of this era was Bramante, who is said to have exhibited the best specimens of the cinque cento style every executed; his cupola of Santa Maria della Grazie built at Milan in 1496 and the Palazzo della Cancellaria at Rome are acknowledged to be [9] amongst its finest examples. — This architect was also the author of the original plan of S^t. Peters at Rome, but which was afterwards altered successively by the Sangallos, Peruzzi, and Michael Angelo Buonarotti.

The fanciful and frivolous style thus brought out of the antique was soon however superseded by the bolder and nobler designs of Angelo, Palladio, Peruzzi and Fontana, all of whom returned to the ancient manner of using larger masses and dispensing with every kind of frippery and superfluous ornament.

Angelo has the reputation of being the first to return to the practise of employing a single order embracing the entire height of the building; but to his predecessors, Bramante and Sangallo must be conceded the praise of having approached much nearer the taste of the ancients in other respects; — the characteristic boldness of Angelo, while it led him to neglect the softer and more delicate elegancies of art, prompted him to [10] direct his genius to the attainment of great and difficult objects; hence we find a want of pure and elevated taste in most of his works; — in the pursuit of the grand and gigantic he often lost sight of the fitness of things, and sometimes even transcended the most obvious limits of propriety. [*To the fact of his never having been humanized by the softening and refining influences of Love and Matrimony may however perhaps be attributed something of the coarseness and extravagance of his ideas; as no one can for a moment doubt that he possessed a most Herculean intellect.*]

The return of a taste for classic architecture in the vicinity of Rome was followed by a general diffusion of the cinque-cento style throughout the Italian states; and scarcely a century had elapsed from its first developements before it had crossed the Alps and spread extensively over France, Spain, Germany and England.

France

It appeared in France during the reign of Louis the XIIth in the beginning of the [11] sixteenth century*, made considerable but awkward progress under his successor Francis the first, and reached something of a national

* Hope's arch. / v. 1, 543

Palazzo della Cancelleria, Rome. Ridolfino Venuti, Accurata, e succinta descrizione topografica
e istorica di Roma moderna *(Rome, 1766). Courtesy, The Winterthur Library: Printed Book and
Periodical Collection.*

character in the time of the second Henry*, under whom a portion of the Cour du Louvre was built by the celebrated Philibert de Lorme.† In the eastern front of this edifice which was erected about a century afterwards from the designs of Claude Perrault, the cinque-cento style was abandoned and a single order applied in the bolder taste of Angelo.

Spain

Revived Italian architecture was introduced in Spain also about the commencement of the 16th century: — it was adopted by Charles the fifth in an extensive addition to the palace of the Moorish kings of Greneda, and in the monastry of Engrazia at Saragossa; — it however became gradually assimilated in that country also to the massy architecture of the more ancient Romans.

Germany

It appeared in Germany in 1550 in a splendid addition to the Heidelberg castle‡ [12] and its course with the Germans likewise tended rapidly to the antique.

England

In England, the first departures from the Gothic were made by John of Padua, who introduced the new grade of Italian architecture with all its native peculiarities about the year 1579. — In 1619 it was adopted by Inigo Jones in the extensive palace at Whitehall, in London, and most other works erected about that period; — but like Angelo in Italy, and Perault in France, this celebrated architect was not long in returning to the grander style practised by the ancients; and in his S^t. Paul's church Covent garden we find a most beautiful development of a single colossal order, equal, if not superior in gracefulness and elegance of proportion to any thing ever erected in Italy.

On the first introduction of classic architecture into England, Gothic and classic forms were often used together, thus producing a mongrel style of composition [13] which exhibits a depravity of taste in that particular period that scarcely has a parallel in any other portion of English history. — M^r. Britton, in alluding to this era says, that "during the intermediate time when one style was growing into repute, and the other sinking in favor there will be found a mixture of both in one building which is not referable

---

* Wood's let / v.1. 95
† Milizia, / v. 1, 350
‡ Hope's arch / v. 1, 594

to either, and which has constituted the greatest problem in antiquarian science."

The Architecture of the time of Queen Elizabeth was of this character — it consisted of a sort of agony which the Roman orders experienced in their struggle with gothic; — and to this peculiar composition of inharmonious forms the term Elizabethan most properly belongs.

M^r. Hakewell in his treatise on Elizabethan architecture contends however that the style which bears the name of the Queen, to use his own words, "is the pure cinque-cento of Italy, unmixed with Gothic forms or Gothic ornaments;" but if it be admitted that such [14] is the fact, then the term Elizabethan becomes worse than useless, as it only serves to confuse the subject by giving the name of Elizabeth to what confessedly belongs to Italy.

Italian architecture it is true prevailed to a considerable extent before the death of the Queen, and so did the heterogeneous jumble of Gothic and classic forms; hence it is obvious that the term Elizabethan can belong properly to no other than the mixed style, and should therefore never be confounded either with the true Gothic or the cinque-cento.

Towards the close of Elizabeth's time the Italian style began to preponderate; — but the era of bad taste through which it had passed loaded it with little conceits and fantastic notions; — grotesque pilasters, shell roof'd niches, and caryatades were introduced without the least regard to beauty or propriety; and about the termination of this age of viciated taste we find the most outrageous medley's of cherubim, lion's [15] heads, bunches of carrots and turnips dangling about the ears of the most shocking distortions, armorial bearings, mythological hieroglyphics &^c the whole catalogue of which may be seen in a single chimney piece in Windsor Castle.

This inharmonious mixture of Italian cinque-cento and English Gothic, which had its origin during the reign of Elizabeth is therefore an unnatural and barbarous association; a chimera of the time, and an evidence of puerile taste.

Inigo Jones is said to have been the first to overcome effectually the prejudices which had previously existed in England against classic architecture, and to establish a taste for the Roman orders; — his palace at Whitehall was built some 15 years after the death of Elizabeth; and in the language of his biographer "magnificence shines throughout the whole, both in the variety and excellence of the proportions, and the convenience and [16] beauty of the apartments."*

Of his church in Covent Garden, which is only 60 feet front by 133 feet deep, Ralph, in his "Critical review of Public buildings" observes,

---

* Milizia's / lives of Archts. / 27.162

though rather extravagantly, "that it is without a rival, and one of the most perfect pieces of architecture that the art of man can produce;—nothing" says he "can possibly be imagined more simple, and yet magnificence itself can hardly give greater pleasure.—This" continues our author "is a strong proof of the force of harmony and proportion, and at the same time a demonstration that it is taste, and not expense which is the parent of beauty."

In the year 1666, fifteen years after the death of Inigo Jones the city of London was almost wholly destroyed by fire; the houses, previous to that time having chiefly been built of wood.—This calamity, if calamity it may be called, brought into action the talents of Christopher Wren, who was then about 34 years of age, and whose [17] previous studies in architecture, and skill in mathematics eminently qualified him for such an emergency.

The taste of this great Architect and Philosopher was however decidedly Roman;—he followed closely in the track of Jones and Palladio, and as the consequence London grew up after the conflagration, in appearance an Italian city, while in strength and solidity it almost equaled the cities of the Nile.

So thoroughly was Sir Christopher's mind imbued with the spirit of Roman architecture that he neglected to study even the styles of his own country, as it is evident from his works that he possessed but a limited knowledge of Pointed architecture:—his restorations of the Abby Church of S^t. Peter at Westminster exhibit a total absence of feeling for anything like Gothic, and his repairs of that beautiful building are ever to be regretted.

"The number and variety of Sir [18] Christopher Wren's works" observes the author of the Parentalia "form such a body of Civil architecture that they appear rather to be the production of a whole century, than of the life and industry of one man."[*]—Besides the great St. Paul's, he built fifty three churches in the city of London forty of which were surmounted by lofty steeples, together with numerous other edifices many of which were of great magnificence.

Had Wren studied his art amid the enchanting productions of Athenian taste, instead of the clumsy and coarser forms of the Roman school, London would have arisen out of her ashes with an elegance and a grandeur scarcely now to be conceived;—but unfortunately for architecture, such was not the case; the mighty mind destined to lead in the restoration of the metropolis had been formed and matured in an atmosphere of Roman taste, and knew no other standard of excellence than that afforded by [19] the ruins of the "eternal city."

The noblest work of this distinguished architect is the celebrated cathedral of Saint Paul's at London,—a building inferior to no structure in the Roman taste in the world except S^t. Peters at Rome, and only inferior

[*] Parentalia / p 343

Christopher Wren, St. Paul's Cathedral (1675-1709). Louisa C. Tuthill, History of Architecture, from the Earliest Times; its Present Condition in Europe and the United States *(Philadelphia, 1848). The Athenæum of Philadelphia.*

to that in point of magnitude: — this master piece of mechanical science and skill, will doubtless perpetuate the name of Wren with accumulating honors to the latest posterity.

The plan of this magnificent structure is that of a latin cross, from the intersection of which rises a dome of 145 feet in diameter, supporting a stone lantern weighing 700 tons: — the cross which surmounts the lantern reaches to the height of 404 feet from the foundation, or about twice the altitude of Christ Church Steeple; — the greatest width of the building is 223 feet, and its extreme length 500 feet [—*a distance about equal to that between Market and Arch streets*].

[20] On the corners of the western front, are two immense towers surmounted by cupolas rising to the height of 210 feet, with a two story portico of coupled columns between them; the entablatures of these porticoes extend around the entire structure dividing it into two stories; and the whole of the exterior is crowded with panels, pilasters, pediments, and the numerous breaks and incongruous forms which characterize Roman Architecture.

The cupola seems to have been designed on entirely different principles from the rest of the structure; its gracefulness, oneness of effect, and majestic bearing, indicate a loftier and more Greek-like train of thought than we find in any other work of Sir Christopher Wren; and one is almost ready to conclude that the great Architect himself had become satiated with the frippery of Roman taste before he designed the embellishments of this beautiful and important feature: — it consists of a plain circular Basement rising about 20 feet out of the roof, and supporting [21] a circular peristyle or colonnade of 32 columns of a composite order surmounted by a continuous entablature; thus forming a beautiful foundation for the Dome. — This portion of S^t. Pauls is unquestionably Wren's most graceful composition; — it exhibits a unity of design — a breadth of light and shade, producing a harmony and repose seldom found in Roman Architecture, while from every distant point of view it forms a majestic centre to the picture of London.

After the completion of S^t. Pauls and the rebuilding of London, architecture declined; and during the latter part of the reign of George the Second, it sunk almost as low as at any previous period of English history; — excepting the names of Kent, Gibbs, and the Earl of Burlington, who successively florished from 1720 to 1780 we hear neither of Architects nor buildings which deserve notice until the accession of the Third George.

The knowledge of Architecture [22] possessed by this monarch qualified him to become an efficient promoter of the art: — while Prince of Wales, in the reign of his grandfather, he studied architecture under Sir William Chambers, and received instruction in perspective from the late M^r. Kirby. — M^r. Elmes mentions that he had an opportunity of examining some of the works of the Royal Student and found them correct, tasteful, and elegant.*

With a mind thus formed for the perception of the beautiful in art, it is not to be wondered at that the reign of George the Third was distinguished as an era of great interest in architecture.

On his accession to the throne he conferred on his preceptor the appointment of Royal Architect, and in the language of Sir Joshua Reynolds "no artist in his time had contributed so much towards the encouragement of the Fine Arts in England as did Chambers."

[23] This favoured artist however followed the Palladian School; although in some instances he beautified and simplified the Roman styles, divesting them of many of their absurdities, and imparting to their proportions a grandeur and a dignity which never appeared in the insipid compositions of his predecessors. — His treatise on "the decorative part of Civil architecture" especially the edition with Papworths notes is decidedly the best text book on Roman architecture extant.

---

* Elmes / p 391

While Sir William was in the zenith of his success, a sad check was put to his career by the introduction of the chaster and more elegant forms of <u>Grecian</u> art; — the graceful developments of Athenian taste were not however sufficient to make head against the prejudices of the Royal architect, and we are told that he pertinaciously adhered to the harsher taste of the Roman school during the remainder of his life. [*The following quotation from his introduction to the work alluded to will show the extravagances of his prejudices.* [24] *He remarks that "none of the few things now remaining in Greece, though so pompously described and neatly represented in various publications of our time seems to deserve great notice, neither for dimensions, grandeur of style, rich fancy or elegant taste of design; nor do they seem to throw new light upon the art, or contribute towards its advancement, not even those erected by Pericles or Alexander, while the Grecian arts flourished most."* * *We should not however consider this as a commentary on the general taste of this famous disciple of the Roman School;*] He looked at the works of the Italian architects "through the telescope of their reputation," and when the lovelier forms of Athenian taste appeared, he examined them too through the same medium, believing nothing pure but what emanated from his Italian favorites: had he visited the classic plains and promontories of Greece, — had he studied the proportions of the beautiful fane of Minerva on the Acropolis of Athens, — become imbued [25] with its enchanting purity of taste, and wandered among the surrounding ruins which seem to pay it homage, he would not have died a Roman.

The first exact and useful measurements of Grecian antiquities were made by Stuart, who has very properly been surnamed the Athenian; — he visited Greece in conjunction with M^r. Revet in 1750, where he pursued the objects of his mission with unremitted industry for more than five years, after which he returned to England and published the first volumn of his antiquities of Athens, which appeared in 1762. This work has established a taste for Grecian chasteness and elegance in Architecture throughout the civilized world; while it has opened a field for antiquarian research beyond all value, many portions of which have already been most ably occupied.

America

The earliest evidences of a taste for architecture in our own country bear date long before the appearance of Grecian [26] art in England, and long after the decline of the Gothic; hence our first notions of scientific building were of necessity wholly Roman, that being the prevailing taste of the Father-land during the entire period of our existence as British colonies. — Remnants of these early efforts of our Fathers in imitating the <u>Roman forms</u> they received from the alembics of the Anglo-Roman School

* Sr. Wil. Cham. / p 15

may still be seen in almost every street of our cities; bearing evidence of no small degree of cultivation in architectural science although confined to the Roman taste.

But a very few years ago every good dwelling house had its heavy Roman cornice with modillions, dentils, or mutules, according to the order affected, and its front door embellished with a well proportioned frontispiece consisting of an arch springing from imposts with columns on either side supporting an entablature and Pediment, all in strict conformity with the principles of some one of the Roman orders.

Many of these frontispieces still [27] remain, but some of the very best of them have been destroyed to make room for the simple round-headed doorways so fashionable for the last few years in most of our cities, but which have now fortunately yielded to a better taste.

A good specimen of these old-time embellishments may be seen around the front door of Willing's Old Mansion at the corner of Third Street and Willing's Alley [*in Philad*ᵃ]; — this frontispiece is also worthy of notice from the fact, that the material of which it is composed is the Portland stone so generally in use in London.

Some of our Public buildings of early date also exhibit a considerable degree of architectural science; but the era in which they were erected being one of evident decline in architecture throughout the world, we find the crudities and absurdities of the Anglo-Palladian school crowded on every design.

One of the best examples of this first period of <u>Americo-Roman</u> architecture is [28] Christ Church in Philadelphia; this venerable edifice was built more than a century ago from the designs of Dᴿ. John Kearsley, and its architecture is probably as good as any thing of its kind, and date in the world; — the proportions of the steeple in particular, are remarkably graceful and elegant. The Roman Doric order seems to have been affected throughout the building, but the columnar division of the interior into nave and aisles, and the general distribution of the Plan, as well as the arrangement of many of the details have evidently been made on the principles of Gothic architecture.

Another building of about the same age is the Old State house, or Independence Hall. — This structure was commenced in 1729 and finished in 1734; and although its exterior possesses but little architectural ornament, its interior decorations are exceedingly bold and effective; — the hall leading through the centre still retains its ancient [29] finish and presents a good specimen of the taste which prevailed in the time of the Second George of England, in the beginning of whose reign it was built.

But this consecrated pile — this birth place of a nation's freedom has higher claims to veneration than any which could be derived from

Old Pennsylvania State House (Independence Hall), Philadelphia (1752).
The Athenæum of Philadelphia.

Architecture alone;—here that glorious phalanx of lofty spirits who planned the beautiful temple of American Liberty, and founded it on the rock of truth and equity, boldly and deliberately, pledged their lives and fortunes in the cause of their country;—within these walls the soul stirring question of Liberty was fearlessly discussed, and the resolution to be <u>free</u> as fearlessly adopted; and from the steps of this edifice the declaration of American independence was first proclaimed in the presence of the American people.—Here have the eloquent and unblenching representatives of a few weak colonies dared to breast [30] the storm against a brave and powerful nation:—here

—"have they taught the spoilers of the land
In chainless hearts what fiery strength lies deep,
To guard free homes."
"Theirs are enshrined names, and every heart
Shall bear the blazoned impress of their worth.
Bright on the dreams of youth their fame shall rise,
Their fields of fight shall epic song record,
And when the voice of battle rends the skies,
Their name shall be their country's rallying word!"

This structure can therefore never fail to awaken the most thrilling associations in every patriotic mind;—it links the heroic age of America with our own times more firmly than any other architectural relic of the Revolution; [*hence the most effective means should ever be employed to protect it from decay or desecration*].

Another example of Americo-Roman architecture worthy of particular remark is the City Hall at New York; — this edifice approaches [31] nearer to the Italian cinque-cento style than to the more ancient Roman, and the high degree of perfection it presents in that peculiar species of architecture, as well as the excellence of its execution is probably unsurpassed by any building of a corresponding style in the world: — it covers a space of 105 by 210 feet and consists of two stories in height resting on a Basement; — the lower story is composed in the Ionic order and the upper one in the Corinthian; — the centre of the pile is surmounted by an attic story crowned with a cupola on which is placed a colossal figure of Justice. — The division of the building into two stories, and the small panels, festoons, and other trifling details mark it as belonging decidedly to the revived Italian or cinque-cento style. — The front and sides of the building are composed entirely of white marble, and the rear of finely wrought sand stone.

The old Bank of the United States [*in Phila*], now the Girard Bank is [32] also a Roman composition, but its merits either as a work of taste, or skill, are not very conspicuous; — its foundations were laid in 1795 and the structure completed in 1798. "Although this edifice" (says Mʳ. Latrobe, in his oration on the Fine Arts,) "is only a copy of a European building of indifferent taste, and very defective in its execution, it is still a bold proof of the spirit of the citizens who erected it, and of the tendency of the community to <u>force</u>, rather than to <u>retard</u> the advancement of the Fine Arts." It is also interesting from the fact of its being the first edifice in this country with a marble front.

The noblest, and the most costly structure in the United States is the Capitol at Washington, and there is probably no Senate house in the world to equal it; but unfortunately it presents a mixture of Greek and Roman features in the details of its architecture which will ever deprive it of the reputation of being a monument of <u>pure</u> taste. — Its defects in this particular [33] have arisen from its having been designed about the time when Grecian Architecture first began to gain ground, and the successive architects who built it having differed in their estimation of attic taste.

The most striking deformity in the general effect of the composition is the ponderosity and inelegance of the centre dome: — the original design for this part of the structure as it came from hands of the tasteful and accomplished architect Mʳ. Latrobe, had a much lower and more graceful curve, and was altogether a more elegant composition [*and had it been executed without alteration it would undoubtedly have presented a sky-line of*

Joseph Francois Mangin and John McComb, Jr.. City Hall, New York (1802-11). The Athenæum of Philadelphia.

transcendent elegance:] — it is therefore matter of surprise as well as regret that the beautiful conception of that great artist was not executed, instead of the immense affair which now crowns the structure, threatening to act as an extinguisher on all below.

This edifice was commenced about the close of the last century, which brings us [34] to the period when Grecian architecture began to attract attention on this side of the Atlantic.

Grecian Architecture

The introduction of a style of building so much more consistent with the genius of our Institutions, and the republican simplicity of our manners wrought wonderful change in every department of the art; — and the great revolution thus produced in the public taste soon outreaching all bounds of moderation, resulted in the adoption of a style of building, particularly in private dwellings, as much too poor and meagre as the former had been too rich and gaudy. — The heavy Roman eaves were wholly dispensed with, and as a substitute 3 or 4 courses of bricks were slightly projected from the face of the wall and gravely called a cornice; — the substantial faced window frames yeilded to a lighter finish called revealed frames (from the latin revello, to draw back, in allusion to their receding from the face of the wall;) window heads were abandoned and a thin strip of iron introduced [35] to support the bricks over the openings; facias, or projections extending across the façade to indicate the several stories were considered so outré that people had them cut out of the fronts even of old houses; and the everlasting round headed doors, were universally adopted, at the expense of the most obvious principles of good taste; thus presenting a façade without the slightest projection except what was made in some instances by thin window sills, and the tasteless apology for a cornice at the top.

Although this revolution in taste was indirectly brought about by the introduction of the chaste and spirited architecture of the Greeks, yet there was no more of Grecian taste in this style of building than there was of Chinese or Egyptian. — The unity of effect so enchanting in Greek architecture seems to have been completely mistaken for simplicity or blankness, and [36] most of our private houses, instead of being constructed in Greek taste as was probably intended, exhibited a sort of blank style to which we are mainly endebted for the brickpile appearance of many of our best streets. This bald and simple mode of building has however given place to a style more consistent with Grecian principles; but which will yet admit of great improvement.

The first marble building erected in this country in the Grecian taste was the Pennsylvania Bank [*at Philadelphia*]; — this edifice was completed in the year 1799 from the designs of the late M.ʳ Latrobe, and presents one of the most beautiful specimens of the greician Ionic order ever executed; — it covers a space of 51 feet in width by 125 in length and the exterior is wholly composed of Pennsylvania marble; — each end of the structure is embellished with a <u>hexastyle</u> or six-columned portico, thus making it a perfect <u>amphiprostyle</u> temple. — The sides are relieved by varied but symmetrical [37] and harmonious openings and projections, and the centre is crowned with a dome and lantern, all in the most perfect proportion. — The beauty with which the arched windows on the sides, and the dome have been introduced is particularly worthy of remark; — it is well known that these features belong more properly to <u>Roman</u> architecture, but the skillful hand of M.ʳ Latrobe has here turned them to <u>Greek</u> account, — they appear like terse and appropriate quotation from another language to express some sentiment which it would seem impossible to illustrate without it.

Those whose standard of perfection in art consists in the accuracy with which a work is copied form the antique, often talk about the incorrectness of a few of the minor details of the order; but no one who has feeling for harmony and proportion — a taste for the chaste and beautiful can look at the Pennsylvania Bank without experiencing a high degree of intellectual pleasure: — that [38] a few trifling deviations from the general practise of the ancients do exist no one will deny, — but the slight errors alluded to seem even necessary to produce the particular expression the artist intended to exhibit; — and the surpassing harmony which pervades the entire composition indicates the workings of a mighty mind throughout the whole.

The distinguished Architect of this beautiful structure, Benjamin H. Latrobe, may be called with propriety the Father of American architecture; — wherever he went we find evidences of his pure and highly cultivated taste; and while a vestage of the building just described remains he will have a monument eloquent in the loveliest proportions, — a memento worthy of his lofty genius.

The completion of the Pennsylvania Bank was followed by the diffusion of a taste for Grecian architecture throughout the country; — M.ʳ Latrobe introduced it [39] himself into several of the states as well as at Washington, and it was not long before Architects generally became converts to its principles, and repudiated Roman forms altogether.

A similar change of taste in favor of Grecian Architecture seems to have taken place wherever the Roman orders had previously been practised, and at this time there is probably no civilized nation to be found, amongst whom the beautiful proportions of the attic models have not been imitated.

Other Styles

The new direction thus given to public taste has had the effect to awaken an interest on the subject of Architecture throughout the world, as well as to quicken the public mind to the perception of the beautiful in whatever mode of building it may be found to exist; — hence the practice of no nation is now exclusively confined to any particular style; — all admire Greek architecture it is true, and all practice it to [40] a considerable extent; but other modes are frequently employed in every country, and for some purposes even with a better effect than could, under like circumstance be attained even by Greek forms.

Egyptian

The massy style of Egypt which has recently been brought up from the shades of forgotten antiquity, by the French expedition, is, for example, far more appropriate for the architecture of Prisons, mausoleums, and military works than any of the more delicate proportions of grecian forms; — this heavy style has already been applied to Prison architecture, particularly in our own country with eminent success; — M^r. Haviland's prisons in New York, Newark, and Trenton, all of which are beautifully executed in cut stone are magnificent specimens of this Herculean style, and serve to show the peculiar appropriateness of Egyptian forms and proportions to Prisons.

Castellated

Castellated architecture has also [41] been introduced into this country as well as Europe for similar purposes, and with evident fitness and propriety; — M^r. Haviland has given us a beautiful and appropriate specimen of this style also in the Eastern Penitentiary: — this noble structure presents a grand and massy castellated façade of nearly 700 feet in length composed entirely of cut stone elegantly wrought; — its embellishments are in the early pointed style of English Gothic and the whole composition is one of faultless consistency.

The Philadelphia county Prison furnishes another example of this species of architecture, in which its adaptedness to such purposes is particularly apparent; — this edifice, which presents a front of more than

300 feet composed of beautifully dressed granite, is likewise castellated, but its decorations are in the Perpendicular, or Tudor style of English Gothic.

Gothic/Pointed

The pointed styles continued to be [42] used though to a limited extent in Ecclesiastical architecture also: — their natural adaptedness to edifices set apart for the worship of that exalted and majestic being whose throne is heaven itself, scarcely admits a doubt; — the peculiar appropriateness of their light and towering proportions to the upward aspirations of the Christians heart, and the sublime and lofty object of his hope, must ever render these developements of Anglo-Saxon genius fit examples for study and imitation in the composition of scared edifices.

No people understood better how to affect the mind with elevated and devotional feelings simply by means of material forms than did the Architects of the pointed structures of England; — they knew that of all other dimensions height made the strongest impression on the human mind, <u>that</u> being the physical property from which the term <u>sublimity,</u> or some kindred metaphor has been adopted in every language: — they discarded [43] therefore all the horizontal lines of classic architecture, and every feature by which the fancy would be checked in its upward flight, they reduced their clustered pillars to fairy-like proportions, and garlanded them with light and delicate foliage, so as to add illusion to reality, and increase the elevating tendency of the style; — no mode of building is therefore so appropriate for ecclesiastical structures as the pointed styles of England; — but unfortunately this species of Architecture has been treated more superficially amongst us than any other, and in truth we have but few specimens to which even the name of Gothic can with any degree of propriety be applied, unless it be employed after the fashion of some writers as a term of reproach: — little attention seems to have been paid to ages or periods, and so absurd are some of the compositions which claim to be Gothic, that portions of every style may often be seen in a single feature; a practice which cannot be too much deprecated, and [44] which ought to be eschewed by every one who attempts under any circumstances to imitate this beautiful style.

[*A late eminent writer, in alluding to the practise of mixing the different grades of Gothic forms in the same composition very justly observes that "whichever period of the pointed style is adopted, good taste as strictly requires that the respective members and ornaments should not be blended together as that <u>grecian</u> and <u>pointed</u> architecture should not be intermixed in the same work."* *

---

* Milner / p 124

The best example of Ecclesiastical Gothic I remember to have seen in the United States is a church recently erected by M^r. Lefever on the Washington Square in New York; this specimen is in the <u>Perpendicular</u> style, and its various features are consistent, while the execution of the tracery and crocketing is particularly spirited: — this building certainly reflects great credit on its tasteful Architect; and there is little doubt that it will lead to most desirable results in [45] promoting a correct taste in this particular species of building.[1]]

Domestic Architecture: Rural, Metropolitan; Urban Planning

The next subject which claims our attention is <u>Domestic</u> architecture; — this branch of the art embraces cottages, villas, and city buildings.

Cottages were originally but small rude tenements, constructed exclusively for the accommodation of laborers; — they were built of the cheapest materials being usually those which were most convenient to their location; hence, their appearance as objects of taste chiefly depended on the natural resources, and the general character of the country to which they belonged. — The peculiar expression thus arising from accidental circumstances has in some measure been preserved in the cottages of the present day, notwithstanding this species of architecture has long since ceased to be appropriated exclusively to the accommodation of the poorer classes. — The picturesque effect of these small rustic structures, shaded by umbrageous folliage [46] and embellished with honeysuckles and ivy, soon led to the employment of similar forms on a larger scale, the most highly decorated examples of which are now called "<u>cottage ornées</u>" or ornamented cottages: — and although in external appearance this species of building bears some resemblance to the cottage style, yet in magnitude, elegance and convenience it possess all the characteristics of villas or mansions.

Old <u>English</u> cottages were generally but one story in height with a steep roof and heavy projecting eaves; they never embraced more than two rooms on the ground floor, and two garrets; the chimneys were commonly carried up on the outside of the house, and terminated with shafts in a variety of fanciful forms; and the windows were usually mullioned, or divided into compartments by vertical pieces of timber.

The cottages denominated <u>cottage ornées</u> followed this rustic style and were made two stories in height, embracing [47] numerous apartments; they were usually ornamented with <u>bay windows</u>, labels over the openings, and other decorations in the prevailing taste of the day.

---

[1] The Dutch Reformed Church, Washington Square, New York, by Minard Lafever, 1839-40.

Villas are insulated rural residences designed for landed proprietors, or for summer retreats in the neighbourhood of populous cities; they are always of much greater extent than cottages, and are generally more elaborate in their architecture; they usually embrace two stories in height, and their magnificence sometimes approaches the grandeur of a palace.

This species of building comes to us from remote antiquity; — the ancient Greeks and Romans in particular practiced it to a great extent; — Pliny the younger says that Laurentum was so crowded with the villas of the Roman nobles that they presented more the appearance of a city, than of detached dwellings; his own Laurentinum villa [48] seems, from the elegant and minute description he has given of it, to have been almost as extensive as a small town, and yet it served him but for a winter retreat; — his Tuscan villa, or summer residence in Tuscany was evidently his favorite abode, and could have been no less magnificent than the one at Laurentum.

Another extensive villa was the celebrated retreat of Marius, which Plutarch says was too luxurious for such a solider; it was situated on the promontory of Misenum near Naples, and was afterwards purchased by Lucullus; — it subsequently came into the possession of Tiberius, who used it as an imperial residence. — This famous retreat of the voluptuous became gradually converted into a strong castle to resist the sea attacks of the Vandals, by whom the rest of the numerous villas situated along the Neapolitan shores were all swept away.

[49] Modern villas have not however any thing like the magnificence and extent of those of ancient times, although the real comforts and conveniences they embrace are no doubt much greater.

Both cottage and villa architecture is found in the present day in greater perfection in England than in any other country; — ideas of comfort and a country life seem to have an inseparable connection in the mind of an English gentleman. [*He turns as by instinct from the sooty town and seeks some pleasant shade where,*
> "purer air
> Meets his approach, and to the heart inspires
> Vernal delights and joy;"
>   where
>   "gentle gales
> Fanning their odoriferous wings dispense
> Native perfumes, and whisper where they stole
> Those balmy spoils."*]

Few who are not [50] engaged in active business are ever contented to live in the smoke and bustle of an English city, while the scenic beauties with which their country abounds invite them on every hand to healthful

---

* Milton, P.L. / 95

A Small Cottage. Andrew Jackson Downing, Cottage Residences (New York, 1842), The Athenæum of Philadelphia.

and intellectual enjoyment—to luxurious repose;—hence England is fast becoming a country of cottages and villas,—an empire of shady groves and highly cultivated gardens
    "where nature multiplies
    Her fertile growth, and by disburd'ning grows
    More fruitful" *

This description of building is beginning to assume an importance in this country also:—there are already many excellent specimens of cottage and villa architecture in the neighborhood of all our large cities, and a taste for the beautiful in art as well as in nature is daily gaining strength.

We come finally to consider that branch of Domestic Architecture which relates to <u>town</u> houses.—Although the means afforded in this discription of building for producing [51] architectural effect are greatly circumscribed by the want of room, and distinct views, yet there are other considerations connected with it which render the subject one of decided importance:—the beautiful suburban villa,—the rural and romantic cottage, may indeed ennoble and delight the mind of the spectator far more than the most perfect specimen of <u>street</u> architecture, but where <u>one</u> sees

* Milton PL / 129

the villa or the cottage, a thousand see the city building, and a thousand minds are in some degree humanized and elevated however unconsciously by its beauties.[1]

Various plans have been resorted to in European cities to improve street architecture by Legislative enactments, but with little success: — Petersburg, for example is all built from designs submitted to, and approved by the Government with the exception of a single street; and that, in 1813 was the only one in the city (as we are told by M^r. Louden[*]) in which there were varied elevations, and as the consequence, the only lively and agreeable [52] portion of the town; the rest being a tiresome repetition of similar forms.

The new part of Edinburgh is built on a still more restricted plan; — all the street elevations are furnished by one Architect, and no builder is permitted to depart a fraction from the prescribed plan without the special sanction of the court; "hence" says the excellent writer just quoted, "it is one of the tamest congregations of buildings in Europe," and "were it not for the external views of the Old Town on one side, and the Frith of Forth on the other, the new town of Edinburgh would be as dull as Berlin."[†] — This monotony is however more than counterballanced by the magnificence of the surrounding scenery, the beautiful situation and grouping of the city, its cleanliness, and the substantial character of its architecture, — a combination of qualities which render Edinburgh one of the loveliest and most romantic spots in the World.

[53] Other European cities have similar, though modified restrictions on their street architecture, but seldom with a desirable effect; — the perfection of this description of building would be, not to have two elevations alike in any one street; as a repetition of similar forms (beyond what may be required for symmetry) in the same composition results invariably in a fatiguing monotony.

The grouping of several houses so as to look like one extensive establishment has, when tastefully designed, a better effect than almost any other description of city architecture, and it is certainly to be regretted that so few attempts have yet been made to embellish our streets by adopting a method at once so simple, economical, and effective. — This plan has been successfully pursued in European cities to a very considerable extent; — in London especially, it presents some of the most attractive specimens of city architecture ever executed. — One block of buildings in particular, called York terrace [54] is so designed as to exhibit nothing at all which would indicate the residence of separate families; — all the entrances are made in the rear and the grounds in front are laid out without division fences so as

[*] Arch. Mag.
[†] Arch. Mag. / v. 1 p. 117

[1] This section can be compared with Walter's article "Street Architecture," *JFI* 1, no. 2 (Feb. 1841), 90-91.

to present the appearance of one large garden: — this however is a plan by no means worthy of imitation, and is here referred to simply to show the care bestowed on this species of building by the Europeans; an expression of unity can as well be given to a group of houses with the doors in front, as it can to a single edifice; — to resort therefore to an expedient like that of York terrace is wholly unnecessary for architectural expression, while its tendency is to deceive the mind as to the purposes for which the buildings are intended, — an effect which should ever be most carefully guarded against.

An expression of unity may be imparted to a row of houses without interfering at all with the idea of their being separate dwellings simply by advancing and elevating the corner [55] and centre buildings beyond and above the rest, and by proportioning the various parts to the magnitude and importance of the entire group: — such a composition, no matter how poor and plain its individual features may be, will always awaken agreeable emotions of taste; it looks like a finished work, — the spectator realizes that nothing can be added to, nor taken from it without destroying its oneness; and even though it may be wanting in the higher graces of art, it possesses qualities on which the mind may dwell with pleasure. — But any attempt to impart a unity of effect to a row of houses which are all alike, and in the same straight line can never succeed: — to borrow a figure from an architectural critic* "such a composition looks no more like one large edifice, than a file of soldiers does like a giant."

As it regards interior arrangements the private houses both of England and America are built on the same general plan, and embrace [56] similar conveniences, but on the European continent a distribution of apartments has been adopted entirely different from what is customary amongst us: — instead of every family occupying separate and distinct house as we do, their buildings are made much larger, and each story is usually appropriated to an entire family.

These mansions are generally built in the form of a hollow square with a court yard in the centre; — the only entrance is through a large archway in front called a porte-cochére or coach-gate; — on one side of this entrance a spacious stairway leading to the several stories, and which is used in common by all the tenants; — on the other side is the residence of the Porter, who generally has charge of the whole house. Each story contains a complete suite of rooms embracing all the apartments to be found in a good English dwelling, including the necessary arrangements for culinary purposes, Bath, and every other convenience [57] requisite for the comfort of a family; instead therefore of placing their dwellings up edgewise in long ranges as we do, they make each story as it were a separate house; — thus

---

* Leeds / arch mag./ v 5 555

dividing neighbours by horizontal lines instead of vertical ones — by floors and ceilings instead of party walls.

Invention in Modern Architecture

Another idea in connection with modern architecture which seems to claim some attention before we close the subject is the popular notion that no invention exists in the present day in architecture, — that every production of modern times is but an imitation of some antique model; — this idea however popular it may be has no foundation in fact; and can only be attributed to a principle of dissatisfaction with things present which has ever characterized the human mind. — If we look back at the progress of architecture through ancient Egypt, Greece, and Rome, and compare it with the advancement of the art in later times we shall find that human ingenuity [58] is by no means on the wane: — During the accumulated ages in which Architecture flourished in Egypt, it was practised comparatively without improvement, after it was once firmly established on a scientific basis; — in Greece, where columnar construction reached its fullest perfection, the principles of the art were few; and we find the same forms copied from ages with scarcely a shadow of alteration; — the same may be said of Rome; and even in England where so much diversity exists in the several periods of the architecture of the middle ages the progress from the coarse and rude Saxon, to the gorgeous perpendicular of the Tudor family (a period of seven centuries) was so gradual as to be almost imperceptible.

If on the other hand we glance at the architecture of the last half century, [59] We shall find a general improvement in the art of building beyond all comparison with any similar period in former ages. — The buildings with which our own cities are adorned present ample testimony on that subject; witness the gracefulness of our steeples and towers, — embellishments never known at all beyond the middle ages, and belonging, in their application to classic architecture exclusively to modern times. — Compare the comforts, and conveniences of the churches of the present day, with those of the houses in which our Fathers worshiped, where heat and ventilation were alike unknown, and where a lady's "foot stove" was as indispensable in Winter as her fan in summer; where half the people sat with their backs to the preacher, and where the height of the pews was so great as to render it difficult for a considerable portion of the congregation to see over them.

In domestic architecture we see also a most decided improvement. The beautiful shop fronts, with their immense plates of glass with which many of our streets are embellished and the old fashioned "bulk windows" with their ponderous sash, a few of which may still be seen, appear as though they were the work of different ages, separated by thousands of years.

None of the architecture of the present day can however be said to posses a decidedly distinctive character amongst any people who mingle with the rest of mankind; nor is it probable that any nation will ever again practice a mode of building peculiar to itself, exclusive of other styles. — The arts of printing and engraving, and the rapidity with which knowledge is every where diffused will undoubtedly prevent such a result; — these arts present every thing which has been rescued from the shades of antiquity, together with all the most important developements of more modern genius, to the view of every civilized people; and as all ideas in matters of taste are dependent on visible objects for their first existence, it is obvious that these [60] arts will ever exert a resistless influence on design even in the humblest departments of decoration. — We shall have to suppose some intelligent nation to be separated from the rest of mankind, and deprived of all recollections of the styles and modes of building which now exist, before we can imagine a people capable of originating a style entirely independent of the forms and proportions which are now familiar to all the World.[1]

It must therefore be obvious, that in the present state of society it would be wholly impossible for any civilized people to resist the influences of the great mass of architectural ideas with which all are now surrounded, so as to admit of their originating any new mode of building superior to, and at the same time independent of, all existing styles and fashions.

It should however be remarked that although the architecture of all the world is now the property of every civilized people, and that the materials for thought [61] in architecture are the same in all countries; still there are peculiarities of climate, — of manners and customs, — and of government which influence the taste of every nation, and which impart a peculiar character to the architecture of each, even in the adaptation of similar principles.

Hence the general diffusion of knowledge, and the subjection of wealth which characterizes our own free institutions must eventually make as great a difference between American and European architecture in point of taste, as that which now exists in the character of their governments: — instead of the magnificence, grandeur, and showy gorgeousness always affected under hereditary monarchies, we shall gradually settle down into a simpler, chaster, more decided taste — a taste like that which marked the triumphant career of Republican Greece, and to which even the severe and equalizing laws of Lycurgus opposed no obstacle; in the language of [62] a celebrated English writer, "the purest system of civil freedom, is creative of the noblest powers of intellectual excellence." *

---

* Shee's Rhymes / on art — note / page 49

[1] The four preceding paragraphs (from "Another idea in connection with modern architecture. . .") are significantly rewritten, with a lengthy page of text added to the back of the page facing [59], and a new section of paper pasted at the top of [59].

Conclusion: Importance of Public Awareness

In this country therefore more than any other, the progress and influence of architecture depend on the estimation in which it is held by the people. — Here we have no nobles rolling in unbounded wealth — no Despot to wield the public treasure at his will; — the people are the nobility — the people are the sovreign; — the wealth is theirs, — the power is theirs, — and on their intelligence and taste rests the character of the nation. Hence a general knowledge of architecture should be diffused in all classes of society; — its <u>history</u>, and its <u>elementary principles</u> ought to form part of every system of popular education, while its <u>poetry</u> and <u>Philosophy</u> should constitute an indispensable branch of collegiate studies.

Such a cultivation of the Public taste would tend to irradiate the social [63] Firmament, — to purify, expand, and ennoble the public mind, — to soften and humanize the sensibilities, — to elevate the standard of civilization, — to adorn and dignify the national character; and to perpetuate the memory of noble and patriotic deeds.

Then rise "Oh favoured land," and brightly stamp thy
    "Mighty image on the years to be" *
"Fame dwells around thee — Genius is thine own;
Call his rich blooms to life — be Thou their sun!
So, should dark ages o'er thy glory sweep,
Should thine ere be, as now are Grecian plains,
Nations unborn shall track thine own blue deep,
To hail thy shore, to worship thy remains;
They mighty monuments with reverence trace
And cry, 'This ancient soil hath nursed a glorious race'"†

---

* Hemans / 166
† Hemans 166

.

LECTURE VI

ARCHITECTURE CONSIDERED AS A FINE ART

Architecture is by no means limited to the mere art of building houses for the comfort and convenience of man; — it aims at nobler ends; — and may be said emphatically to stand pre-eminent among the peaceful arts; — with them it sheds the richest lustre and most enduring honours around the national character; — it refines and ennobles the mind of man — vivifies his imagination — expands his ideas, and produces a purity of thought — a glowing and tender sensibility, whence he derives some of his sweetest and purest pleasures.

The existing remains of ancient architecture speak for themselves of the value of

Erectheum, Athens. James Stuart and Nicholas Revett, The Antiquities of Athens *(London, 1762-1816). The Athenæum of Philadelphia.*

LECTURE VI
ARCHITECTURE CONSIDERED AS A FINE ART

Introduction[1]

[1] Architecture is by no means limited to the mere art of building houses for the convenience of man; — it aims at nobler ends; — and may be said emphatically to stand pre-eminent among the peaceful arts; — with them it sheds the richest lustre and most enduring honours around the national character; — it refines and ennobles the mind of man — vivifies his imagination — expands his ideas, and produces a purity of thought — a glowing and tender sensibility, whence he derives some of his sweetest and purest pleasures.

The existing remains of ancient architecture speak for themselves of the value of [2] the peaceful arts: — In the lasting monuments of Egyptian power and skill, are left to be seen the most magnificent memorials of departed generations — here are landmarks of ages that have long since passed away, — documents to verify the historic page, — triumphs of art, by which we may catch the mysterious spirit of other times, and imagine to ourselves the brightest days of oriental splendour. — If we turn to Attica, we behold the unfading enchantment of a Parthenon, a Theseum, or an Erectheum, and a hundred other gems of art that tell of the elegance and refinement of ancient Greece, in stronger language than all the graphic descriptions that historians have ever penned. — In Rome, the eternal city, we find the mighty spirit of the past shed over the ruins of the majestic

---

[1] In contrast to the first five lectures, to which Walter made (for the most part) specific and definable changes, alterations, additions and deletions, Lecture VI remains as a work in progress, giving the reader little sense of when Walter edited the document, or at what level of completion he left the essay. This lecture's abbreviated length (about half that of the other five), different labeling and absence of the precise dating in Walter's hand suggests that this may in fact be a later manuscript, perhaps dating to 1860 when Walter presented ten shorter lectures drawn from the original six before an audience at the Columbian College in Washington, D.C.

Colosseum — the famous Pantheon of Agrippa — the triumphal arches, and crumbling temples, to which the sages of ancient times were accustomed to resort, [3] — all of which bear witness to the truth of Roman story. — Herculaneum and Pompeii are also indebted to the peaceful arts for all the thrilling interest that has attended their <u>disinterment</u>.

Influence that Architecture Exerts as a Fine Art on the Mind

My principal object in the present lecture, is to consider the immediate influence that Architecture exerts, as a fine art, on the mind: — We shall therefore be naturally led to a consideration of the <u>sources of beauty in art</u>, and the <u>effect</u> that beauty has upon the understanding.

Our subject being inseparably connected with the philosophy of the human mind, we shall be under the necessity of discussing it metaphysically.

Every individual who has studied the nature, or watched the operations of his own mind, is aware of the great influence that external objects exert over its powers, even when it is not particularly [4] dwelling upon them; — objects that surround him become insensibly associated with whatever thoughts may be passing in his mind and produce, according to their appearance, an exalting, or a debasing effect upon his ideas; — thus, in recalling the thoughts which have engaged him at some particular time, he unavoidably recalls the scenes or objects which were before him at that time: — or in recalling the scenes to his memory, he recalls the thoughts that attended them, though there was probably no necessary connection existing between them: — He moreover finds, that his thoughts have been ennobled and enlarged by association with magnificent scenery, or that they have become degraded and contracted by association with mean and inharmonious objects.

Those therefore who have cultivated a taste for the fine arts, find that their [5] ideas become purified, raised or expanded, according as they are surrounded with that which is beautiful, harmonious or vast; — hence he who unites with this sensibility a philosophic mind, will naturally delight to surround himself with as many of the beauties and sublimities of nature and of art, as the circumstances in which he is placed in life will admit; — not that he may be absorbed in continually contemplating them, but, that by their association, his thoughts may have a pure and lofty tone, by which he receives a vigour to reach — a power to grasp things of higher import: — he finds that such associations expand his views of existence — of the wisdom and power of GOD, and of the mysteries of nature and of mind.

We can have no better evidence of the influence of external objects upon our minds, than the fact that all our [6] thoughts are composed of ideas or mental images and that all ideas are in the first instance communicated to us through the medium of our senses: — ideas may therefore be called the atmosphere, as well as the food of the soul, upon the quality and purity of which, depend its healthfulness and vigour.

If then, such is the influence of external objects upon our intellect, it becomes a matter of great moment, that we should so regulate the order and appearance of things that are within our power, as to cause them to produce a favourable impression upon our minds.

It is contended by some that the beauty of an elegant object is enhanced by being brought in contrast with one that is mean, and contemptible: — hence inferring that unsightly things are unobjectionable under certain circumstances; both reason and observation would lead us to a contrary conclusion; — the presence [7] of inharmonious compositions under any circumstances is always calculated to degrade the mind, and render it unfit for contemplating more perfect forms: — as well might we suppose that the charms of a delightful piece of music would be increased by occasional interruptions of discordant sounds, as to imagine that a beautiful composition in architecture would be improved by association with discordant and inharmonious objects.

Cultivation of Public Taste

From these considerations it is evident that a cultivation of the peaceful arts exerts the happiest influence on the mind; — it becomes therefore a matter of the highest importance that a taste for their enjoyment be generally diffused through society.

It should also be remembered that artists alone, with all the skill and judgment of a Phidias, a Raphael or a Michael Angelo, could make no head against the crudeness of uncultivated [8] taste; — if the millions who look upon their works, are blind to every beauty, and regardless of all the silent harmony and poetry of art, their labour will be of little consequence.

If then, our progress as a nation, in the peaceful arts depends upon public taste, which again depends upon some knowledge of the principles of art, and if such progress be an object worthy of ambition, it is certainly desirable that the public taste should be cultivated. — And here permit me to remark, that such cultivation is especially important with regard to architecture; as that, more than any other art, bears palpable witness to the refinement and civilization of a people.

Principles of Architectural Composition; Primacy of Beauty

The principles of composition in Architecture necessarily depend upon the end which that art is intended to effect; its object may therefore be [9] embraced in the terms <u>utility</u>, <u>durability</u>, and <u>beauty</u>.[1]—The principles of <u>utility</u> determine the situation, dimensions, arrangement, and local relations of buildings;—that of <u>durability</u>, the mode of their construction, and the nature of their materials;—and that of <u>beauty</u>, their appearance as objects of taste.

The first two of these principles are entirely of a practical, or mechanical nature; we shall pass them over, and limit ourselves to the consideration of architectural composition, with reference alone to the production of beauty. The subject being one that requires a systematic train of thought to comprehend it I propose to consider it under the following heads.

Unity of Design/The Whole

The first principle in all compositions having any claims to beauty, is that of producing a combination of harmonious forms so as to present a <u>unity of design</u>, usually called by artists <u>a whole</u>: the necessity of this leading feature in composition is manifest from the fact, that [10] every object we look at produces some sort of a distinct sensation on the mind and that we are incapable of attending to more than one sensation at a time; it is also equally clear that by judicious arrangement, a single sensation may be produced as well by a number of objects as by one alone:—suppose for example that all the blocks of marble necessary to construct an edifice like the United States bank were prepared for their respective places in the building and then strewed promiscuously over a piece of ground, so that they could only be looked at separately; it is evident that each stone would produce a separate impression, making as many different sensations as there were stones;—now imagine all these pieces to be piled up together in a heap so that they might be observed by a single glance of the eye, it is clear that one sensation only would be produced; thus we find that in architectural compositions <u>contiguity</u> is an indispensable principle.[2]

Again, suppose the heap of stones to be so large, and the spectator so near to it, as to prevent him seeing the whole at one glance, [11] he would then experience confused sensations; he would see the pieces nearest to him individually, and those farthest from him in masses, without being able to see the heap as an entire object:—this supposition shows the necessity of adjusting the dimensions of the object, and the distance from

---

[1] Standard English translation for the Latin *firmitas, utilitas,* and *venustas* first outlined by Vitruvius, *De architectura* I.2.1.

[2] Walter's original example was a generic "perfect temple." At some point he chose the more specific model of the Second National Bank of the United States (Strickland, 1818-24).

Benjamin Henry Latrobe, The Bank of Pennsylvania, Philadelphia (1798-1800). John Haviland, Biddle's Young Carpenter's Assistant (Philadelphia, 1837). Courtesy, the Winterthur Library: Printed Book and Periodical Collection.

which it will generally be viewed, to the powers of human vision: — These examples illustrate two subordinate principles in the formation of a whole: — contiguity and distance.

Although the different form and finish of objects, produce different impressions on the mind, yet each impression is separate and distinct, whether it be agreeable, or the reverse; — if we again refer to the pile of marble blocks, and suppose them to be contiguous, and at such a distance from the eye so as to be comprehended at one glance, we have, as I before remarked a single sensation; — but if we further suppose [12] these stones to have been put together by skillful mechanics so as to present to our view a beautiful edifice, which for the purpose of giving you a tangible idea we will assume to be the US Bank, then we experience an entirely different sensation, although still included in the one impression produced by the whole.

We may next suppose this building to be composed of variegated marble; — this will not interfere at all with the idea of a whole, though it will give a different effect to the sensation produced by it; — If we further suppose the stones in the building to be alternately composed of dark and light marble, may still viewed as a whole: — but if we go further and suppose the lower half of the building be composed of white, and the upper half of black marble, the mind would then in that case receive two distinct and opposing sensations, and the composition could not be said to be a whole: — Thus we arrive at two familiar principles in the production of beauty; to wit, the necessity of the unity of the whole, and the necessity of the contiguity of the parts that [13] compose it.

Effect/Expression

This principle, important as it is in producing an agreeable ensemble, is far from being the only thing to be attended to in architectural compositions; — a mass presenting one smooth unvaried surface, however imposing it might be from its size, or its gracefulness of contour, would produce but one kind of idea in the mind; — the first general impression might be good, and the distant view full of grandeur, but upon closer inspection it would excite but a repetition of the same idea, and become wearisome from its monotony: — hence it is evident that no architectural composition can be truly beautiful unless its parts are so arranged as to produce an effect, or expression in the whole, that will bear analysis, and afford materials for contemplation.[1]

---

[1] The following paragraph appears on the page facing [13] but is lightly crossed out:

Although the first impression produced by a building, or any other object is certainly the most lasting one, it is nevertheless necessary to arrange the parts which produce that impression so as to allow the mind when it descends from contemplating the whole mass, to dwell upon the minutia with equal pleasure—hence an unbroken contour similar to pyramids of Egypt or a smooth unvaried surface like the sides of hundreds of our

Having demonstrated that a unity of the whole, and a contiguity of the parts [14] are essential principles in the production of beauty in Architecture, we shall proceed to consider the nature and properties of effect, or expression.

Effect in Architecture is that quality which gives lustre to all other qualities; it attracts, and retains the attention of the beholder to the object, and renders the whole composition agreeable;—This quality may be considered as arising from a judicious combination of projecting and flat surfaces, relieved by graceful mouldings, and harmonized by symmetry of form, and appropriateness of colour:—The most pleasing and brilliant contrasts of light and shade spring from these varied combinations, and produce a striking, and a beautiful expression.

The forms of the masses composing the elevation of an edifice, are therefore of primary importance in producing architectural effect: —these forms should [15] always be so disposed as to give the idea of a perfect whole, not only from the front of the building, but from every attainable point of sight:—such a composition would present a different aspect from every position the spectator might assume;—consequently a succession of different, but kindred sensations would be produced in the mind, continually creating new and agreeable combinations of ideas: —one prevailing character of form should be evident in every part of the composition;—all the features should bear such a relation to each other, and to the whole, as to appear as though they were the production of one mind, they should seem like portions of the same general thought.

Variety

From these considerations it is evident that a limited use of the means of variety is important to the production of architectural effect;—this quality therefore, when introduced without interfering with the principles of unity, is always found to enhance [16] the beauty of the composition;—but when practised to excess, it never fails to produce the same mental inaction that arises from the want of it:—a multitude of small parts—beautiful perhaps in themselves, but profusely crowded together—will always excite a confusion of ideas, by which the mind is unfitted for examining and judging of the design:—thus an attempt to create effect by an excess of variety, invariably fails of its object.

(cont.)

city houses can never produce but one kind of idea in the mind, and it matters not how beautiful that idea may be it will invariably become monotonous and tiresome, it therefore follows that unless a building possesses other qualities than a unity of design, important as this principle most certainly is, it will come far short of affording gratification to the spectator.

Symmetry

In resorting to the principles of variety under any circumstances, the strictest regard should be had to symmetry; — this quality harmonizes all other qualities, and without it, every attempt to produce an architectural whole would fail.

Symmetry is understood to be nothing more than one half of an object, consisting of a combination of different parts being exactly similar to, or a reflection of the other half: — There are no forms therefore, that [17] may not be employed in a symmetrical composition, provided that those forms are repeated on each side of a common centre.

Intricacy & Harmony

Some of the most pleasing impressions produced by variety, may be included under the terms Intricacy and Harmony.

The chief property of intricacy is to engage the eye and the mind by exciting the curiosity in search of that which is unseen, but which is yet apparently discoverable, — it impels the spectator to think, while harmony renders his thoughts agreeable, by leading his imagination more clearly to the concealed object.

A combination of these two qualities is strikingly evident in the form of a column: — notwithstanding the beholder can see but one half of the circumference at the same time, his imagination fills up with certainty the entire column, and he realizes its circular form as satisfactorily as though he has examined it all around; [18] thus the harmonious form of the column renders its intricacy an agreeable quality.

In harmony — in intricacy — and in every modification of variety — or in all architectural compositions, the beauty of which depends chiefly upon form, the essential principle will be found to be contrast.

Color[1]

The next subject that claims our attention, is the influence of colour in producing architectural effect: this quality is of the greatest importance, not only in preserving the character of other qualities, but in giving unity of expression to the whole composition.

The application of colours has been very erroneously considered as a mere matter of abstract fancy, altogether unimportant to the beauty of an edifice; — hence we hear of "fashionable carpets" — "fashionable paper hangings" &c. — the stamp of fashion, or the gloss of novelty seems to

---

[1] Remarks in this section reflect Walter's article "On Chromatics as Pertaining to Architecture," *JFI* 2, no. 1 (July 1841), 32-37.

have [19] been in almost every instance, the governing principle in the decoration of every description of Architecture.

This total disregard of science in the application of colours, has not been confined to interior arrangements alone, but the exterior appearance of our city houses generally, affords practical illustration of the most palpable inattention to this subject: — In every building, whether it be composed of bricks or stone, there are of necessity several colours; it is therefore important, in order to keep up a unity of design,[1] that all the colours that may be employed, be harmoniously arranged, and that one prevailing tint of the same general character be assumed throughout; — thus, if the front wall of a house were faced with marble, and the sides and back composed of bricks, the brickwork should either be roughcast, or painted of the same general tint as the marble; — or if the front [20] were composed of bricks, and the sides roughcast, as is often the case, then the whole should be painted: — The glaring colour of bricks under any circumstances is objectionable, but when brought in contrast with roughcasting, or large surfaces of marble, in the same building, the unity of the design is invariably destroyed. If bricks could be banished altogether from our street architecture or covered with stucco or paint I have no doubt that the benefit to society would be incalculable.[2]

[*It cannot be denied, that location or economy, frequently makes it necessary to construct the different sides of a house with different materials, but good taste always demands in such cases, that those materials be harmonized by some general and agreeable tint.*]

Certain principles are implanted in our nature, by which harmonious combinations of colour, produce an effect upon the eye, similar to that which is produced on the ear by harmonious music; — hence a variety of colours harmoniously arranged, even [21] though they be unconnected with any idea of utility, will produce an agreeable effect on the eye, and if not so arranged, the effect will always be unpleasant: — harmony of colour, should therefore be studied in every composition having any pretensions to beauty.

Uniformity & Regularity

Uniformity and Regularity are also essentially requisite to the production of beauty in Architecture: — The idea of a whole could never be attained without these qualities, and by them, the works of art, are distinguished from the works of nature.

Without uniformity in the composition, and regularity in the arrangement of the component parts of an edifice, all attempts to produce

[1] The phrase "a unity of design" replaces the original phrase "the idea of a whole."
[2] Walter added this last sentence on the page facing [20].

agreeable sensations in the mind of the spectator, would prove fruitless:
— These principles are the first which display themselves in the efforts
of man, in building — and are [22] indispensably necessary in every
architectural composition.

It should be recollected however, that none of the principles upon
which the production of beauty in art depends, are capable of abstract
application; — Uniformity and Regularity would therefore, if applied
independent of other equally important qualities, invariably tend to
monotony: — suppose for example, a row of buildings to be constructed, in
which all the houses are exactly alike, the doors and widows all uniform,
and regularly disposed, and every feature arranged with the greatest
regularity; it is obvious that in such a composition we could have no idea
of a perfect whole; — we could conceive of no beginning, or ending, — any
number of houses might be taken away from one end of the row, and the
remaining part would have as much claim to the character of an entire
composition, as it had before, [23] or the houses might be extended ad
infinitum, and still the idea would be unchanged: — now if we suppose the
introduction of variety and symmetry, and imagine the centre houses of the
row to be raised higher than the rest, — and the buildings at each end to be
finished with pediments, or attics, of uniform design; — or suppose the ends
and centre to advance a small distance beyond the intermediate houses, it
is evident that Uniformity and Regularity would be preserved, while the
idea of a perfect whole would be clearly conveyed to the mind by means
of variety and symmetry: — If either of the ends of such a composition were
removed, uniformity, regularly and symmetry would be destroyed, and
the remaining mass would be imperfect; or if another house were added to
either end, the idea of imperfection would again be conveyed to the mind.

From these considerations we infer [24] that uniformity and regularity
are essential qualities in the production of an architectural whole, when
judiciously combined with other principles of beauty; but when employed
separately they produce monotony.

Recognition of Human Ingenuity

These qualities are also important when considered in reference to
the means they afford, of recognizing the efforts of human ingenuity:
— Artificial objects will never excite admiration as works of art, unless they
are easily recognized as such; hence it is obvious, that architectural beauty
can never be attained, by closely imitating nature; nor can rural scenery be
rendered beautiful by confining it within the bounds of Uniformity and
regularity: — Nature displays her sublimest imagery — her grandest and
most imposing scenery in wild and romantic loveliness, while art requires
the square, the compass, the plummet and the line, in all her works.

Natural objects may suggest all the [25] ideas of an architectural composition, but exact imitations of nature, are altogether inconsistent with the character of art:—In the details of Architecture, (especially in its sculptured ornaments,) natural forms, such as foliage and flowers are frequently imitated,—these however, are rendered unobjectionable, and characterized as works of art, by the artificial regularity with which they are disposed, and the uniform colour of the materials of which they are composed.

If works of art were excellent in proportion as they approached an exact imitation of nature, then would the perfection of art be found only in a perfect resemblance of natural objects; and we should experience the same sensations in viewing foliage or statuary, as we would in beholding corresponding objects in nature.—It is therefore evident that an actual facsimile of nature, is not required [26] to constitute a perfect work of art.

M^r. Louden, in his excellent treatise on composition in Architecture, very justly observes that "the essential distinctive principle of works of art is, that they are evidently the creation of man." [*]

An artist might possibly construct an artificial tree in a hedge-row, or on a lawn exactly similar to surrounding trees, or he may imitate the form of a horse so perfectly as to deceive the eye of the most critical observer; but, it is evident that in this he would display no creative power whatever; the nearer he approached to nature, the less easily would art be detected, and consequently no satisfaction would be experienced by the spectator, different from that afforded by the original:—but if the exact resemblance of a tree were portrayed on canvas, or the noble form of a horse, wrought in marble in beautiful proportion, it is obvious that the spectator [27] would enjoy feelings of an entirely different character;—he would look on these objects as the work of his fellow man, and not as nature, or counterfeits of nature;—he would trace the development of human genius and admire the work only as a production of art.

The sublimer objects of nature receive their interest from loftier and far holier associations;—the wild confusion, and imposing grandeur so often displayed in natural scenery, seldom fail to excite in us the purest sentiments of infinity; by which our mind are raised to the contemplation of "beauties of eternal duration." The soul here takes an upward flight; it soars from the visible to the invisible, and finds itself in the unbounded fields of intellectual enjoyment;—it looks through nature up to nature's GOD.

---

[*] Loudon / architecture / magazine / vol. 1 p 281

Simplicity

The next quality in architectural composition to which I invite your attention [28] is simplicity:—this principle, although of an entirely negative character, has been considered by some, as the very soul of architectural beauty. We frequently hear of "dignified simplicity"— "chaste simplicity,"—"elegant and graceful simplicity," and other similar expressions, which may all be correct in a qualified sense, but which seem to convey an idea that simplicity is a quality of peculiar excellence.

Much of the misunderstanding of this principle, has arisen from its having been confounded with coexisting features in nature;—The ocean, for example, is said to convey an idea of "simple majesty;" but if we separate the idea of the vastness of the ocean from its simplicity, we have certainly no other quality left to admire;—a fish pond possesses all the simplicity of the ocean, and only wants its vastness to produce the same effect upon the mind.[1]

[29] The same reasoning may be used in reference to the simple grandeur of a lofty mountain, but in both these instances, although simplicity is an important quality we find it wholly dependent on other qualities for effect.

No one will deny, that the simple and the grand frequently stand connected; but it is obvious wherever this is the case that all our impressions are produced alone by the grand: and that the grand is the result of size, which becomes effective, just in proportion as the form of the beholder is by comparison reduced to insignificance.

The properties of simplicity are frequently confounded with other qualities by which a total misunderstanding of the term is produced, we often hear, for example, of the simple majesty of the ocean or the simple grandeur of a mountain, but in both these instances if we separate the idea of vastness from the objects we have nothing left to admire—a fish pond is as simple as the ocean and the peak of Teneref is not so simple as a little hillock; it is therefore evident that the term simplicity will never admit of abstract application, and can only be considered as a comparative and indefinite quality. Hence we say with propriety, that some works are too simple, too poor, or too complex, but absolute excellencies admit of no such comparative expressions as they can never be carried to extremes; —no [30] work of art was ever yet too grand, too graceful, or too harmonious; these qualities being absolute.

The very fact therefore that simplicity is a comparative and indefinite quality invalidates its claim to absolute excellence in architectural compositions.

---

[1] The following notes appear on the page facing [28] and seem to correspond with this paragraph:
   in fact it [simplicity] *can be considered, aesthetically speaking, as nothing more than blankness and poverty. . . . As a late writer on architecture observes,* [by our identifying beauty with simplicity] *we should have a rule that would terminate in a reductio ad absurdum constituting that most beautiful which is most blank.*

Thomas U. Walter, Philadelphia County Prison (Moyamensing), Philadelphia (Main Building 1831, Debtors' Apartment 1835). J. C. Wild, Panorama and Views of Philadelphia *(Philadelphia, 1838). The Athenæum of Philadelphia.*

While however we consider simplicity as a character of comparative and uncertain value, to be regarded altogether in a negative sense, we would not by any means assert that it is at all times the reverse of excellence,—we regard it as exerting the same negative influence in architectural composition as the cypher does in decimals;—it gives and receives significancy from the integral terms with which it stands connected.[1]

Simplicity is therefore valuable only where it promotes a desired expression of some absolute principle, as in the architecture of Prisons, mausoleums &ᶜ. in which [31] great apparent strength, or solemnity is required;—but when the character of firmness, or gravity, becomes less requisite, and the character of elegance more desirable, it is obvious that the necessity of simplicity ceases.

It may perhaps be objected, that the more closely we follow the dictates of simplicity, the more likely we shall be to render the productions of art intelligible, and its images susceptible of being at once apprehended by the eye, and permanently impressed on the memory; —All these advantages however, are necessarily insured by a regard to the principles of unity.[2]

The praise that the Parthenon, the Theseum, and other works of Grecian art have received on the ground of simplicity, should rather be ascribed to a unity of design;—nothing could be richer than the frieze and cornice of a grecian doric portico, yet the oneness of thought that evinces [32] itself in the whole structure, leads the spectator frequently to credit simplicity, with that which in reality belongs to unity.[3]

Limits of the Principles

Although a beautiful work of art will generally be found to contain, (in a greater or a less degree,) all the qualities we have described, yet the power of producing all that may be called beautiful, is by no means limited to these principles;—As far only as the beautiful comes within the scope of our reason, may we fix rules that cannot consistently be departed from;—but there are other qualities in design, which produce certain effects upon the mind, that are totally undefinable; and by which we form and arrange the various members of architecture, so as to enhance the

---

[1] On the page facing [30] Walter noted his indebtedness to a "Mr. Trautwine" and his "excellent treatise on simplicity with the citation "107 vol. 1."

[2] On the page facing [31] Walter rewrote this section, suggesting a shade of difference in his thinking:
Some may perhaps object that the greater the simplicity of a work of art, the more easily it be understood and the more permanently impressed on the memory – but these effects are perfectly attained by the principles of unity and harmony and are not at all dependent on simplicity.

[3] On the page facing [32] Walter wrote
It is therefore not the simplicity of the grecian Doric order that awakens agreeable emotions of taste but its unity of design.

pleasure produced by the definable qualities, and give grace and elegance to the composition.

[33] A mere knowledge therefore, of those qualities that address themselves to the human reason, will never enable the Architect to [*rise superior to the rank of an imitative builder; or render him capable of producing compositions having any claims to novelty or gracefulness.*

The Architect of imagination alone can] administer to the intellectual enjoyment of those who look upon his works; — out of difficulties he frequently "starts" beauties, — and obstacles that would be considered "by scale and compass" as insurmountable, are often the sources of original elegancies, that none but an imaginative mind would ever coin.[1]

Conclusion

If then, the science of architecture is of so intellectual a character, the study of its beauties becomes exalted, in proportion as its intrinsic merits are understood: — Hence, the more widely its principles are diffused, and the [34] more generally they are studied, the greater will be its influence upon the public taste, and the nobler will be, the monuments that are destined to bear to after ages the spirit of the times in which we live.

---

[1] On the page facing [33] Walter elaborates in the following incomplete thought:
rules may give him confidence but they can never give him taste and invention; they are acquired only by a profound study of his art the one practice gives him and the other [breaks off]

APPENDIX A
CITATIONS AND SOURCES

The extent to which Walter cited particular source material, referenced historical events, alluded to mythological narrative, quoted from poems, and referred to historical, contemporary, and mythological individuals in the course of each lecture reveals the high importance he placed on the erudition and also the extent of his background reading and research for the series. Identifiable sources, publications, writers, people, mythic figures and deities noted in the text and marginalia of the lectures are listed here with their specific locations noted in brackets. First editions are assumed and utilized unless an alternate edition was known to have been used by Walter. Rather than including comprehensive descriptions and biographies, this index emphasizes each entry's relevance to the lectures. Walter's spelling, which is usually identical to contemporary spelling, is preserved. Dates are AD unless noted otherwise.

Abel [I: 52, 53] Dr. Clarke Abel (1780-1826), chief Medical Officer to the Embassy of Lord Amherst to the Court of Peking and Canton from 1816 to 1817. In that role he gathered the material which appeared in his *Narrative of a Journey in the Interior of China, and of a Voyage to and from that Country, 1816 and 1817* (London: 1819).

Abraham [IV: 24] Biblical figure (ca. 2500 BC) and progenitor of the Jewish people.

Adrian (see **Hadrian**)

Æneas [III: 2, 3] Son of Anchises and Venus, hero of Virgil's *Aeneid*, cousin of Troy's King Priam, soldier. After the Trojan war he lead a band of refugees to Italy and became the founder of Roman culture and the Julian gens.

Aeschylus (see Eschylus)

Agarthacus [II: 58] Agatharcos of Samos, third-century BC author. His writings on scenic perspective for theatre are known only through such second-hand sources as Vitruvius.

Agrippa [III: 33, 41] Marcus Vipsanius Agrippa (64-12 BC), Roman soldier and statesman. He was responsible for significant construction projects in Rome, including baths, an aqueduct and the original Pantheon, which burned, making way for Hadrian's famous domed structure of the same name.

Alaric [IV: 3] Alaric I (ca. 370-410), King of the Visigoths and occasional ally of Rome. He led the Roman army against the Huns in 394. After renouncing the allegiance in the following year (after the division of the empire and subsequent defeats in Italy) he successfully sacked and captured Rome in 410.

Albert, Archbishop [IV: 14] English ecclesiastic consecrated to his post in 767; died 779. After a fire of 741 he rebuilt the church of St. Peter at York.

Alexander [I:39, 40; III: 30; V:24] Alexander the Great (356-323 BC), son of Philip II, King of Macedonia (see **Macedonian King**). He conquered the mighty Persian empire and most of the known world. Decisive battles included those against Darius III of Persia at Issus (333 BC), Egypt (332 BC), Nineveh (331 BC) Babylon, the center of Mesopotamia (330 BC). His infamous sack of the Persian capital of Persepolis took place in 331 BC.

Alexander Severus [III: 52] Marcus Aurelius Alexander Severus, Roman emperor (r. 222-35) who lead an expedition against the Persian king **Artaxerxes** in 227.

Alfred [IV: 15] Alfred the Great (848-899), youngest son of King Æthelwulf, who defeated Danish invaders as king of the English kingdoms (r. 871-899).

Alwalid [IV: 60] Umayyad Caliph. Al-Walid is credited with starting the history of Islamic architecture with his patronage of the Great Mosque in Damascus, which he built in its present shape between 708 and 715.

Amati [IV: 57] Carlo Amati (1776-1852), Italian architect and writer, was involved with the hurried completion of the façade of Milan cathedral between 1806-13 at the behest of Napoleon.

Anaxagorus [II: 58] Fifth-century Greek philosopher and director of a school of philosophy in Athens. Vitruvius records his authorship of a lost treatise on perspective.

Ancus Martius [III: 34] Legendary fourth king of ancient Rome (ca. 640-616 BC), credited with having significantly enlarged the city's area.

Angelo (see **Michael Angelo Buonarroti**)

Anthony [III: 41] Mark Antony, Marcus Antonius (ca. 82-30 BC), active supporter of Julius Caesar who battled Octavianus (**Augustus**) for power after the Emperor's death. After their division of the government he went to Asia, where he established his legendary partnership with Cleopatra.

Antoninus Pius [III: 34, 56] Titus Aurelius Fulvus Boionius Arrius Antoninus (86-161) Roman emperor who enjoyed a lengthy reign (139-161).

Apis [I: 12, 13] In ancient Egyptian religion, originally a fertility symbol associated with the creator-god Ptah which developed into a sacred bull seen as a protector of the dead.

Apollodorus [III: 35] Apollodorus of Damascus (first third of 2nd c.), Greek architect who completed several of the most extensive works in the Imperial capital, including Trajan's Forum, Column, and Markets. According to tradition, he was executed after mocking Hadrian's architectural efforts.

Apostle of the Gentiles (see **Paul**)

Appius Claudius [III: 31] Popular Roman politician (ca. 340-ca. 273 BC). He was responsible for legal and social improvements for the landless and lower classes as well as both the first paved road and aqueduct in Rome.

Arch. Antiq. (see **Britton**)

Arch. Mag. (see **Loudon**)

Aristides [II: 3B] Although history records many people by this name (including an Athenian Christian philosopher, a painter of Thebes, and a Greek musician), Walter was probably referring to a fifth-century Athenian patriot and defender of liberty (d. ca. 468 BC) who earned his nickname ("the Just") through a distinguished military career.

Artaxerxes [III: 52] Also Ardashir I, Persian king (r. 226-42) who declared his country's independence in 226 and extended the empire's limits.

Asiatic Researches [I: 35] Journal of the Asiatic Society of Bengal (Calcutta), founded in 1784 and comprised of thirty Europeans dedicated to investigating the geography and culture of Asia. Their journal *Asiatick Researches* was published 1788-1839.

Athena (see **Minerva**)

Augustus [I: 24, 25; II: 11, 14, 41] Originally Caius Octavius, became Caius Julius Caesar Octavianus (Octavian) upon his adoption by the Julian gens in 44 BC; later granted the title Augustus by the senate in 27 BC after succeeding Caesar as the first Roman emperor. His biographer, Suetonius (ca. 69-after 122), recorded in *The Divine Augustus* the emperor's famous boast that he had found Rome a city "of brick and left it of marble." Setting new standards for architectural patronage in the capital, Augustus (63 BC-14 AD) completed numerous works and improvements during his long reign (r. 31 BC-14 AD), including the Theatre of Marcellus, Maison Carrée (Nîmes), Ara Pacis, Forum of Augustus and Temple of Mars Ultor.

Baal [I: 9B] Pagan deity worshipped throughout the ancient world in a variety of manifestations.

Bard of Avon (see **Shakespeare**)

Barrow [I: 52] Sir John Barrow (1764-1848), English statesman who accompanied the first British ambassador to China as comptroller of Lord Macartney's household and recorded this experience in *Travels in China: containing descriptions, observations, and comparisons, made and collected in the course of a short residence at the Imperial Palace of Yuen-min-yuen; and on a subsequent journey through the country from Pekin to Canton* (London: 1806).

Bede [IV: 12] The Venerable Bede (672/3-735), Catholic historian, theologian, and author many works, including *The Ecclesiastical History of the English People*. Walter's read parts of this history within Henry Gally **Knight's** *Architectural Tour in Normandy*.

Belus (see **Nimrod**)

Belzoni [I: 22, 27, 29] Giovanni Battista Belzoni (1778-1823) made a living in circuses before embarking on a career as an archaeologist during an 1815 expedition to Cairo. With a hydraulic machine of his own invention he removed a colossal stone head of Ramesses II from Luxor and delivered it to the British Museum. Two years later he discovered the tomb of

Pharaoh Seti I in the Valley of the Kings, and in 1818 was the first person to penetrate into the second pyramid of Giza. He recorded sundry exploits in the two-volume *Narrative of the Operations and Recent Discoveries Within the Pyramids, Temples Tombs, and Excavations, in Egypt and Nubia* (London: 1820). In it he mentions a "Capt. Cabilia," who has left no other mark in available historical documents.

Benedict Biscopius, Abbot [IV: 12, 13, 3B] Benedict Biscop (ca. 628-90), English monk who founded the monasteries of Wearmouth and Jarrow; also the abbot of St. Peter's, Canterbury. Significant through his famous pupil, Bede. Knight recorded his introduction of glass art into Britain (see **Knight/Night's Normandy**).

Bentham [IV: 13] The Rev. James Bentham (1708-1794) authored several works, including a *Historical Remarks on the Saxon Churches* which was reprinted as one of several articles (by Rev. Thomas Warton, Capt. Grose, and the Rev. John Milner) in *Essays on Gothic Architecture* (London: 1808); it is this compilation which Walter read.

Bernini [III: 51] Gianlorenzo Bernini (1598-1680), widely recognized as the most outstanding sculptor of the 17th c. and credited as a main instigator of the Italian Baroque style in architecture. His complex designs conjoined architecture, sculpture and painting in some of the most emotive church projects of the Counter-Reformation. Bernini became the favored architect of a series of popes starting in the mid-1620s.

Blodget [III: 24] Samuel Blodget (Blodgett) Jr. (1757-1814), merchant and economist. As an "amateur" architect he designed the Bank of the US in Philadelphia (1795), significant for its all-marble façade and Palladian portico.

Boabdil [IV: 69] Last Moorish king of Granada (d. ca. 1527, r. 1482-3 and 1486-92). The last of a dynasty of twenty kings, he was forced to surrender Granada to the Catholic monarchs King Ferdinand and Queen Isabella in 1492.

Boniface IV, Pope [III: 43] (d. 615) Significant in architectural history for effecting the first transformation of a pagan temple into a place of Christian worship in Rome after persuading Emperor Phocas to convert the Pantheon into a church (dedicated to the Virgin Mary and all the Martyrs) in 608 or 609.

Bramante [III: 5] Donato Bramante (ca. 1443-1514), Renaissance architect, painter, and engineer. Responsible for many papal works, Bramante devised the original plan for the rebuilding of St. Peter's Basilica in the first decade of the sixteenth century under Pope Julius II.

Britton [IV: 51; V: 8, 9] John Britton (1771-1857), English art/architectural historian. Beginning in 1801 Britton produced a series of publications that focused on architecture and ultimately transformed the study of medieval architecture into a serious archaeological approach. Walter read at least *The Architectural Antiquities of Great Britain* (**Archt. Antiq.**), 5 vols, London, 1807-26.

Brunelleschi [V: 8] Filippo Brunelleschi (1377-1446), Florentine Renaissance architect, engineer and sculptor. Most famous for his ingenious solution for constructing the dome of Florence Cathedral, Brunelleschi is recognized as the first architect of the Italian Renaissance for his many classically-derived works starting in the 1420s.

Bulwer's Pompeii [III: 58 fn.] Popular fictional account, *The Last Days of Pompeii* (London: 1834) by Baron Edward Bulwer Lytton (Edward George Earle Bulwer-Lytton, first Baron of Lytton; 1803-73). Later a member of Parliament, Bulwer wrote many popular historical novels noted for being well researched.

Burlington, Earl of [V: 21] Richard Boyle, 3rd Earl of Burlington and 4th Earl of Cork (1694-1753), patron, collector, and architect. Lord Burlington was most influential in his outstanding sponsorship of Palladian publications and architects. During travels in Italy he collected drawings by **Palladio** and **Inigo Jones** and later sponsored their publication and an accurate translation of Palladio's treatise which remains in print; he was largely responsible for **William Kent's** success.

Byron [II: 12, 62 fn.; III: 9] George Gordon Byron, Lord Byron (1788-1824), English Romantic poet. Walter draws from two of his poems. The lengthy "Childe Harold's Pilgrimage" (1812-18), was the result of Byron's travels in Spain, Malta, Albania, Greece and the Aegean and includes evocative descriptions of physical locations, cultures and attitudes. In 1813 he published a more exotic narrative poem set in Turkey, "The Giaour."

Cabilia (See **Belzoni**)

Cain [I: 5B] Biblical figure, first son of Adam and Eve, recorded to have built a city which he named after his first son, **Enoch**.

Caldeleigh, Robert A. [IV: 45 (endnote)] Robert A. Caldeleugh, listed as a "gentleman" in contemporary Philadelphia directories.

Caligula [I: 25; III: 11, 32] Caius Caesar Germanicus (12-41 AD), Roman emperor (r. 37-41). Referring to the little boots he wore as a child, his appellation is oddly quaint considering the cruel reputation he gained after becoming emperor after the death of **Tiberius**. An energetic builder, he was responsible for beginning the Aqua Claudia, reconstructing the Theater of Pompey, and building a harbor for grain supply and a circus.

Callimachus [II: 22] Kallimachos (fl. 2nd half of 5th c BC), Greek sculptor probably from Corinth. **Vitruvius** honored him as the originator of the Corinthian capital.

Cambyses [I: 24, 41] Cambyses II (d. 521 BC), son of **Cyrus the Great** and King of ancient Persia (r. 529-521 BC); invaded Egypt ca. 525 BC.

Canaan [I: 42] Fourth son of **Ham**, grandson of **Noah**, and founder of the peoples known as the Canaanites in western Palestine.

Caracalla [III: 45, 52] Marcus Aurelius Antoninus (188-217), ruthless Roman emperor (r. 211-17) who murdered his brother to avoid sharing power after the death of his father, **Septimius Severus**.

Cassiodorus [IV: 5] Flavius Magnus Aurelius Cassiodorus Senator (ca. 490-ca 585), Roman statesman. After erecting a monastery (Vivarium) on his own estate he retired to the life of a monk, during which he produced several written ecclesiastical and historical works, the latter focused on the Romans and Goths.

Cecrops [II: 5B] In Greek mythology, a primeval half-man and half-serpent being who was the legendary founder and first king of Athens.

Ceres [II: 7] Roman goddess of agriculture; corresponds to Greek Demeter.

Chambers, Sr. Wil. Cham. [III: 17, 18, 20; V: 22, 24 fn.] Sir William Chambers (1726-1796), British architect and author. Prior to his royal posts as architectural tutor for George, Prince of Wales, and later the royal architect in the Office of Works, the Scottish architect was especially well-traveled for his day. As a merchant in the East India Company he made three voyages to the East in the 1740s. With this experience he published books on Chinese Buildings and Oriental Gardening, but his best known work is the *Treatise on Civil Architecture* (London: 1759). (Walter read the fifth edition of the revised *Treatise on the Decorative Part of Civil Architecture*, with notes and an essay added by John B. **Papworth**; London: 1836.)

Chandler Ionian An. [II: 8 fn., 47] Richard Chandler (1738-1810), archaeologist. He was sent to Greece in 1764 by the Society of Dilettanti which five years later published his multi-volume *Ionian Antiquities* (London: 1769), co-authored with Nicholas **Revett** and W. Pars.

Charles I [IV: 5B] (1600-49) King of England in the Stuart line (r. 1625-49); deposed and put to death.

Charles V [V: 11] (1500-58) King of Spain (r. 1516-56) and Holy Roman emperor (r. 1519-56).

Charles the Simple [IV: 46] Charles III (879-929), King of France (r. 898-922).

Childe Har. (see **Byron**)

Cicero [II: 57] Roman orator, lawyer, politician, and philosopher (106-43 BC), widely read and highly regarded as one of the great thinkers of antiquity through the nineteenth century.

Claudius [III: 11, 32, 44] Tiberius Claudius Drusus Nero Germanicus (10 BC- 54 AD), Claudius I, Roman emperor (r. 41-54). During his reign he built the harbor at Ostia, and finished (and named after himself) an aqueduct begun earlier by **Caligula**.

Clovis [IV: 9] Clovis I (ca. 456-511), King of Franks (r. 481-511) and king of France (r. 508-11). First king of all France and first true ruler of the Merovingian dynasty; also a Christian convert.

Constantine [I: 24, 25; III: 12, 46] First Christian Roman Emperor, Constantine I, Constantine the Great (ca. 272-337). He granted tolerance for Christian worship in 313 and in 330 moved the capital of the Empire to Byzantium, which he renamed after himself, Constantinople.

Court of Naples [III: 59] Most famously lead by William Hamilton, British ambassador to the Court of Naples, starting in 1763, excavations of Pompeii were undertaken well past the mid-nineteenth century.

Cortez [I: 54, 60] Hernán Cortés (1485-1547), Spanish conqueror of Mexico in the years around 1520. After returning to Spain in 1528 to receive the title of marquis he went back to Mexico in 1530 and lead the first European expedition to lower California in 1536.

Cressy and Taylor [IV: 56] Edward Cresy (1792-1858) and George Ledwell Taylor (1788-1873), British architects. Their European travels of the late 1810s culminated in the two-volume *Architectural Antiquities of Ancient Rome* (London: 1821-22), which bears striking resemblance in content and organization to Antoine Desgodetz' earlier *Ancient Buildings of Rome* (London: 1682; first published under the title *Antiques de Rome dessinés et measures très exactement*).

Cush [I: 7B] In the Bible, a descendant of Ham.

Cyrus [I: 11B, 8, 38, 39, 40] Son of **Cambyses** I, Cyrus the Great (ca. 590 –529 BC), father of Cambyses II and founder of the Persian Empire. Cyrus conquered Lydia and Babylon and united Media, Sardis, Lydia, Babylonia, the neo-Babylonian empire and central Asia into an imperial structure. He was buried in a royal tomb of his own construction at the royal residence in Persia, which he built.

Dallaway [IV: 4B] Rev. James Dallaway (1763-1834), author of *A Series of Discourses upon Architecture in England from the Norman Æra to the Close of the Reign of Queen Elizabeth* (London: 1833).

Dardanus [I: 14B] Legendary son of Zeus and Electra, founder of Troy (originally Dardania).

Darius [I: 8] King Darius I (Darius the Great, ca. 558-ca. 486 BC), Persian monarch. His otherwise undefeated army was overwhelmed by the smaller Athenian force at the Battle of Marathon (490 BC).

David [I: 46] Old Testament king of Israel (d. ca. 970 BC, r. ca. 1010-970 BC). As told in the Bible, David was divinely ordained king and allowed to prepare for the construction of the Temple in Jerusalem, the actual building of which was left to his son and successor, **Solomon**.

Del Rio [I: 57, 63] Capt. Antonio Del Rio (1745-ca. 1789), Spanish soldier and explorer. Serving in Central America in 1786, he was sent by the king of Spain to make an examination of the ruins in Guatemala. His discovery of Palenque lead to a manuscript translated into English by Dr. Pablo Felix Cabrera and published after his death as *Description of the ruins of an ancient city discovered near Palenque, in the kingdom of Guatemala, in Spanish America* (London, 1794).

Democritus [II: 58] Greek philosopher (ca. 460-ca. 370) and author of a lost book on perspective.

Demosthenes [II: 4B] Regarded as the greatest orator in Athens, if not the entire ancient world. Through powerful, eloquent orations Demosthenes (384-322 BC) encouraged the Greeks to unite against their common enemy, Philip (II) of Macedonia.

Denon [I: 22] Vivant Denon (1747-1825), French draftsman, engraver, author, diplomat, collector, and director general of museums. After accompanying Napoleon during his Egyptian invasion Denon produced one of the most influential books on Egyptian antiquities, *Voyage dans la Basse et la Haute Egypte* in 1803.

Dio Cassius [III: 35] Cassius Dio Cocceianus (ca. 164-ca. 235 AD), Greek senator and author of an 80-book history of Rome from its foundations through the early 3rd c. (the time of his death). Written in Greek, the book is now only partially extant.

Diocles [II: 30] Greek mathematician (2nd c. BC) who invented the *cissoid of Diocles*, an algebraic curve and tool for cube duplication, based on intersecting parabolas.

Diodorus of Sicily [I: 12B, 21, 23, 28, 55; II: 7, 10, 57] Sicilian writer (ca 90-21 BC). His compiled historical vignettes (including those about African Amazons and the lost city of Atlantis), collected while traveling through Asia and Europe, culminated in his *Bibliotheca Historica* (*Historical Library*).

Dionysius [III: 2, 36] Dionysius of Halicarnassus (late 1st c. BC) Greek rhetorician and historian. As a teacher in Rome he was one of the most famous of ancient critics. His longest work, the 20-book *Antiquities of Rome*, chronicles the history of Rome to the third c. BC.

Dœdalus [II: 7]   Legendary Greek craftsman and inventor of great ingenuity. As architect to King Minos on the island of Crete he built the palace at Knossos and the Labyrinth to house the Minotaur. To escape imprisonment he crafted wings of wax which lead to the infamous death of his son Icarus, who flew with them too close to the sun.

Domitian [III: 11, 37, 41] Titus Flavius Domitianus (51-96), Roman emperor (r. 81-96) and son of **Vespasian**. Domitian came to power after the death of his older brother **Titus**, and as emperor completed or restored many public buildings, including the Capitol, Colosseum, and a great palace on the Palatine.

Dorus [II: 18]   Mythical ancestor of the Dorians, who were one of the three main groups of people of ancient Greece.

Dyer [III: 47] John Dyer (1699-1757), Welsh painter and poet, author of "The Ruins of Rome" (1740).

Edward I [IV: 30] "Edward Longshanks" (1239-1307), King of both England (r. 1272-1307) and Scotland (r. 1291-92 and 1296-1307).

Edwin [IV: 13] Also Eadwine (ca. 585-633), English ruler; king of Northumbria (r. 616-33).

Elgin [II: 60, 61] Thomas Bruce, 7th Earl of Elgin; Lord Elgin (1766-1841). British Ambassador, (in-) famous for purloining the Parthenon marbles in 1806 and conveying them to Britain.

Elizabeth; Elizabeth I [V: 13, 15] Queen of England (1533-1603, r. 1558-1603) and last ruler of the House of Tudor.

Elmes, Elmes lectures [II: 22 fn., 58 fn., 60, 60 fn., IV: 32] James Elmes (1782-1862), British architect, civil engineer and author of several volumes on the arts and architecture. Most significant for Walter is his *Lectures on Architecture, Comprising the History of the Art from the Earliest Times to the Present Day* (London: 1823), as well as the fact that a young **John Haviland** was apprenticed in Elmes' architectural office.

Emilius Lepidus [III: 34] Marcus Aemilius Lepidus (d. 152 BC), Roman consul who constructed the Via Emilia in 187 BC.

Enoch (see **Cain**)

Eschylus [II: 4B, 58] Aeschylus (ca. 525-456/5 BC), tragic dramatist credited with introducing the second actor in drama, winner of twelve victories at the Great Dionysa, known through only seven existing plays of an estimated ninety.

Ethelbald [IV: 14] Aethelbald (d. 860), King of England (r. 858-860).

Euclid [II: 59] Mathematician, teacher and scholar from Alexandria, probably educated at **Plato's** Academy in Athens. Euclid (323-285 BC) compiled mathematical knowledge that established the axiomatic method as the standard followed by mathematicians to the present in his most influential work, the 13-volume *Elements*.

Euripides [II: 38; III: 6] Athenian playwright (late 480s-407/6 BC), the third of the triad of great Attic tragic poets including **Aeschylus** and Sophocles. His ninety plays broke from patterns founded on traditional religious and moral values and heroic formats by allowing both non-idealized heroes, princes, and contemporary Athenians to speak in everyday language about ordinary experiences. Walter cites his play "Iphigenia in Tauris," in which Iphigenia is Agamemnon's daughter, Orestes is her brother, and Pylades Orestes' friend.

Felibien [IV:.3B, 4B] André Sieur des Avaux et de Jàversy Félibien (1619-95), French administrator, art historian and critic. Walter read, from among his many works of criticism and theory, the third edition of his *Principes de l'architecture, de la sculpture, de la peinture et des autres arts qui en dépendent* (Paris: Coignard, 1699), originally published in 1676.

Field [VI: notes] George Field (ca. 1777-1854), English chemist and writer of several books on color chemistry which were standard guides for artists through the nineteenth century. *Chromatics, or an Essay on the Analogy and Harmony of Colours* (London: 1817) details a scientific explanation of color, and explains analogies between color, line, sound, language, idealism, and the harmony of the universe.

Fontana [V: 9] Domenico Fontana (1543-1607), Italian architect and engineer. One member of a large family involved in art and architecture, Fontana was renowned mostly for his organizational and engineering feats when removing and re-erecting the ancient obelisk in St. Peter's square, part of Pope Sixtus V's building program.

Fortunatus [IV: 3B] Saint Venantius Fortunatus (530/40-ca. 600), priest in Gaul, later bishop of Poitiers, and as last of the Gallic Latin poets, writer of lengthy poems and hymns. Fortunatus recorded his travels among people and events of the church, describing both the consecration of buildings and their architectural details, as well as the celebration of feasts, including the elevation of Gregory of Tours to the position of bishop.

Francis I [V: 11] Originally Francis of Angoulême (1494-1547), later King of France (r. 1515-47).

George II [V: 21, 29] George Augustus (1683-1760), King of Great Britain and Ireland (r. 1727-60).

George III [V: 21, 22] Grandson of George II, king of Great Britain and Ireland (r. 1760-1820). As a prince George III (1738-1820) studied architecture with **Chambers**.

Giaour (see **Byron**)

Gibbs [V: 21] James Gibbs (1682-1754), Scottish architect. Gibbs exercised his enthusiasm for the Italian Baroque in both public and private buildings, and became especially well known through his publications, *A Book of Architecture* (1728) and *Rules for Drawing the Several Parts of Architecture* (1732).

Gregory of Tours [IV: 3B] Saint Gregory of Tours (538/9-593/4), French historian and bishop of Tours (from 573). Among other religious writings, his ten-book history of the Franks is important for its account of contemporary events.

Gunn [IV: 24] Rev. William Gunn (1750-1841), ecclesiastic and author who seems to have coined the term "Romanesque." Gunn wrote the *Inquiry into the Origin and Influence of Gothic Architecture* (London: 1819).

Gwilt, Gwilt on the Origin of Cary. [II: 31] Joseph Gwilt (1784-1863), British architect and prolific author of architectural books, encyclopedias, and editions of **Vitruvius** and **Chambers**. His brief (16-page) pamphlet entitled *A Cursory View of the Origin of Caryatides* (London: 1822) discusses the original of use of the human form as a vertical support in Egypt, India (Elephanta), and Greece.

Hadrian, Adrian [III: 35, 41, 52]   Publius Aelius Hadrianus (76-138), nephew of **Trajan** and emperor of Rome (r. 117-38). As emperor Hadrian ordered the construction of a lengthy fortification in England (Hadrian's wall) and completed many significant buildings, including the concrete-domed Pantheon and his own villa at Tivoli.

Hakewell [V: 13] James Hakewill (1778-1843), English architect and author of books on English and Italian architectural history, including *An Attempt to Determine the exact character of Elizabethan architecture, illustrated by parallels of Dorton House, Hatfield, Longleate, and Wollaton, in England; and the Palazzo della Cancellaria, at Rome* (London: 1835).

Hallam on the Middle Ages [IV: 17 fn.]   Henry Hallam (1777-1859), English jurist and author of *View of the State of Europe During Middle Ages* (Philadelphia: 1821).

Ham [I: 4, 14B]   One of Noah's three sons (including Shem and Japeth). Ham was cursed for ridiculing his father. His descendants were believed to have settled along the Mediterranean and Egypt and southward into the rest of Africa (see Gen. 10:6-20).

Haviland, John [I: 21; II: 48; III: 18; V: 40, 41]   English-born architect (1792-1852). Haviland trained under James **Elmes** and in 1816 emigrated to the US where soon established himself as a skilled expositor of the main revival styles of the day. As Professor of Drawing at the Franklin Institute he instructed a young Walter. In addition to his many built works he is remembered for his revival style buildings, innovations in penitentiary design, and the *Builder's Assistant* (1818), the first American architecture book to detail the Greek and Roman orders.

Haydon on the Elgin marbles [II: 60]   Benjamin Robert Haydon, historical painter (1786-1846) and author of the two-volume *Lectures on Painting and Design* (London: 1844-46, 2 vols.).

Hemans [I: 65; II: 15, 29, 60]   Felicia Hemans (1793-1835), best-selling poet in England and America and the leading female poet of the early nineteenth century. Her success came from capturing emotion and popular sentiments in poems like "Modern Greece," which Walter quotes.

Henry II [V: 11]   Son of Francis I (1519-59), King of France (r. 1547-59).

Henry III [IV: 5B]   King of England (1207-72, r. 1216-72).

Henry VII [IV: 39] King of England (1457-1509, r. 1485-1509) and founder of the Tudor dynasty.

Henry VIII [IV: 35] King of England (1491-1547, r. 1509-47).

Hermogenes [II: 47] Hellenistic architect and theorist (fl. Late 3rd –early 2nd c.) who designed the temples of Bacchus (or Dionysius) at Teos and of Artemis at Magnesia on the Maeander. Admired and cited by **Vitruvius**, Hermogenes extended a great influence on the development of Roman architecture.

Herodotus [I: 4B, 8B, 9B, 10, 11B, 11, 27, 28, 30, 43; II: 7, 57; III: 29] Greek historian (484?-425 BC) who is credited as the discipline's originator. Exiled from Halicarnassus for conspiring against Persian rule, he embarked ca. 457 BC on a long tour through Asia Minor, Babylonia, Egypt, and Greece, developing sound firsthand knowledge of the entire ancient middle East. In 443 BC he settled in southern Italy, devoting the remainder of his life to completing the *Historia* (Greek for "inquiry"), a comprehensive study of ancient customs, legends, history, and traditions in Greece, Scythia, the Medes, Persia, Assyria, and Egypt, within a moral tone that posits east against west.

Hesiod [II: 57] With **Homer**, one of the most ancient of known Greek poets (fl. ca. 8th c.), a central representative of the early epic.

Hiram [I: 43, 47] Phoenician ruler and king of Tyre (969-936 BC) who provided the famous cedars of Lebanon used by **Solomon** in construction of the Temple at Jerusalem.

Homer [I: 11; II: 6B, 35, 57; for **Iliad** see II: 35 fn.] Greek poet (ca. 850 BC), author of the earliest and greatest works of Greek literature, the *Iliad* and *Odyssey*.

Hook's Rome [III: 4 fn.] Nathaniel Hooke (ca. 1690-1763), classical historian and author of the multi-volume *Roman History: From the Building of Rome to the Ruin of the Commonwealth* (London: 1738-71).

Hope's archt. [IV: 23 fn., 25 fn.; V: 11 fn.] Book by British patron, collector, connoisseur, designer and writer Thomas Hope (1769-1831). Hope's eight-year Grand Tour in Europe and the Near East started in 1787; he returned to Greece in 1799, France and Italy in 1802-3 and in 1815-7. These extensive studies led to several books, including the one Walter read, the two-volume *Historical Essay on Architecture* (London: 1835).

Horace [IV: 1B] Quintus Horatius Flaccus (65 BC-8 BC), satirical Roman poet and lyricist. Accomplished in both Greek and Roman literature, Horace completed books of *Satires, Epodes, Odes, Epistles,* and *Ars Poetica* between 35 BC and 13 BC. Walter's interest in Horace seems to concentrate on his portrayal of Rome's Augustan age, a time of peace when the arts flourished.

Horatius Coles (Heratius Cocles in the original manuscript) [III: 34] Horatius Cocles, legendary hero of ancient Rome. To repulse the attack of Lars Porsena and the Etruscans (who marched against Rome to reinstate the exiled **Tarquinius Priscus**), the Romans retreated across the Sublican Bridge, which Horatius defended while his army demolished it. After swimming to safety, Horatius was honored with a statue in temple of Vulcan.

Hoskins, Hoskins treatise [II: 22 (fn.) III: 31; IV: 24] George Alexander Hoskins (d. 1864), explorer and author. After his travels in Ethiopia in the early 1830s Hoskins returned to Britain and wrote *Travels in Ethiopia. . . illustrating the antiquities, arts, and history of the ancient kingdom of Meroe* (London: 1835), which includes lesser-known monuments in Nubia and Ethiopian art.

Humbolt, Hum. [I: 56, 58 n., 59 n. 60, 60 n., 61 n., 62 n., 63] Baron Alexander von Humboldt (1769-1859), German naturalist and adventurer, one of founders of modern geography. His travels, experiments, and knowledge transformed western science in the nineteenth century. Although most of his publications centered on natural philosophy and geography, at least a few extended to a topic of Walter's interest, the antiquities and former inhabitants of the ancient Americas. Walter likely read *Researches, concerning the institutions & monuments of the ancient inhabitants of America* (London: 1814).

Ictinus and Callicrates [II: 4B] Iktinos and Kallikrates (both 5th c. BC) Greek architects in Periclean Athens. The pair have been ensured lasting fame for their roles in designing the Parthenon (447-438). Iktinos additionally designed the Telesterion at Eleusis (ca. 430) and the Temple of Apollo at Bassai (ca. 430-400), and wrote (with a certain Karpion) a lost treatise about the Parthenon. Kallikrates designed the Temple of Athena Nike on the Athenian Acropolis and fortifications between Athens and Peiraeus.

Iliad (see **Homer**)

Inacus [II: 5B] In Greek mythology, a personified river god and hero of Argos.

Ionian Antiquities (see **Chandler**)

Irving, Washington [IV: 69, 69 fn., 70] [IV: 69, 69 fn.] Washington Irving (1783-1859), American writer. Irving was the first American to be recognized abroad as a man of letters. As a diplomat he was assigned to the embassy in Madrid in 1826, after which he wrote *The Alhambra: a series of tales and sketches of the Moors and Spaniards* (Philadelphia: 1832). In addition to this, Walter read the work which brought him his early fame on both sides of the Atlantic, *The Sketch Book of Geoffrey Crayon, gentn* (New-York: 1800). This collection of sentimental and satirical stories includes "Rip Van Winkle" and "the Legend of Sleepy Hollow."

Isaiah [I: 8, 9 fn.] Ancient prophet and author of biblical book containing prophecy about the downfall of Babylon (see especially Isaiah 13).

Isis [I: 12, 19] In ancient Egyptian religion, daughter of sky goddess Nut and earth god Geb; sister and wife of **Osiris**, mother of Horus. Isis is depicted in human form, crowned either by a throne or by cow horns enclosing a sun disk.

Ivanhoe, Author of (see **Scott**)

Jabel [I: 5B] Jabal, descendant of **Cain**; supposedly the inventor of portable tents, perhaps of skins, to suit his nomadic way of life. (see Gen. 4:20.)

Jerome [IV: 3B] Well-traveled ecclesiastic (ca. 340-ca. 420) whose literary works include biblical studies, theological problems, history, letters, and translations.

John of Padua [V: 12] Enigmatic sixteenth-century figure in English architectural history known through written records to have held the royal office of Deviser of Buildings in the 1540s. **Walpole** credited him with the introduction of "regular architecture" into England.

Jonah [I: 12B] Biblical figure, famous for his excursion in the belly of a great fish. Jonah included in his biblical writings (see Jonah 3) a description of the Assyrian capital of Nineveh, from which Walter drew.

Jones, Inigo [V: 12, 15, 16, 17] English architect, designer, and painter (ca. 1573-1652) under the house of Stuart. Jones introduced classical architecture into England after his first-hand examination of ancient and Renaissance classicism in Italy, in particular the architecture of **Palladio**. His pioneering studies paved the way for the Anglo-Palladian revival of the 1720s. His fame was secured in both buildings and a posthumous publication by William **Kent** (sponsored by Lord **Burlington**), *The Designs of Inigo Jones* (2 vols., London: 1727).

Julius Caesar [III: 10] Caius Julius Caesar (100-44 BC), Rome's first de facto dictator (r. 49-44) — and not the first Roman emperor, as he is called by Walter — famously assassinated on the Ides of March. During his military career Caesar lead the Roman army to significant conquests in Gaul, Germany, Britain, and Egypt. (For Shakespeare's eponymous play, see **Shakespeare**.)

Juno [III: 36] In ancient Roman mythology, goddess of women and marriage, wife of **Jupiter**, and queen of the gods, based on Greek Hera.

Jupiter [II: 7, III: 41] In ancient Roman mythology, King of Gods and husband of Juno, corresponds to the Greek Zeus. As Jupiter Ultor his character as the Avenger is emphasized.

Justinian I [IV: 9] Justinian the Great (483-565), Byzantine emperor (r. 527-65). Justinian was the empire's most significant architectural patron, leading the construction of the great church of Hagia Sophia (532-37) in addition to other projects.

Juvenal [I: 13] Decimus Junius Juvenalis (fl. 1st-2nd c. AD), Roman satirist. Best known for works that communicate through anger and irony, including his sixteen *Satires* (ca. 100-128 AD), which criticize Rome's decadence and moral corruption.

Kearsley, Dr. John [V: 28] English physician (1684-1772). After emigrating to Philadelphia by 1719 Kearsley gained prominence in the Assembly and as a vestryman for Christ Church. As a man of taste he became involved in two of the city's most significant building campaigns: Christ Church, and the State House (later Independence Hall, for which he served on the building committee and directed construction).

Kent [V: 21] William Kent (1685-1748), English architect, painter, landscape gardener and designer. Groomed by Lord **Burlington**, Kent became one of the leading expositors of the Anglo-Palladian style through both his buildings (Holkham Hall, 1734) and publications (*Designs of Inigo Jones*, 1727).

Ker Porter [I: 39] Robert Ker Porter (1777-1842), history painter. The former court painter in St. Petersburg achieved a highly advantageous marriage and knighthood by the early 1810s. In the years around 1820 he traveled extensively through Russia, Sweden, Portugal, and Spain, publishing on all those countries. Significant for Walter were Ker Porter's 1817 expeditions to Persia, Baghdad and western Asia Minor, during which he focused on correcting errors in earlier travelers' drawings of the famous antiquities. These accounts were published in *Travels in Georgia, Persia, Armenia, Ancient Babylonia, &c. &c. during the Years 1817, 1818, 1819, 1820* (2 vols., London: Longman, 1821-22).

Kirby [V: 22] John Joshua Kirby (1716-1774), English painter. Kirby instructed the Prince of Wales (later George III) in perspective, after attracting the crown's attention through a book he authored on the subject in 1754.

Knight, Henry Gally (See **Night's Normandy**)

La Comte [I: 50] Louis-Daniel Le Comte (1655-1728), French missionary. In 1685 he sailed with five other Jesuit mathematicians to Siam (present-day Thailand) and China, later authoring several publications, including these translations in English: *Memoirs and observations topographical, physical, mathematical, mechanical, natural, civil, and ecclesiastical: made in a late journey through the empire of China* (London: Benjamin Tooke, 1697).

Laborde [IV: 63, 66 fn., 71] Comte de Alexandre Laborde (1773-1842), explorer and author. Walter enjoyed access to the encyclopedic and gorgeously illustrated two-volume folio set *Voyage Pittoresque de l'Espagne* (Paris: 1806-1820) .

Lamartine [I: 6B; III: 55, 55 fn.] Alphonse de Lamartine (1790-1869), statesman-politician, poet and historian, author of modern French histories and biographies. Lamartine achieved international success with his *Pilgrimage to the Holy Land/Voyages en Orient* (1833, 1835), a poetic and thoughtful account of his travels with strong theological and philosophical overtones.

Latrobe [V: 32, 33, 36, 37, 38] Benjamin Henry Latrobe (1764-1820), English architect. Latrobe emigrated in 1796 to America where he introduced the Neo-Classical style through his Bank of Pennsylvania (1798-1800) and other landmarks. Latrobe trained William Strickland (who subsequently instructed Walter), and published one of the first lectures on the arts in America: *Anniversary Oration, Pronounced before the Society of Artists of the United States* (Philadelphia: 1811).

Layard [I: 13B] Sir Austen Henry Layard (1817-94), British adventurer, archaeologist and diplomat. Layard explored and excavated in Mesopotamia, most importantly the ruins of Nineveh, between 1842 and 1851, eventually depositing his Assyrian collections in the British Museum. He published several books, including two volumes on Nineveh (*Nineveh and Its Remains* and *The Monuments of Nineveh: from drawings made on the spot*, both 1849), and *Discoveries in the Ruins of Nineveh and Babylon* (London: 1853).

Le Brun [I: 37] Cornelis de Bruijn (c. 1652-1726/7), explorer and author. Known for accurate descriptions and drawings, the Dutch de Bruijn examined and drew details of the principle antiquities in the East. His book of 1698, *Reizen van Cornelis de Bruyn, door de Vermaardste Deelen van Klein Asia*, was translated into French in 1700 as *Voyages au Levant* and into English in 1702 as *A Voyage to the Levant: or Travels in the Principal Parts of Asia Minor*.

Leeds arch mag [V: 55] W. H. Leeds' article "Design for a Villa Comprising Two Distinct Residences," appeared in *The Architectural Magazine* (vol. 5, no. 58 (December 1838): 554-64), edited by **Loudon**. Leeds also wrote books, like *Rudimentary Architecture* (London: 1854)

Lefever [V: 44] Minard Lafever (1798-1854), architect and author. Born in France, Lefever was trained as a carpenter before emigrating to New York by 1828. There he became a prolific architect and author of popular architectural books, several of which ran to multiple editions through the century, including *The Young Builder's General Instructor* (1829), *The Modern Builder's Guide* (1833), *Beauties of Modern Architecture* (1835).

Ligorio [III: 51] Pirro Ligorio (ca. 1513-83), Italian architect, painter, draughtsman and antiquarian. Ligorio worked for Pope Pius IV at the Vatican and in the gardens for his Villa d'Este at Tivoli.

Linschotten [I: 33] John Huyghen Van Linschoten, Dutch explorer. Walter records the visit of a Lindschotten to Elephanta in 1759, likely Linschotten, who actually made the trip in 1579, publishing his record of the voyage in 1592; English translations followed starting in 1598, entitled *The Voyage of John Linschoten to the East Indies* (1579-1592).

Livy [III: 36] Titus Livius (59 BC-AD 17), Roman historian. His *History of Rome* spans from the foundation of the city in 753 BC to 9 BC, and was the primary source of information about Rome until the 18th century.

Lorme, Philibert de [V: 11] French architect and writer (1514-70). One of the founders of the classical style in France, Philibert de L'Orme synthesized Roman and French traditions in his architecture. Of his writings, *Le Premier Tome de l'architecture* (Paris: 1567) was the most comprehensive in the 16ᵗʰ c. in France.

Loudon; Loudon architecture magazine (Arch. Mag.) [V: 51, 51 fn., 52 fn.; VI: 26, 26 fn.] John Claudius Loudon (1783-1843), Scottish garden designer and writer of over a dozen books on landscape gardening and gardens, country residences, horticulture, and agriculture, founded and edited the first periodical dedicated to architecture. *The Architectural Magazine* was published for five years, 1834-39.

Louis XII [V: 10] King of France (1462-1515, r. 1498-1515).

Lucian [I: 12; IV: 1B] Greek writer and rhetorician (ca 120-after 180). His works influenced the development of satiric dialogue.

Lucretius [IV: 1B] Titus Lucretius Carus (ca. 94-55 BC), Roman poet and philosopher, author of the famous didactic poem "On the Nature of Things."

Lucullus [V: 48] Lucius Licinius Lucullus Ponticus (ca. 110 BC-58 BC), Roman epicure and general.

Luke [I: 11] Physician, evangelist and Gospel author. His comments on the learning of Moses appear in Acts 7.

Lycurgus [I: II: 11] Possibly-legendary Spartan legislator. Responsible for all military and political institutions and laws, he founded Sparta's *eunomia*, or "good order," ca. 800 BC.

Macartney [I: 52] Lord George McCartney (1737-1806), British ambassador to China. Several members of his entourage wrote books on their experience in China, including Sir John **Barrow's** *Travels in China* (1804) and *Voyage to Cochin-China* (1806) and Sir George Staunton's *Authentic Account of an Embassy from the King of Great Britain to the Emperor of China* (1797).

Macedonian King [II: 4B] Philip II (382-336 BC), King of Macedon (r. 359-336 BC). His swift conquests across Greece spurred **Demosthenes** to denounce him in his *Philippics*. Killed when preparing to attack Persia, his consolidated kingdom was the basis for the even more extensive campaigns lead by his son, **Alexander** the Great.

Maderno [III: 51] Carlo Maderno (ca. 1555-1629), architect. One of the most prominent Italian architects at the beginning of the seventeenth century and the favorite of Pope Sixtus V, Maderno was appointed architect of St. Peter's in 1603, in which office he completed the basilica's nave, narthex, and façade.

Magna Grecca (see **Wilkins**)

Marcellus [III: 5, 6] Marcus Claudius Marcellus (ca. 268-208 BC), five-time Roman consul and general. His successful campaigns against Gaul, Sicily and Syracuse are recorded in his biography by **Plutarch**.

Marius [V: 48] Gaius Marius (ca. 157 BC-86 BC), Roman general and politician. His six-year civil war against Sulla began in 88 BC.

Mason's Garden [IV: 27 fn.] William Mason (1725-1797), English poet, painter, hymnist, and musician wrote *The English Garden*. A blank-verse didactic poem in the manner of **Virgil**, **Horace**, and **Milton**, it was published in four books between 1772 and 1782.

Michael Angelo Buonarotti [III: 51; V: 9, 11, 12] Michelangelo Buonarroti (1475-1564), Italian sculptor, painter and architect. Widely considered the greatest practitioner of these three visual arts, Michelangelo created many of the canonical Renaissance works during his professional career which spanned over 70 years, including the ceiling of the Sistine Chapel (1508-12), the tomb of Julius II (1505-19), the Campidoglio (1540s), and the design for St. Peter's dome (1558-64).

Milizia, Milizia's lives of Archts [V: 11 fn., 16 fn.] Francesco Milizia (1725-1798), Italian writer. His biographical encyclopedia of architects, *Le vite de'* *più celebri architetti* (Rome, 1768) was subsequently translated as *The Lives of Celebrated Architects, Ancient and Modern* (London: 1826). The author's selection of architects and theoretical introduction revealed his bias against the Baroque and helped form the taste of later architects in favor of sixteenth-century classicism.

Milner [IV: 13, 46 fn.; V: 44 fn.] The Right Rev. John Milner (1752-1826), English priest, historian, writer. His *Treatise on the Ecclesiastical Architecture of England during the Middle Ages,* 1811 (London: J. Weale, 1835), cross-references a number of Walter's sources, including **Bede**, **Bentham**, **Dallaway**, and **Warton**.

Milton, P.L. [V: 49 fn., 50 fn.] John Milton (1608-1674), one of the greatest English poets, wrote *Paradise Lost* (1667), as a retelling of a biblical story that could rival the epic works of antiquity. The poem was reprinted frequently through the nineteenth century.

Minerva [II: 13, 15, 35] Roman goddess of war and wisdom (adapted from the Greek Athena). Born full-grown from Zeus' head, she became the patron deity of Athens after winning a famous contest against Poseidon. Her status was celebrated every four years with the Panathenaic procession, which included all free citizens of Athens and honored the goddess as the city's patron divinity. Walter and his authors often referred to the Pantheon's titular deity as Minerva rather than Athena.

Mizraim [I: 14B] Biblical figure. Son of **Ham** and grandson of **Noah**, Mizraim led a colony into Egypt, where he founded a kingdom which lasted nearly 1700 years. Consequently, Mizraim is the name generally given by the Hebrews to the land of Egypt.

Montezuma [I: 54] Moctezuma (ca. 1480-1520), Aztec emperor. His despotic rule encouraged his enemies to ally with Cortés, leading to his death during Aztec/Spanish warring.

Moses [I: 5B, 6B, 11, 13, 44] Old Testament prophet and lawgiver. Moses lead the Israelites out of Egypt and presented them with the Ten Commandments. His description of the ark built by **Noah** and the city & tower at Shinar are recorded in the book of Genesis, one of the five books of the Bible (the Pentateuch) of which he is believed to have been the author.

Neibhur [III: 12 fn.] Barthold Georg Niebuhr (1776-1831), German historian and son of **Karsten Niebuhr** (see below). His three-volume

History of Rome (1811-32) is credited with establishing the modern scientific historical method. His text related individual events to political and social institutions of ancient Rome, and recreated the past in terms understandable to the modern reader.

Neibuhr [I: 33] Karsten (Carsten) Niebuhr (1733-1815), German traveler in Arabia, India, the Persian Gulf and Tigris River, Palestine, Syria, and Constantinople. The elder Niebuhr authored many accounts of extensive travels in the eighteenth century, including *Travels through Arabia and other Countries in the East* (2 vols., Edinburgh: 1792).

Nero [III: 11] Nero Claudius Caesar (37-68), Roman Emperor (r. 54-68). Nero's egotism and extravagance were manifest in his Domus Aurea or Golden House, construction on which was halted upon the emperor's forced suicide.

Nerva [III: 11] Marcus Cocceius Nerva (ca. 30-98), Roman emperor (r. 96-98). Responsible for starting Rome's greatest territorial expansion (to be concluded by **Trajan** and **Hadrian**), Nerva also sponsored building activity in Rome, including granaries and the Forum Transitorium begun by Domitian.

Nights' Normandy [IV: 13 fn.] Henry Gally Knight (1786-1846) wrote *An Architectural Tour in Normandy, with some Remarks on Norman Architecture* (2nd ed., London: 1841).

Nimrod [I: 7B] First king following the biblical flood and builder of many cities, including Nineveh. He founded his kingdom at Babel, the city he built and in which he reigned until the division of tongues, after which it was called Shinar. Also known as Belus, Nimrod was proclaimed a deity by his son, Ninus.

Ninus (see **Nimrod**)

Noah [I: 7B, 42] Biblical figure. In Genesis, builder of the ark constructed with divine direction to save his family from a catastrophic flood.

North American Review [II: 40 fn.] Periodical founded in Boston, published 1815-1940 and resumed in 1968. First focusing on literature, in the later nineteenth century it included current affairs and politics.

Olympidorus [III: 45] Olympiodorus of Thebes (fl. AD 425), Greek pagan historian and geographer.

Orford, Lord (see **Walpole**)

Osiris [I: 10, 12] In ancient Egyptian religion, son of sky goddess Nut and earth god Geb; brother and husband of **Isis**; legendary ruler of predynastic Egypt and god of the underworld. Depicted in human form wrapped as a mummy, holding the crook and flail.

Ovid [III: 2] Publius Ovidus Naso (43 BC-17/18 AD), Roman poet. His accounts of Greek and Roman myths remain the standard accounts.

Palladio [III: 17, 32; V: 9, 17] Andrea della Gondola, (1508-80), Renaissance architect. Christened "Palladio" by his humanist patron Trissino, he is best known for villa designs and a treatise, one of the most significant and successful ever: *I quattro libri dell'architecttura* (Venice, 1570), continuously in print through the present day.

Pallas [III: 2] Soubriquet of **Athena**, meaning maiden or youth.

Papworth [V: 23] John Buonarotti Papworth (1775-1847), member of an English family of architects and author/editor of books on design, gardening, and country dwellings. He published Walter's preferred edition of **Chambers'** *Decorative Part of Civil Architecture* (1836).

Parentalia [V: 18, 18 fn.] Ostensibly a history of the Wren family, this book includes the collected writings of Sir **Christopher Wren**, and was published in 1750 by his grandson, Stephen.

Paul ("Apostle of the Gentiles") [II: 4B] Originally Saul of Tarsus before his conversion, Biblical figure (ca. 10- ca. 65) and author of at least nine books of the Bible. His three extensive missionary journeys to reach the gentiles lead him throughout Asia Minor and Greece, including Athens (ca. 51-53 AD).

Pausanias [I: 3; II: 8, 15, 28, 46] Greek geographer, traveler and author (fl. ca. 160 CE). His comprehensive guide books to Greece include great detail of sites and monuments blend art history, mythology, geography and history.

Pericles [II: 3B, 15C, 29] Greek Athenian statesman (ca. 490 BC-429 BC), patron of the Parthenon and other buildings on the Acropolis. Credited for instituting reforms that advanced democracy, Pericles also established a truce between Athens and Sparta, leading to years of peace during which he sponsored artists, architects, dramatists and musicians to develop the artistic splendor of Athens.

Perrault, Claude [V: 11] French physician, theorist and architectural designer (1613-88). His architectural writings, which began as a translation of Vitruvius, became fundamental to the contemporary side of the Quarrel of the Ancients and Moderns in the French Academy of Architecture. The fact that his contribution to the design of the Louvre's east façade (probably more the work of architect Louis le Vau and decorator-architect Charles le Brun) is perhaps overestimated should not detract from his contribution to architectural theory.

Peruzzi [III: 51] Baldassare Peruzzi (1481-1536), Italian architect, painter, and draughtsman. Considered a transitional figure between the Early and High Renaissance, he practiced chiefly in Rome and Siena.

Petronius [III: 31] Gaius Petronius, Roman military leader under **Augustus**. His successful invasion of Nubia took place in 23 BC.

Phidias [II: 4B, 15C] Pheidias (ca. 490-430 BC), Athenian sculptor. Although his work survives only in written descriptions and copies, he remains one of the most famous classical Greek sculptors, famous for his cult statues in the major temples in Greece, including the one of **Athena** in the Parthenon.

Philoponus, Johannes [IV: 3B] John Philoponus (ca. 490-570), Christian philosopher. His *Against Aristotle on the Eternity of the World* defended the idea of a creator God. Less-weighty topics of his include essays on glass and plaster frames.

Plato [I: 11, 55; II: 3B, 4B] One of the most influential philosophers in the history of Western civilization. Greek philosopher (ca 429-347). Disciple of **Socrates** and teacher of Aristotle, Plato founded the philosophical school called the Academy. His prolific writings include the *Republic* and the *Timæus*.

Pliny [I: 23, 26, 28; II: 7, 15, 57; III: 31, 36, 44, 45; IV: 2, 1B] Caius Plinius Secundus, Pliny the Elder (AD 23-79), military leader and author. Of the many works which he produced during his time as a writer at the end of is life, only the encyclopedic *Historia naturalis* (*Natural History*, completed in 77), remains. Its thirty-seven books include comment on the nature of the physical universe, including essays in astronomy, geography, medicine, zoology, botany, agriculture, and also a brief history of the fine arts.

Pliny the Younger [V: 47] Caius Plinius Caecilius Secundus (61/62 – 113), lawyer and nephew of **Pliny the Elder**. His ten books of letters on a variety of subjects include literature, politics, domestic news, cotemporary history, and morality, and also an essay on villa life.

Plutarch, Plut. [III: 5, 6, 37; IV: 1B; V: 48] Greek philosopher and biographer (ca. 46-ca. 120 AD). Plutarch traveled through Athens, Egypt and Italy, and lectured at Rome. He completed studies on Athens and Rome, and treatises on moral philosophy. His greatest achievement is considered the *Parallel Lives*, which demonstrates individual virtues and vices in the lives of great men.

Pocock [I: 29] Rev. Richard Pococke (1704-1765), English traveler. For five years Pococke traveled in Egypt, Palestine and Syria, leading to his *Description of the East and Some Other Countries* (2 vols., London: 1743 and 1745).

Pompey [III: 52] Cnaeus Pompeius Magnus (106-48 BC), Roman general and politician. He was the third member of the First Triumvirate with Caesar and Crassus.

Porsena [III: 34] Semilegndary king of Etruria (ca. 500 BC; see **Horatius**).

Priest [I: 59 fn.] Josiah Priest (1788-1851), American explorer and author. His investigations into and speculation about North America's pre-Columbian civilizations culminated in *American Antiquities and Discoveries in the West* (Albany: 1834), which posits that a partially-civilized nation, completely separate from contemporary native Americans, were responsible for the America's antiquities.

Proclus [I: 55] Poet, philosopher, scientist (410/12-485). Born in Constantinople and schooled in Alexandria and Athens, where he taught at the Academy, Proclus wrote commentaries on **Plato's** works and theological texts.

Procopius [III: 32; IV: 2] Byzantine historian (b. late fifth c., d. after 562). Considered one of the greatest of late Greek historians. Among his many works, his eyewitness accounts of **Justinian's** reign (especially "Justinian Buildings," completed 558-9), are most pertinent.

Prospero (see **Shakespeare**)

Publius Victor [I: 24] Probably the author of *De regionibus urbis Romae libellus aureus, in Venerabilis Bedae presbyteri de temporibus* (Venice, 1509), translated by the nineteenth century as *Topographical Description of Rome.*

Pythagoras [I: 11] Greek philosopher and mathematician (ca. 582-ca. 500?). A strong influence on **Plato**, Pythagoras established the scientific foundation for mathematics, accomplished advances in astronomy (as the first to consider that the earth was a globe revolving with other planets around a central element) and made great discoveries in geometry, including the hypotenuse theorem.

Pytheus [II: 47] Pythius, Pytheos (fl. ca. 370-330 BC), Greek architect. Said to have built the Mausoleum at Halicarnassus and Tempe of Athena Polias in Priene, Pytheus is also significant as possibly the first major Greek architectural theorist. His activities as a writer are recorded by **Vitruvius**.

Quatremére de Quincy [II: 25 fn.] Antoine-Chrysostome Quatremére de Quincy (1755-1849), French writer and theorist. His book *An Essay on the Nature, the End, and the Means of Imitation in the Fine Arts* (*Essai sur le nature: Le But et les moyens de l'imitation dans les beaux-arts,* Paris: 1823), trans. J. C. Kent (London: Smith, Elder & Co., 1837) was influential to Walter's thinking, especially Lectures II and VI.

Ralph [V:16] James Ralph (d. 1762), author of *A Critical Review of the Publick Buildings, Statues and Ornaments, in and about London and Westminster* (London: 1734).

Raphael [III: 51] Raffaello Sanzio/Santi (1483-1520), Italian painter, draughtsman and architect, one of the greatest European artists. As one of most famous painters in Italy during the High Renaissance, Raphael completed numerous canonical altar pieces and portraits, and decorated the papal apartments in the Vatican.

Rennel [III: 29] James Rennell (1742-1830), English cartographer, geographer and oceanographer. As a historical geographer he wrote a blend of military history, geography, traveler's account, and comparative (ancient vs. modern) geographies, on such subjects as **Cyrus'** expedition to Babylon, on the topography and plain of Troy, and **Xenophon's** retreat, and on **Herodotus**. Walter probably was reading his *Geographical System of Herodotus Examined and Explained* (2 vols., London: 1830).

Revet [V: 25] Nicholas Revett (1720-1804). (see **Stuart Athens**.)

Reynolds, Sir Joshua [V: 22] English painter, collector, and writer (1723-92). The foremost portraitist in England during the eighteenth century, Reynolds was also first president of the Royal Academy in London. His *Discourses on Art* were delivered to students and members of the Academy between 1769-90 and subsequently published through the twentieth century.

Rich [I: 9, 9 fn.] Claudius James Rich (1787-1821), English traveler and scholar. After mastering many languages, including Latin, Greek, Hebrew, Syriac, Persian, and Turkish, he traveled through Constantinople, Alexandria, Egypt, Damascus, Bombay, and Baghdad in various governmental posts from 1804, studying the geography, history and antiquities of each. The fruits of his exploration on the remains of Babylon resulted in an English publication, *Narrative of a Journey to the Site of Babylon in 1811* (London: 1815).

Richard II [IV: 35, 36] King of England (1367-1400, r. 1377-99) and last ruler of the House of Plantagenet; deposed.

Robert the Pious [IV: 46] Robert II, Robert the Wise (ca. 971-1031), King of France (r. 996-1031). Prolific builder of churches and monasteries.

Rolla [IV: 46] Rollo (855-931), Scandinavian Viking turned Norman duke. After his attack on Paris and Chartres in 910 he negotiated a peace with King Charles III of France that included his baptism, after which he was known as Robert and took charge of Normandy, establishing a barrier against further invasion.

Rollin [I: 9B, 23] Charles Rollin (1661-1741), French rhetorician. Written in his retirement, his series of histories were republished in Walter's day, including the sweeping *Ancient History of the Egyptians, Carthaginians, Assyrians, Babylonians, Medes & Persians, Macedonians, and Grecians* (originally 1730-38; 8 vols. Philadelphia: 1805).

Romulus [III: 3] One of legendary twin brothers, sons of a human mother and Mars, and namesake of Rome. Set afloat in a basket which came to rest on a bank of the Tiber, Romulus and his brother Remus were first nursed by a female wolf and later raised by a shepherd. After Romulus' murder of his brother, he is said to have established the city in 753 BC and reigned as its first king.

Sallust [I: 26]   Caius Sallustius Crispus (86-35 BC), Roman historian and politician. One of the first people to write monographs focused on specific events and people, his *History of Rome* exists in fragments.

Sangallos [III: 51; V: 9]   Italian family of artists. The two most prominent family members were Giuliano da Sangallo (ca. 1445-1513) and his nephew Antonio da Sangallo (1484-1546). Guiliano was an innovative architect and woodworker in Florence, the favorite of Lorenzo de Medici. Antonio, as architect, engineer, urban planner, landscape designer, draughtsman and theorist, famously assisted Raphael in the design and construction of part of St. Peter's.

Sat. XV   (see **Juvenal**)

Saturn [II: 7]   In Roman mythology the god of fertility and agriculture, parallel to the Greek Cronus (Kronos).

Scamozzi [III: 17]   Vincenzo Scamozzi (1548-1616), architect, theorist, writer, and most prominent of **Palladio's** followers. One of northern Italy's leading architects in the seventeenth century, he authored several treatises which were republished in English through Walter's day.

Scott [IV: 33]   Sir Walter Scott (1771-1832), Scottish novelist and poet. Considered the father of both the regional and historical novel for such books as *Ivanhoe* (1820), which reconstructs twelfth-century England.

Semiramis [I: 8] Ninth-century Assyrian Queen. Semiramis ruled through the abdication of her husband and in the stead of her son as absolute monarch for decades. A great builder, she directed the construction of defensive walls, towers, and gates around Babylon.

Senaca [II: 57; IV: 1B] Seneca the Younger, Lucius Annæus Seneca (ca. 4 BC-65 AD), Roman philosopher, dramatist, and statesman. First sent to Rome from Spain to study philosophy, he later became tutor and then advisor to **Nero**.

Septemius Severus [III: 47, 56]   Lucius Septimius Severus (146-211), Roman emperor (r. 193-211). After leading successful campaigns in Syria, Byzantium, Mesopotamia, and Gaul, he died during an incursion into Britain and was succeeded by **Caracalla**.

Serlio [III: 17] Sebastiano Serlio (1475-ca. 1555), Italian architect, theorist and painter. Serlio is perhaps less known for his buildings than for his books (written from 1537-84 and published erratically), which were some of the most important during the Renaissance.

Sesostris [I: 25] Sesostris I, Egyptian king and second ruler of the XII Dynasty (r. 1972-1928 BC). According to recent research, his obelisks remain standing in Heliopolis. The one that Walter describes is actually a 72-foot high red granite obelisk raised during the much later reign of Psammetikos II, the third king of the 26th Dyn. (r. ca. 595-ca. 590 BC), and which was conveyed to Rome by **Augustus**.

Sextus Rufus [III: 44] Secretary under Roman emperor (of the east) Valens (r. 364-78) and author of a Roman history published through the eighteenth century.

Shakespeare [III: 11] The "Bard of Avon," William Shakespeare (1564-1616), the greatest of English playwrights. Author of *Julius Caesar*, written in 1599, from which Walter quotes [III: 11 fn.]. Walter also refers to Prospero [II: 60], the main character in *The Tempest* and a great lover of arts and books as well as magician. Both works were published and republished in numerous editions through the nineteenth century.

Shee's Rhymes on Art [V: 62] Martin Archer Shee (1769-1850), Irish painter and writer active in England. His influential *Rhymes* (1805; Philadelphia: 1815) argues for national patronage of artist.

Sidon [I: 42] Eldest son of **Canaan** and grandson of **Ham**; founder of great Phoenician city and port named after himself (Gen. 10:15).

Simond [III: 59] Louis Simond (1767-1831), French-born American and successful New York merchant. Following his journeys abroad he wrote *A Tour in Italy and Sicily* (London: 1828).

Sketch book, Author of (see **Irving**)

Smirk [IV: 33] Sir Robert Smirke (1780-1867), British architect. Best known as a leading Greek revivalist, he designed the British Museum (1823-46) and directed what was probably the most profitable practice of his day. His restorations at York Minster were conducted between 1830-32.

Socrates [II: 3B, 4B] Greek philosopher (469-399 BC). Generally regarded as one of the greatest thinkers of all time, Socrates did not write, but his ideas were recorded by his most famous pupil, **Plato**, and in the memoirs of **Xenophon**.

Solomon [I: 43, 44, 46, 47; III: 52] Son of King David and successor to the throne of Israel (r. ca. 1015 BC to ca. 975 BC). He was esteemed for his wisdom, his biblical writings and significant building campaigns, including his own palace and the Temple in Jerusalem.

Solon [I: 11, 55] Athenian statesman and legislator (638?-559? BC), considered founder of Athenian democracy.

Sonnerat [I: 34] Pierre Sonnerat (1748-1814), French naturalist who traveled to New Guinea, Dutch East Indies, the Philippine islands, and China. Walter is probably drawing from his three-volume *A Voyage to the East-Indies and China performed by a order of Lewis XV between the years 1774 and 1781* (Calcutta: 1788-89).

Spelman's Glossary [IV: 48] Sir Henry Spelman (ca. 1564-1641), English historian and philologist, first published his *Glossarium* in 1626.

Stephanus [III: 52] Stephanos of Byzantium, fifth/sixth-century grammarian who compiled a study of Greek place names.

Stephen [IV: 20] Etienne, Count de Blois (ca. 1097-1154), King of England (r. 1135-54).

Stephens [I: 23, 29, 64] John Lloyd Stephens (1805-52), American author and explorer. He recorded the adventures and findings of his extensive travels in Europe, the Mid-East and Central America in several volumes, including two Walter read: *Incidents of Travel in Egypt, Arabia Petraea, and the Holy Land* (2 vols., New York: 1837) and *Incidents of Travel in Central America, Chiapas, and Yucatàn* (London: J. Murray, 1841). The latter provided the first accurate and reliable descriptions of Maya ruins in southern Mexico and northern Central America and enjoyed great popular success. Even so, the former was widely praised and was the more widely read of the two, remaining in print for over forty years.

Strabo [I: 9B, 10B, 24, 43; II: 57; III: 31; IV: 1B] Greek geographer and historian (ca. 63 BC-ca. 23 AD). His 17-volume *Geography*, in which he compiled passages from earlier geographers, mathematics, physics, political theory, and history, is the only extant study of civilizations and countries known to both Greeks and Romans during the reign of **Augustus**.

Stuart, (James); Stuart Athens [II: 8 fn., 10 fn., 14 fn., 15C fn., 30 fn., 31 fn.] James "Athenian" Stuart (1713-88) and Nicholas **Revett**, English architect-archaeologists. The duo's travels in Athens to measure and record the famous antiquities was supported by the Society of Dilettanti and resulted in one of the most influential architectural publications of all time, the four-volume *Antiquities of Athens* (London, 1762-1818).

Stuart, (Robert); Stuart dic; Stuarts Dic.; [IV: 12, 12 fn., 65 fn., 70 fn., 71 fn.] Robert Stuart, architect and engineer, author of a highly inclusive three-volume *Dictionary of Architecture* (London: Jones & Co., 1830, 3 vols.).

Swinburn [IV: 65 fn., 70] Henry Swinburne (1743-1803), gentlemanly traveler and author of popular travel books. Of his publications on European voyages, Walter drew from his *Travels through Spain, in the years 1775 and 1776* (2nd edit, London: P. Elmsly, 1787. 2 vol.).

Tarquinius Priscus [III: 36] Lucius Tarquinius Priscus (616-579 BC), son of a Greek colonist and the fifth legendary king of Rome. He established the Circus Maximus, built the great cloacae, and most famously founded the great Etruscan monument, the Temple of Jupiter Capitolinus.

Tarquinius Superbus [III: 36] Lucius Tarquinius Superbus (534-510 BC), son of **Tarquinius Priscus** and the last of the legendary seven kings of Rome. His violent and ruthless reign lead to the entire family's expulsion and then to the establishment of the Republic in 509 BC.

Theodoric [IV: 5] Theodoric the Great (ca. 454-526), king of the Ostrogoths (r. 471-526). Theodoric lead the armies in a successful campaign to conquer Italy in the years around 490. His long rule was characterized by his respect for Roman institutions and the Romans themselves; his repairs to harbors, roads and public buildings also bolstered his success, as did alliances with the kings of the Franks, Visigoths, Vandals, and Burgundians.

Theophrastus [IV: 1B] Greek philosopher (d. 287 BC) and immediate successor of Aristotle in leadership of the Lyceum. What little of his work remains includes writings on fire, odors, stones, and winds.

Thomson [II: 17] James Thomson (1700-48), Scottish poet. A forerunner of the Romantic movement, Thomson found fame in his four-part "The

Seasons" (1726-30) and later with "Liberty" (1735-36), a tribute to Britain. Walter excerpted the latter in his history of the Greek orders.

Thucydides [II: 15C] Greek historian (ca. 471 BC-ca. 400 BC) and author of a fragmentary history of the Peloponnesian war between Athens and Sparta (431-404 BC) in eight books.

Tiberius [III: 34; V: 48] Tiberius Julius Caesar Augustus (42 BC-37 AD), second Roman emperor (r. 14-37). Upon succeeding his stepfather **Augustus**, Tiberius curtailed luxury expenses, and did not share Augustus' enthusiasm for architectural patronage.

Titus [III: 11, 26, 37, 38, 40, 41] Titus Flavius Sabinus Vespasianus (38-81), eldest son of **Vespasian** and Roman emperor (r. 79-81). Known for his generosity, he dedicated the Colosseum begun by his father, constructed public baths, provided lavish spectacles, and assisted Pompeii and Herculaneum after the eruption of Mt. Vesuvius in 79. His fierceness in battle is recorded in the arch erected for him by **Domitian** (r. 81-96), which commemorates his capture and destruction of Jerusalem in 70.

Trajan [III: 11, 35, 41] Marcus Ulpius Trajanus (ca. 53-117), first non-native Roman emperor (r. 98-117). Trajan built in a manner that expressed the greatly enlarged extents that the empire experienced under his rule, constructing the largest of imperial forums (including a temple, basilica, libraries, and markets), completed by 117 by **Apollodorus** of Damascus. His 100-ft. tall honorific column records his campaigns against Dacia (modern Romania, in 101-03 and 107-08).

Tubal-Cain [I: 5B] In the Bible, a descendant of **Cain** who is recorded as having great skill with metals, specifically brass and iron (Gen. 4:22).

Urban VIII [III: 42] Maffeo Barberini (1568-1644), elected pope in 1623. His widespread building projects included the new Palazzo Barberini, several new churches and the restoration of others, including the decoration of St. Peter's interior, including **Bernini's** baldacchino which was cast of bronze removed from the Pantheon.

Vasari [IV: 50] Giorgio Vasari (1511-1574), Italian painter, draughtsman, essayist, architect, and collector. He wrote the *Vite de' piu eccellenti pittori, scultori e architetti (Lives of the most Eminent Painters, Sculptors and Architects,* (1550; the enlarged 2nd ed. of 1568 is the basis for later editions and translations) which, although not the first such chronological biography, was the earliest to include a critical history of artistic style.

Vespasian [III: 11, 37, 38]   Titus Flavius Vespasianus (9–79), Roman emperor (r. 69-79).   An energetic builder, he completed the Colosseum (Flavian Amphitheatre), Flavian palace, Forum and Temple of Peace and restored the Capitol.

Victor [III: 39]   Sextus Aurelius Victor, fourth-century Roman author of *De viris illustribus urbis Romae (The Lives of the Illustrious Romans*, ca. 360), which existed in Walter's day at least in seventeenth-century English translations.

Vignola [III: 17, 51]   Jacopo (Giacomo) (Barozzi da) Vignola (1507-73), Italian painter, architect and theorist. He wrote the *Regola delli cinque ordini d'architettura* (Rome: 1562), a succinct illustrated treatise on the five orders which enjoyed immense popular and academic success in its multiple translations across the centuries.

Virgil [IV: 1B]   Vergil, Publius Vergilius Maro (70 BC-19 BC), acknowledged as the greatest Roman poet. Writer of pastoral poems and didactic texts, he is best known for his national epic *The Aeneid*, written by 19 BC for **Augustus** and considered a classic even in his lifetime.

Vitellius   [III: 37]   Aulus Vitellius (15-69), short-term Roman emperor. Infamous for his gluttony, Vitellius enjoyed only a nine-month reign in 69, the end of which was marked by an attack on Rome lead by **Vespasian** that resulted in the burning of the city, including the ancient temple of Jupiter.

Vitruvius [II: 18, 21, 22, 27, 29, 30, 58; III: 14, 17, 18, 44] Marcus Vitruvius Pollio, (ca. 70-ca. 25 BC) Roman architect and author under **Caesar** and **Augustus**. Vitruvius' fame as a writer far outstrips any distinction as a builder. His *De Architectura* (17 BC or after) is the only complete treatise on architecture to survive antiquity; it alludes to several lost writings on Greek architecture, is an important source for Roman architecture, its discovery in the fifteenth century was an impetus behind the Renaissance, and virtually all architectural treatises to the modern period reference it in one way or another.

Walpole (Lord Orford) [IV: 25]   Horace Walpole (1717-97), English author and member of parliament 1741-67. In 1747 Walpole acquired a country house, Strawberry Hill, where he built a rambling Gothic castle as a setting in which to entertain his many creative and learned friends and as a site for a printing press begun in 1757. His signature contribution to literature is the early "gothick" novel, *The Castle of Otranto* (1765). He also published letters and essays on the arts and other subjects, many of which were gathered in *Walpoliana*, published in many forms in Europe and America from 1783 through the 1820s.

Warburton, Bishop [IV: 25] William Warburton (1698-1779), English bishop and author, most of whose work was ecclesiastical in nature. Walter likely learned of his theory on the pointed arch (and his own later dismissal of it) from secondary sources, in particular Thomas **Hope** and Horace **Walpole**.

Wilfred [IV: 13,1 4] St. Wilfrid (634-ca. 709) English churchman who traveled with Benedict **Biscop** before 661, when he became abbot of Ripon, in 663 its bishop, and later of Hexham.

Wilkins, Wilkins Vitruvius [II: 9 fn.] William Wilkins (1778-1839), highly successful English writer, collector, and as architect an expositor of the archaeological Greek Revival and Tudor Gothic styles. His travels in Italy, Sicily, Greece and Asia Minor gave him material for a large and fine folio, *The Antiquities of Magna Graecia* (Cambridge: 1807). In 1809 he prepared a translation of books 3-6 of **Vitruvius** which was published 1813-17 as *The Civil Architecture of Vitruvius*. In this large folio book, with hefty theoretical intro (76 pages long) Wilkins compiled his learning from a variety of ancient and modern sources — Burke, Knight, Price, Aristotle, Pliny, Thucydides — and was a main source for Walter.

Wilkinson [IV: 2B] Sir John Gardner Wilkinson (1797-1875), founder of British Egyptology. Wilkinson made five long trips to Egypt between 1821 and 1856, during which he devised a chronology for the New Kingdom dynasties and also the numbering system still used in reference to the twenty-one tombs in the Valley of the Kings. Walter read one of the most popular of his works, *A Second Series of the Manners and Customs of the Ancient Egyptians Including their Religion, Agriculture, &c.* (3 vols, London: 1841).

William I [IV: 10, 46] William the Conqueror (ca. 1027-87), ruler who lead the Normans into England where they successfully deposed the recently-crowned King Harold at the Battle of Hastings in 1066. William became king and reigned until his death.

William of Malmsbury [IV: 17] English monk, librarian at Malmesbury, and historian (ca. 1090-ca. 1143) who both collected and wrote. His most famous book, *The History of the Kings of England* (1125-42) is considered an essential study for the period leading up to the reign of the Norman king

Stephen. It was translated from Latin into English for several editions through Walter's life time.

Winkleman [II: 15C] Johann Joachim Winckelmann (1717-68), German art historian. Through his numerous writings on ancient sculpture Winckelmann redefined the history of art and introduced the idea of stylistic frameworks; he is also credited with bolstering the idea of Greek art's and cutlure's superiorotiy. Walter used Winckelmann as a source for his commentary on Greek architectural sculpture, especially the work of **Phidias**.

Wood's Let.; Woods letters from Greece [II: 14 fn.; V: 11 fn.] Joseph Woods (1776-1864), British architect and author of *Letters of an Architect, from France, Italy, and Greece* (London: 1828, 2 vol.).

Woods Palmyra, Robert Wood [III: 53, 53 fn., 54] Robert Wood (1717?-1771), British traveler and antiquarian. In 1751 Woods studied, measured and recorded the ruins of Palmyra, later publishing them in several volumes: *The Ruins of Palmyra, otherwise Tedmor, in the Desart* (which Walter cites; London: 1753); *The Ruins of Balbec, otherwise Heliopolis in Coelosyria* (London: 1757); and *The Ruins of Palmyra and Balbec* (London: W. Pickering, 1827).

Wordsworth [III: 61; IV: 29] William Wordsworth (1770-1850), English Romantic poet of the Lake District, author of the "Ecclesiastical Sonnets" (1821-22) from which Walter draws.

Wren, Christopher [V: 16, 18, 19, 20, 21] Sir Christopher Wren (1632-1723), geometer, scientist and as architect, leader of English Baroque school, best known for his rebuilding of London's churches, most importantly St. Paul's, after the fire of 1666. Wren's papers on architecture were published posthumously as *Parentalia* (London: 1750) by his grandson, Stephen Wren.

Wyatt, James [IV: 39] English architect (1746-1813) whose practice included both preservation efforts and new buildings in a variety of revival styles. He was appointed Surveyor of Westminster in 1776.

Xenophon [I: 12B] Greek general and historian (ca. 434 BC-ca. 355 BC). Xenophon served in the Athenian cavalry during the Persian civil war (401 BC-387 BC) during which he gained notoriety as the elected commander of the "Ten Thousand." This group fought their way through 1000 miles of unknown territories to reach Greece in early 400 BC. The book he wrote based on the exploit, *Anabasis*, made his name and fortune at a young age.

Xerxes [II: 28] Xerxes I, Xerxes the Great (ca. 519 BC-465 BC), King of Persia (r. 486 BC-465 BC). The "Persian Portico" erected at Sparta (mentioned by **Vitruvius** in Book I, ch. 1:6) was a monument to the successful overthrow of the Persians at the Battle of Platea in 479 BC.

Zenobia [III: 54] Queen of Palmyra (called Tedmor in the Bible; d. after 274). Ruling as regent for her son, she made Palmyra a leading power in the East by expanding its territories into Asia Minor, Syria, and Mesopotamia. Her downfall began with a successful campaign into Egypt (269) which Rome perceived as a threat. Rome crushed the campaign, invaded Palmyra, and in 272 brought Zenobia to Rome where she and her son were pensioned and exiled.

APPENDIX B
THE LOST RENDERINGS

In spite of the accomplished hand Walter applied in watercolors for his own architectural projects, it appears that he did not paint the large watercolor renderings displayed during his lectures. Instead he sketched designs that were then passed along to others for their production. The twenty-two drawings were so essential to the lectures that Walter felt unable to accept invitations to lecture when he did not have access to them. None of the drawings is known to survive; indeed, most went missing during Walter's own lifetime. Some were deposited in the Drawing School of the Franklin Institute, where they were generally well cared for. Two large images, one of the Athenian Acropolis and the other of the Temple of Isis at Dendera, were lost for about twenty years between a Sunday School lesson at the Spruce Street Baptist Church in Philadelphia and their rediscovery in the "rubbish" of the Franklin Institute's attic. What happened to them after the 1870s is unknown.

The watercolor illustrations that Walter displayed in the course of his lectures are known only through his references within the text of the lectures and in occasional correspondence. The following letters record Walter's efforts to locate the drawings, and are in the collection of Letterbooks in the Thomas U. Walter Collection at the Athenæum of Philadelphia:

> *Walter to G. Parker Cummings, 6 Aug. 1859*
>
> *Walter to G. Parker Cummings, 10 Aug. 1859*
>
> *Walter to William Hamilton, 27 Dec. 1859*
>
> *Walter to George W. Samson, 10 Mar. 1871*
>
> *Walter to G. W. Samson, 20 Mar. 1871*

Lecture I: On Ancient Architecture (four drawings)

1. Elevation of Temple of Isis at Dendera (I: 16, 22)

This drawing was one of two (the other being the view of the Athenian Acropolis for Lecture II) that went missing after Walter's Sunday School lesson. Before it was recovered Walter had it redrawn by his draftsman in Washington, Augustus Schoenborn (Samson, 10 Mar. 1871).

2. The Foliated Order of Egyptian Architecture (I: 17)

3. The Isis Order of Egyptian Architecture (I: 17)

4. The Plain or Robust Order of Egyptian Architecture (I: 17)

Walter describes these drawings as the "3 Egyptian columns," some of his most "indispensable" to the Lectures (Cummings, 6 Aug. 1859). As opposed to the Greek and Roman Orders, these were "full" orders showing the entire columns, including the shafts. Walter estimated them at "6 or 8 feet high. . . these were very large and elaborate." For a time he allowed their use in the Franklin Institute to "decorate" the model room (Cummings, 10 Aug. 1859). They were among the drawings Walter most wanted to retrieve: "These are all I care very much about; the rest I can draw on a black board" (Hamilton, 27 Dec. 1859).

Lecture II: On the Architecture of Ancient Greece (seven drawings)

1. The Acropolis (II: 12)

Walter's image of the Acropolis in Athens must have been truly spectacular, measuring "some 6 by 10 feet. . . one of the most perfect scenes I ever saw in distemper" and based on the panoramic view in Stuarts and Revett's *Antiquities of Athens*. Like the Egyptian Orders, it was left at the Franklin Institute "to embellish the rooms, and for use in the drawing school," then used them for a lecture to the Sunday School at Spruce Street Baptist Church in Philadelphia (Cummings, 10 Aug. 1859). He found it twenty years later at the Franklin Institute, much defaced (Samson, 20 Mar. 1871).

2. The Parthenon: Plan and Elevation (II: 13)

Like the view of the Acropolis, this too was based on plates from Stuart and Revett (Samson, 20 Mar. 1871).

3. The Doric Order of Greek Architecture (II: 17, facing 32, facing 34, 37)

4. The Ionic Order of Greek Architecture (II: 17, facing 32, facing 42)

5. The Corinthian Order of Greek Architecture (II: 17, facing 32, 48)

All drawn from examples in the *Antiquities of Athens,* Walter's Athenian examples were as follows: the Doric of the Theseum, the Ionic of the Temple on the Illisus, and the Corinthian of the Temple of Lysicrates. Walter later regretted the manner in which he portrayed the Greek (and also Roman) Orders, having made them on separate pages so that their relative scale could not be compared, and also to have left out the column shafts (Samson, 20 Mar. 1871).

6. Construction Diagram (II: facing 19)

The context of Lecture II suggests that this diagram illustrated the derivation of Greek masonry from carpentry as described by Vitruvius in Book 4 of *De architectura.*

7. Temple "Orders" (II: 53)

This drawing portrayed the several plan types as described by Vitruvius in Book 3 of *De architectura.*

Lecture III: On the Architecture of Ancient Rome (five drawings)

1. The Tuscan Order of Roman Architecture (II: 13, 16)

2. The Doric Order of Roman Architecture (II: 13, 18, 19)

3. The Ionic Order of Roman Architecture (II: 13, 21)

4. The Corinthian Order of Roman Architecture (II: 13, 23, 24)

5. The Composite Order of Roman Architecture (II: 13, 24)

Like his images of the Greek Orders, the five Roman orders were illustrated on separate sheets and with bases, capitals, and architraves without the full shaft (see above).

Lecture IV: On the Architecture of the Middle Ages (six drawings)

1. The Saxon Style of English Medieval Architecture (IV: 11, 12)

2. The Norman Style of English Medieval Architecture (IV: 11, 18)

3. The Early Pointed/Early English Style of English Medieval Architecture (IV: 11, 21, 22)

4. The Decorated English/Pointed Style of English Medieval Architecture (IV: 11, 29)

5. The Florid Pointed Style of English Medieval Architecture (IV: 11, 35)

Perhaps taking his cue from Britton's works, which often assembled parts and details of different buildings into single compositions, Walter blended different buildings in his medieval diagrams which he described as "façade" drawings (Samson, 10 Mar. 1871). As he explains in Lecture IV, the "Norman" drawing blends details from Chichester Cathedral and St. Albans; the "Early Pointed" drawing blends details from Dereham, Beverly, and Salisbury; the "Decorated English" blends details from Worstead Church, Norfolk, Beverly Minster and York Cathedral. Another source further describes the second drawing as "Norman interlaced arches" (Samson, 10 Mar. 1871).

These were among Walter's most useful and prized drawings, described as "very large and elaborate" (Hamilton, 27 Dec. 1859) and "indispensable to my proceeding" in accepting invitations to lecture (Cummings, 6 Aug.). He described them as being "some 6 feet by 8 or 10 each. . . they were specimens of <u>Saxon</u>, <u>Norman</u>, <u>early pointed</u>, <u>Decorated</u>, and <u>florid Gothic</u> architecture — I made the designs myself and paid Russell Smith $30 each for painting them; I still have the designs, and if the diagrams were not found, will have them reproduced here. These. . . [were] the best of the lot" (Cummings, 10 Aug. 1859).

6. Lombard architecture (IV: 52, 54, 55)

In Lecture IV Walter explained this drawing blended details from San Zeno at Verona, the Duomo of Piacenza and San Michele at Pavia.

Lecture V: On Modern Architecture and Lecture VI: Architecture Considered as Fine Art

The lecture manuscripts do not indicate the use of drawings in the final two lectures.

Appendix C
Walter's Notes on the Fine Arts

Departing from the established course of the lectures, the back pages of Lecture VI seem to begin another notebook which Walter wrote simply by turning the lecture booklet over and upside down. It is a curious blend of information, starting with a laundry list for Morley's Hotel, Trafalgar, London. There follows four pages on the subject of "light" and two pages on the subject of "harmony." These are notes that perhaps Walter intended to work into Lecture VI, or into articles for the Franklin Institute, since some of the ideas seem to reflect his article "On Chromatics as Pertaining to Architecture."[1] Lastly, Walter recorded a series of notes on taste and harmony which appear to be germane to the content of Lecture VI, and are recorded here as they appear in the manuscript:

good taste is nearly allied to moral and intellectual excellence as its opposite is to physical, sensual and mental degradation. Field p 385 vol. 2

Harmony consists in relation, and springs from the reunion of that which is naturally one, or identical—the feeling or perception of harmony is a perception or relation or reason,—a natural logic—a consciousness of truth or unity—and the more intimate and comprehensible such unity is, the nearer to perfection is the harmony. 159 vol 2 Field

[*Nature itself seems to be impatient of the discord that prevails in many of the works of man.*]

How beautifully the effects of Harmony are displayed in the romantic ruins that embellish the crumbled and time worn fanes of other days—every flaw and fissure that natural decay or violence has made, is sweetly decked with vegetal beauty; and all their crudeness is toned down and glazed with time.

---

[1] Walter, "On Chromatics as Pertaining to Architecture" *JFI* 2, no. 1 (July 1841), 32-37.

APPENDIX D
WALTER'S WRITINGS ON ARCHITECTURE

The extensive Walter Collection at The Athenæum of Philadelphia is the archival resource for Walter's office records, diaries, journals, office notes, drawings, letterbooks, and other personal and professional effects. Other archives which include significant Walter material include Girard College (Philadelphia, PA), the American Institute of Architects Library and Archives (Washington, DC) and the Architect of the Capitol (Washington, DC).

Walter's published works are as follows:

Books (with J. Jay Smith)
A Guide to Workers in Metals and Stone. Philadelphia: Carey and Hart, 1846.
Two Hundred Designs for Cottages and Villas. Philadelphia: Carey and Hart, 1846.

Articles
"Architecture." *JFI* 1, no. 1 (Jan. 1841): 11-12.
"On Chromatics as Pertaining to Architecture." *JFI* 2, no. 1 (July 1841): 32-37.
"A Description of the Eastern Penitentiary, of the State of Pennsylvania, designed and executed by John Haviland, Esq., Architect." *JFI* 2, no. 2 (Aug. 1841): 118-20.
"A Description of the Philadelphia County Prison, and the Debtors' Apartment. Designed and Executed by Thomas U. Walter, Architect." *JFI* 2, no. 3 (Sept. 1841): 189-91.
"On Glass as Applied to Architecture. — Extract from a Lecture on the Architecture of the Middle Ages, delivered before the Franklin Institute, by T. U. Walter, Professor of Architecture, December 10, 1840." *JFI* 1, no. 4 (May 1841): 266-67.
"The Orders." *JFI* 1, no. 3 (Apr. 1841): 194-96.
"Street Architecture." *JFI* 1, no. 2 (Feb. 1841): 90-91.

INDEX

Numbers in italics refer to illustrations. For names of individuals and texts cited within the lectures, see also Appendix A. For individual buildings, see place names.